The Water The Woman and The Wine

Contents

All Bible scripture and passages taken from the "King James Version" – *Public Domain*

"The Water, the Woman, and the Wine"

Dedication

It is with great joy I have life and breath to write this book. Had it not been for the Lord who was on my side, I would have been consumed long before the birth of this book. I would like to thank my wife, Ginger, who has stood by my side through lean and hard times. Through seasons of near impasses, she has been a pillar of strength and encouragement to me. A faith that moves mountains she possesses indeed. Thank you for believing in me when life was most trying. A vision and a dream of a life after the struggle, we together shared, now has become reality. Truly, God saved the best for last. I also would like to thank my parents, Reverend Dr. Ronald and Janice Beady for their unending quest in the pursuit of Christ likeness. While growing up in a Christian home, they together modeled the life of the One in whom they placed their faith. Dad and Mom, thank you for modeling for me the faith that would help forge my personal beliefs and faith. I can think of one statement to sum up their provided Godly parental upbringing - "As good as it gets."

Mom, though you are not here in body and are by Jesus' side, you are here with me in spirit and I know you are proud. I wish you could have been here to read it, as you were an avid reader and my spiritual friend. I also thank those whom along the way played seeming to be insignificant roles in my Christian life. It is them whom God used over the years to help bring clarity to an otherwise abstract calling. These Saints of God, while unbeknownst to them, offered key insight into the master plan God had for my life. May we not overlook those to whom no fanfare is given; yet, take the time to simply be in their God ordained place. It is these whom God uses to connect the dots of our life and speak a word in due season. Even though they may be faceless and nameless at times such as a shopper in the store, a tire salesperson, or simply a newspaper boy, they nevertheless share in the success of one named believer. Finally, thank you to Lee Anne who stepped in and took on a monumental job editing when I needed someone the most. Your kindness, keen eye and sharp pen have completed this work. You are a God send and I am indebted to you!

The Water The Woman and The Wine

Introduction

Please travel with me on a journey back in time, to a land and setting that to most would seem like another planet. We will look at a beautiful story, the Son of God "Emanuel" coming to earth and dwelling among us. To most, it seems as if God would have shown up on the scene in a blaze of glory, angels as ministering flames of fire leading the charge, engulfed in a radiant power filled light, swooping down on earth in rank, marching and singing in cadence "The King of Glory is now come." *The Lord of Glory, who was and is, and is to come, has come to your world. Bow and bend your knee; fall prostrate before His holiness.* I believe not only did the disciples, Sadducees, Pharisees, and all the religious Zealots of the day feel like the God of all the universe would show up in this fashion, but we feel like He should as well. That was not the case; it was not then, and it is not now. God is not a Genie in a bottle; He is not a lucky rabbit's foot nor is He an object that we can rub in order to coax Him out that He might perform a magic trick. All of us desire for God to be, at times, what He is not. This thinking is off base and from our own self-will. We want to be in control. We want to control who, what, and how matters are accomplished in our life. We want to control time and possess the power to see what we want to transpire in a sphere of time - or when we believe it should happen. We spend a lifetime trying to manipulate time for our personal benefit and arrange matters that seem important to us. Yet, God is the complete opposite. He asks us to: "Seek ye the Kingdom of Christ first, and then all these will be added unto us." All of what we have desired will transpire in time; however, in our mind, priorities need attention. If we rearrange our thought-process ensuring God to be first it is then that time falls into place. We chase

1

time, yet all too often, have unchecked issues remaining at the end of the day. God holds our time!

In the gospel of Luke the 10th chapter, we find an account of Jesus meeting a woman named Martha as He entered a certain village.   There were no bright flashing metropolitan lights just a small obscure unnamed village. Yet, it is a story that has profound power and gives a good glimpse into the heart and mind of God. This story will serve a pre-cursor to the subject matter of this book. Contained within is the knowledge of what is important to the Lord, yet, somehow seems to escape most of our understanding while we live our busy lives; let us read.

> *And as they went, it happened that He entered into a certain village. And a certain woman named Martha received Him into her house. And she had a sister called Mary, who also sat at Jesus' feet and heard His word. But Martha was distracted with much serving. And she came to Him and said, Lord, do You not care that my sister has left me to serve alone? Therefore tell her to help me. And Jesus answered and said to her, Martha, Martha; you are anxious and troubled about many things. But one thing is needful, and Mary has chosen that good part, which shall not be taken away from her. Luke 10:38-42*

Mary was on to something. Jesus did not tell her to forgo helping her sister, yet something inside of her saw the importance of not letting the moment slip by. Somehow she was able to see past the carnality of household first impressions, for the thought of pressing into the moment - sitting at the feet of the Christ. I like the fact that she let everything else go that she might utilize the full opportunity that was made available to her. She saw time through the eyes and heart of God, and she was not willing to be denied even if it meant having to deal with a not-so-forgiving sister. No, not this time: *"I am not going to scurry around the house helping you cook and clean. He is here now, I must learn now, while He is here. I must talk with Him now; I must fellowship with Him now, Martha. That can wait."* We all too often follow the pattern of Martha. We invite Jesus into our lives; we reach out and bring him to our dwelling space only to get distracted by the cares of life and the rudiments of the world. This should not be!

We somehow need to refocus: We must find a way to become Christ-centered instead of self-centered. We must ensure that we do not allow one visitation to slip through our grasp.

We will follow the story in detail of how priorities were out of order, how God is a God of order, and how God is not only the author of time but also the redeemer of time. God is God alone. He does not need our help, yet He extends an invitation to partake in this Holy union. God united and yoked with mankind through covenant relationship. What a sight it must have been to see God manifest in the form of flesh attending a wedding. We have the thought that God should be off doing some Holy thing like healing the sick, raising the dead, or causing blind eyes to be opened. We do not picture our Lord taking time out of His busy schedule to go to a wedding. A fact is, that this passage of scripture we will explore conveniently leaves out vital information. We, from reading this passage, never learn what the names of the parties taking part in matrimony are. We do not know where they come from, and we do not know the length of their engagement. So much detail is left unrecorded. We must read into it, and draw our own conclusion to the validity of their love for each other. It would seem that we would be apt to draw a more adequate conclusion as to the importance of the miracle if we would have known whose wedding we are attending. This is not the case. We must place our focus on the perfection of the anointed hand that recorded the event and penned this passage of scripture. We want to control all aspects of life; however, God asks us to trust him in ways that seem completely foreign to our intellect. As you read the pages of this book you will find yourself immersed in an ancient historical event that holds volumes of truth today.

I invite you to journey with me through the pages of, "The Water The Woman and The Wine."

The Water The Woman and The Wine

John 2:1-11 And *the third day there was a marriage in Cana of Galilee. And the mother of Jesus was there. 2 And Jesus and His disciples were both invited to the marriage. 3 And when they lacked wine, the mother of Jesus said to Him, They have no wine. 4 Jesus said to her, Woman, what do I have to do with you? My hour has not yet come. 5 His mother said to the servants, Whatever He says to you, do it. 6 And there were six stone waterpots there, according to the purification of the Jews, each containing two or three measures. 7 Jesus said to them, Fill the waterpots with water. And they filled them up to the brim. 8 And He said to them, Now draw out and carry it to the master of the feast. And they carried it. 9 When the ruler of the feast had tasted the water which was made wine (and did not know where it was from, but the servants who drew the water knew), the master of the feast called the bridegroom. 10 And he said to him, Every man at the beginning sets forth good wine, and when men have drunk well, then that which is worse. You have kept the good wine until now. 11 This beginning of miracles Jesus did in Cana of Galilee. And it revealed His glory. And His disciples believed on Him.*

Chapter 1

It's About Time

To everything there is a season, and a time for every
purpose under the heavens: Ecclesiastes 3:1

It's all about time. We read from the man of wisdom, Solomon, the author of the book of Ecclesiastes, that everything has a time. All that God has set in place is done so in its own time. God is not bound by time, for He is without beginning or end. Nevertheless, everything He does is done so in its own time. Let us draw from the book of Genesis and follow the creation of what we call **time**.

> *And God said, Let there be light. And there was light. And*
> *God saw the light that it was good. And God divided*
> *between the light and the darkness. And God called the*
> *light, Day. And He called the darkness, Night. And the*
> *evening and the morning were the first day. Genesis 1:3-5*
>
> *And God said, Let there be lights in the expanse of the*
> *heavens to divide between the day and the night. And let*
> *them be for signs, and for seasons, and for days and*
> *years. Genesis 1:14*

Not only did God create light, and not only did God divide the light and darkness into night and day, but He also created a pattern we follow called time. Reading through the account of creation, we do not find where He created "time" or even *used* the word time. What we do find is where He simply divided night and day, hung two lights in the sky, one for night and one for day. Man through his God-governed intellect formulated what we now call hours in the day, for which we are able to draw our current method for keeping time. 2 Peter 3:8 reveals to us God's concept of time as compared to ours: "One day with the Lord is as a thousand years, and a thousand years as one day." So we stand back and say, "What?" It's hard for us to wrap our mind around the concept of time in contrast with the Lord's. It's difficult for us to understand that God views everything from the vantage point of eternity. This viewpoint is a perpetual existence as it relates to God's created beings. We were born, we had a beginning, and we have an appointment with death. It is appointed unto every man once to die...(Hebrews 9:27). However, that is not the end, we are rushing headlong toward our eternal existence, whether it is living eternally with Christ or in eternal judgment.

Again I want to draw your attention to time and the significance of it. It is costly, it is valuable, and it must be guarded. If we are not careful, we will forget that with each passing day we are losing time. Though once created to live eternally in this earthly garment (flesh), because of the fall of mankind in the Garden of Eden, we now find ourselves in a race with an eternal clock while in this earthly tent.

So teach us to number our days, so that we may bring a heart of wisdom. Psalms 90:12

Life is not to be lived haphazardly, nor is it to be lived indoors for fear of the sky falling. Jesus said in the 10th chapter of the gospel of John that He has come to give life and to give it to us more abundantly. He uttered this truth directly after He spoke of our adversary desiring to destroy our life. God does not want us to walk around in fear, yet He does want us to know that we have a limited amount of time on earth. It is one of my greatest beliefs that the Lord wants us to know we were created with purpose and fashioned in his image. Additionally, we are to work the works of righteousness. The Lord gave us the example of working in our season and in the time we are given. There is no greater truth than to know that we can pattern our life after the master Teacher. Read and listen carefully to the following words, and again see the pattern that Jesus is setting for us.

I must work the works of Him who sent Me, while it is day. Night comes when no man can work. As long as I am in the world, I am the Light of the world. John 9:4-5

We move in and out of time. All of us have an opportunity that is given to us. No one can take this window, this time from us; yet we can give time away and never regain it. Even during the most unimaginable seasons of setbacks and bewilderments that life can dish out, time must be given attention to. We still have a time that God will give us to be effective and not on a limited scale. God wants for you to prosper; or shall I say prosper the word in you, and for that word to go out and accomplish what He intended. I stand on the principal that everyone has a God-breathed reason for being alive, and as long as we stay true (i.e. follow the leading of the Lord), we will all arrive ultimately at our intended destination. This intended destination or place is what God has designed us for. I stand, flat footed, refusing to give any ground to the enemy of our soul, refusing to give any suggestion that he can take me out of the palm, hand, and plan of God. This solid ground, faith-driven thinking allows the impossible to abound for us.

I want you to know you are on a collision course with your God-breathed destiny and it's all about time. It's time for you to stand up! It's time for you to get up! It is time for you to arise to the knowledge that God is on your side. He cares for you and He desires fellowship with you. Regardless of whether you feel life has robbed you of time, God is still a redeemer of time.

Hear the words given to the church at Ephesus by the Apostle Paul:
See then that you walk circumspectly, not as fools, but as wise, redeeming the time, because the days are evil. Ephesians 5:15-16

Here, an alarm is sounded. The watchman on the wall trumpets with fervency to stand up and take notice. We, as the redeemed of the Lord, should not walk around with an attitude of business as usual. No! Not now. We don't have the time to slack.

We must be about the Father's business. We must redeem the time. We must know or admit that we have but a few days upon this earth. *I must make the best of the time allotted to me.* I must make the best of everyday. I am not getting any younger. I need to utilize the life God has given me. The Apostle Paul tells us in Ephesian's 5 to walk as if we know we have purpose. We must walk circumspectly, to be cautious to look around. Stand up, take notice; things are not just going to fall into place. I must redeem the time. I must make a strategic, tactical approach to my time. I have "a time." *This day I awaken to the knowledge that God has given me time. I've been given time to breathe, time to read, time to pray, time to place my plans on paper, time to care, time to love, time to try one more time. God, today I am going to redeem the time You have given me. Yesterday I wasted time on negative thinking. I gave away vital, valuable time to things that do not add to your kingdom. Yesterday, I could see where I should have planned better, where I should have invested better, with the time you have given me. Today, Lord, I take a more direct approach. I ask, "Lord, where can my time best be utilized?"*

I believe most could attest that the older you get, the shorter the days seem to be. Age has a way of getting our attention, especially when you walk to the mirror in the morning or after a hard day's work. We see that time has passed. Where have the years gone? I can hear the question that is asked so often, "God, do I have the time to accomplish all that You have shown me, all that You have placed within my heart? God, it feels at times, the more I try, the more I get behind with the time that I have. It seems there is not enough time in the day to get done all that I need to accomplish. Lord, look how much time has passed and I seem to be no further along than I did five years ago."

We all wrestle with time. This wrestling is an epic struggle - not with the forces of darkness, but with time. "God, will I blossom in my time?" "Will I have enough time to finish?" I hear the voices echoing throughout time of those who feel they have come near the end of their life or time, feeling like they never accomplished all that they wanted to see happen. Many have asked the question and find themselves pondering, "Did my life matter? Did what I put my hands to matter, or did what I tried to do count for anything?" I doubt few arrive at that point wishing they had attended more board meetings, traveled in bigger business entourages, or made one more sales call.

No, this is not the case. We, as humanity, desire to have sowed into something we feel will last long past our departing this earth. Seeds we have sown into our children and into our friends and family - we desire we would have done something that would have mattered. A cry goes out from the heart of God, "Redeem the time!" A pleading that is made to not sit by idly waiting for the right time to make a move. No! Stand up, move toward Christ and know that He will, through you, redeem time. He will make what's in your hands to prosper. God will prosper you in your way.

At times, we feel what we are doing doesn't matter. It seems like we are going through the motions and there seems to be no real progress, nothing of merit. I sense, as I write these words, God wants you to know that He values your efforts, He values the time you've given on His behalf. I feel we need to be reminded that when we yoke ourselves to the gospel that we become co-labors with Christ. He values our dedication. Anytime that you commit toward His kingdom and the building of it, there is value and no waste in the efforts you put forth. Everything you have given up for Him, He will redeem your time, or plainly stated, at a place in time that God has ordained, there will be a return. God tells us in His word whatever we give up or give away for the sake of the gospel, He will return a hundred-fold (see Mathew 19:29, Mark 10:30). Wow, what a thought! If I give of my time to the Lord, it will be for a good cause, and as an added benefit, I will get a bountiful harvest or return.

At times, we feel like it's not happening quickly enough. Years have passed, and we seem to still be in the same situation or the same predicament as we have always been. I feel the Lord wants us to know that in His time it will not only happen *for* us, but also *through* us. Yes! He wants to use our gifts, our talents and our availability. He wants to do a work through our lives. Gone is the notion that He only wants to use us in short, laconic appearances.

9

No, to the contrary, He has a bigger and better plan. Even if you've seen success in a past season, He wants to take you higher. He has made the way for others to be blessed by the giving of our purposed time. God will make it count and it will add up to more than what appears on the surface. Galatians 6:9 tells us to not get weary in well-doing, for we shall reap if we faint not. A picture is painted showing a block of time may pass in the giving of our time without seeing any good come from it. Just because year after year passes without noticeable change or benefit, it is not a reason to quit. Time and the passing of it are not excuses to quit in what we were given to do. The fact is, we are getting closer to our reward with each day completed. You are rushing toward your blessing, but you must not get weary. You must not lie down and slumber, or get tired in the fight.

Listen… resist the temptation to cash in the chips and coast. No. Do the opposite. Stand up, buckle up, and know every year, every month, every day, and every passing moment that you have labored for, or in the Lord, will be rewarded. Rest assured your labor is not in vain. If you find yourself at a place where you feel exasperated by the passing of time and the weight of the season, know God has seen your labor of love and it is all in God's time. Everything is in the plan of God, and in God's great scheme of time, He will bless you. He will prosper you. He will position you for His purpose and for His plan. Don't be disheartened. Don't allow the enemy to cast down your hope and dreams. If you still have breath, God has given you time. Redeem that time given to you, and know that He is working with and for you. He is on your side. He cares and loves you and wants you to know you are not out of season. You are right on time, and He will bring you into your season.

In the story we are exploring, it is Jesus' first public miracle - the turning of water into wine. The second chapter of the Gospel of John gives an account in fashionable detail as to the occurrence of His first public display of power. This is the first time the Son of the living God has chosen to uncover His power over the laws of nature and mankind. We pick up in verse one with the words, "On the third day." This was a set place in time; a time that was chosen by the Lord for Him to begin to reveal himself not just in word, but now in deed. "On the third day." I can tell you by simple observation that there is always an importance of time with God. The writer of the Gospel of John records the importance of the chronological order of events of the public ministry of Jesus even to the recording of the day that Jesus preformed this first of many miracles. Let's examine the significance of "the third day" in scripture.

Jonah was in the belly of the great fish three days. Jonah 1:17 *Esther, on the third day, went before the king.* Esther 5:1 *On the third day, Joseph spoke to his brothers after having them under lock and key.* Genesis 42:18 *He spoke to them with his identity hidden and told them "if you do this, you will live."* God spoke to Moses and uttered these words in Exodus19, "*And be ready for the third day. For the* third day *Jehovah will come down in the sight of all the people upon Mount Sinai."*

Jesus was in the heart of the earth three days. It was that triumphal morning, the third day that our Christ rose from the grave. There is significance in time with the Lord. And so it was true, when on the third day, Jesus' miracle ministry on earth launched upward. This was accomplished when He chose do the simplest of tasks. Is *there anything too hard for God?* On the third day, Jesus was invited to attend a wedding. We are not privileged with being given the names of those getting married; in fact, it seems to be such an unimportant detail. The greatness of Jesus' first public miracle has little to do with the parties getting married or so it seemed. Nevertheless, He chose to work his first miracle for eyes to see and the tongue to taste in the miracle of Jesus turning the water into wine, *John chapter 2.*

He chose to do to it on the third day, not the second, not the fourth or fifth, but on the third day. This quickly should peak our attention and settle in our mind a solid fact: God is not in heaven randomly allowing or disallowing matters to happen in our life. We are on a timetable with God. He chose to live His life on this earth in precise sequence - not ahead, nor behind, but rather precisely on time. I will be the first to tell you my understanding of time is only based on my understanding of who God says He is. I don't, nor do I believe anyone has a complete grasp of time except that there is a

God who works time to his benefit, even if we don't understand. After all, He is God and he chooses to do as he pleases.

This is where trust and faith collide. We must be attentive, and we must work while there is light, but we must also allow God to be God. Even if he chooses to move ahead or behind our schedule, we must not point accusing fingers as if he is out of the sequence of his own time. There are two examples that I will present, and I am positive we all can relate to. I would like to call the first the "Lazarus Syndrome." At times we feel like Jesus did not show up when we thought he would, or when we thought he should. In the Gospel of John we read the story that plays out as Jesus is in "trying ministry times." The fame of His ministry has begun to ruffle the feathers of the Jews, who liked all their own religious attention. Now this Galilean was stealing the show. A spirit of jealousy began to arise within them and they were ready to kill Jesus. Jesus receives word that his friend Lazarus is sick and is dying. His response to the news was, "This sickness is not unto death." *John 11:4* Jesus was not bound by time, but those who brought word and those who were beside Jesus believed otherwise. They saw Lazarus lying upon his deathbed, sickness ravaging his frail body. They believed with their entire heart saying within, "Jesus, if you do not get here soon he is going to die."

I love the discourse that takes place. It almost seems as if Jesus goes from one subject to another. He is concerned for His friend that is dying; yet He is also concerned for His lost sheep that were in Judea. He had just gotten word that His friend is dying. Scripture tells us that He loved Lazarus, yet He desired to go to Judea. His disciples seem perplexed at this statement. "Hey Jesus, wait a minute! You want to go to Judea where they are plotting and planning to kill You. The last time You were there You narrowly escaped with Your life. Why wouldn't You want to go to the place where You are loved? Lazarus is sick. Mary is there waiting for You, Martha is too. Jesus, don't You think we should wait until things quiet down before we try to go back to Judea? Shouldn't we wait until a better time? "

Scripture instructs us that He waited two more days. What is it that Jesus waited two more days? I believe whole-heartedly that Jesus wanted to accomplish two things among others: One, he wanted to build their faith, and two; He wanted to show that He was not bound by time. Jesus was not bound by time, even by the death of one of his saints. I draw my conclusion from Him teaching his followers about time with direct relation to verse nine of the eleventh chapter of John. He asks them, "Are there not twelve hours in the day?" He goes on to ask them questions about walking in the day and the night. Then He abruptly says, "Our friend Lazarus sleeps; I go that I may wake him." It almost appears that He waited until it was too late. By all accounts, both Martha and Mary that had the same response to Jesus. They spoke the grief stricken words, "Jesus if you had been here my brother would not have died." Without a doubt they believed he was dead, and by all accounts Lazarus *was* dead. To all who saw, and according to all present, he was dead. They did not understand who was with them, He whom they knew by personal relationship. This was not a passing friendship. No, I think not. This is the same Jesus who came to their house. The same house of Mary, and the same Martha's house I wrote about in my forward.

Yes, Jesus knew them personally and had spent time with them. From this we know why they were so deeply wounded. I can hear their hearts cry, "Jesus, I thought we were tight! I thought you loved us! I thought you cared? You told us that You loved us. Jesus, if You had come when we called, this would not have happened to our brother." This same cry rises from the voices of others who do not understand the sovereignty of God. These voices are those who know and knew God personally, and yet they cry as Martha and Mary did. "Why did you let this happen to him, her, and me? I do not understand. I served you, I went to church, and I gave my money. You told me You loved me, and yet You delayed Your coming. You were too late Jesus. You should have been on time, and this would not have happened! Jesus, I just do not understand how you could have let this happen. We spent so much time together; did it really mean anything to you? Did I and my family really mean anything to you?"

Can you hear all the questions? I bet we could all put ourselves in their position and, without a doubt, we would be pressed not to react in a similar fashion. There is the possibility that some have reacted in this same matter in their life already. Yet Jesus said to Martha, "Your brother will rise again." I find it rather refreshing that the very woman he spoke to about having many troubles is the very woman He redeems. Jesus asks her, "Do you believe?" and she tells him, "Yes Lord, I believe that you are the Christ, the Son of God who has come into the world." Wow, what a second chance and what a third opportunity at getting it right!

God is so patient with us that even when it seems like we cannot get it right he provides *yet* again. God does this so our faith might be built and increase. In John 11verse 33, we find the account of Jesus seeing Mary weeping. He then groaned within himself and asked where they laid him (Lazarus). Verse 35, the shortest in our bible, says that "Jesus wept," and the Jews said, "See how He loved him!" This is true, Jesus did love him even more than we comprehend - God *is* love. But I submit to you that he wept for more than the passing of his friend. Jesus groaned within himself; he was upset in more ways than one. Over and over in scripture Jesus makes statements concerning our faith: *"O Ye of little faith...",* *"If you would have the faith of....", "It is by your faith...".*

Jesus was upset that they were mourning the passing of their brother, who, in verse four He declared, "This sickness was not unto death." In their mind and in our mind, it appears Jesus was incorrect and He missed that one. By all accounts, naysayers could claim that he, Lazarus, died. I believe the record needs to be corrected and state that when Jesus makes a proclamation and says, "This sickness is not unto death," He means what He says. No pulse? Too bad! Cold lifeless body? Not a problem. Mourners gathered around to watch what Jesus would do. Jesus was saddened at their lack of faith at what He previously said concerning Lazarus' present state. He told them that Lazarus was not going to die, and they thought His timing was off in arriving to pray for poor Lazarus. All together it has been four days since Lazarus died - dead, stiff as a board, and by now not smelling so sweet. Jesus asks the profound question, "Where have you laid him?" As a direct result of the statement,

"Could not the one who opened eyes, keep this one from dying?" Verse 38 says Jesus groaned again within himself. Two times He groaned within Himself over the lack of faith from a people whom he loved.

Jesus said he was sleeping. The crowd said he's dead, and Martha, stumbling again, said, "By now he stinks. He's been dead four days." Jesus said this sickness is not unto death.

Jesus, standing at the tomb of His sleeping friend, commands the stone to be rolled away and stands confident in stating, "Father, I know you hear me." With a loud voice He called, "Lazarus come forth!" Out walked a dead man who was bound head and foot, but was not bound by time! It is never over until Jesus says it is over.

By now you are asking, "What does this time matter have to do with the wedding?" I submit to you that it has *everything* to do with it. Mary, the mother of Jesus, comes to Him and says, "They have no wine."

Jesus replied, "Woman, what does your concern have to do with me?" He then makes the statement, "My hour has not yet come." A precise time had not occurred. He did not move on her command, but in divine order. Rest assured, He was moved by the statement she made in desperation, yet he was not going to move out of order or out of time. I like to say he was 'power under control.' Jesus was not a loose cannon. He did not go around wielding a scepter in hand beating at the air. Jesus was a man under control and He would see the fruit of His restraint. Jesus' hour had not yet come, though it was coming. It had not *yet* come. Soon everything would change, but at this exact moment His time was not yet fulfilled. This gives us a good glimpse into waiting on our time. Our time for our calling, our anointing, and our gifting will manifest but it will happen in the Lord's time. When the time is right He will launch you into the deep. You must know that there is "the waiting time." The word of God says about Jesus, that when growing from childhood, "He grew in the grace and in the knowledge of the Lord." *Luke 2:52*

15

For thirty years, the Son of the living God walked, talked and breathed. He ate and slept, but never performed one public miracle until after the age of thirty. Many want to shake the world right away upon receiving salvation and a ministry calling. While this is good and healthy, not everyone is on the same time as God. God wants us to have zeal and passion, but the danger of discouragement lurks when open doors do not happen in the time frame we believe they should.

Obstacles and hurdles can be discouraging when trying to launch into ministry or when trying to use gifts early in ones Christian walk. For some, the discouragement even leads to the point of permanent retreat. Forever walking away is possible if you do not understand, "It's all about time." Jesus waited on His time. He did not move before His time had come. I echo *Galatians 5:5 - For we through the Spirit wait for the hope of righteousness out of faith.*

There are times when we just have to wait. There is a time and season for everything, but there are times when we must wait. Waiting is a monumental task at times, but we must keep hoping, and at times *waiting*, until our time. Faith, hope and time make for an awesome trio - the one who will ultimately go out in power and might is the one willing to allow all three to occupy their life. Jesus did just that. He did not move out of time when His mother came to Him and made a pleading implication, even though she was on to something. There is one thing Mary knew for certain. She knew her Son was special. The angel, Gabriel, had come to her in a dream and told her she was highly favored among women. Now, thirty years later, she finds herself at a wedding with her Son, the creator of the universe. As of yet, He had not moved in power except through His profound knowledge of scripture and his un-paralleled wisdom. Yet, I believe, she sensed something was about to change. She was stirred in her spirit, sensing there was something great that was about to happen. Hear this: She was discerning the time. Mary knew that now there were men that were not only following her cousin's son, John the Baptist, but Jesus as well. Now Jesus comes to this wedding and there are men that are following her Son on their own free will.

16

I believe this got her excited! She had waited a long time for her Son to stand up and take His rightful place. All her life she had known that He was different - not just by the word from the angel, but she knew without a doubt she had not had sexual relations with any man. The angel showed up and dropped the bomb on her and she replied, "How can this be? I know not a man." She knew from the beginning that He was a special son. Now she sees something that is starting to happen, something changing like a vehicle that is shifting gears and beginning to accelerate. This same type of change or shifting is happening in the ministry of her Son. I can see the Son of the living God walk in the House. Mary has been there for hours helping out, and now her Son has arrived and men are flocked around Him. She knew something was about to happen. Never before do we find where she asks anything of Him, but this time was different. Boldly, she walked up to Him and said, "They have no wine!" I can almost see the glimmer in Jesus' eye, the slight tilt of His head, and the strength of His stance. He without stutter replies, "What does your concern have to do with Me? My hour has not come!" Yet, we read that she tells those serving, "Do what He says to do." Mary was observant of the time. She, herself, was beginning to operate in a ministry or period of time that she had never walked previously. Jesus' reply seemed to rebuke her, yet she does not appear shaken by His response. I believe that she was confident in her Son - in who He was, and also who He claimed to be. Mary now had the opportunity to watch what she had waited so long for. Jesus was coming into His time. She sensed it.

As never before, this seemed to be the perfect time, in front of everyone. Mary possibly sought redemption from a lifetime of harassment from friends and family. To those who knew her, they had knowledge of her predicament. It seemed clear, they could do the math. Nine months of pregnancy and their marriage date - things didn't add up.

Controversy swirled over whether the child was conceived out of wedlock. We, as humanity, in our modern day society, know all too well how difficult it is to live down the rumors, especially with family and friends. It seems those whom we think would be the

17

first to understand are the ones who stand in direct opposition of the healing process. I'm sure every time Mary walked into a room or took a stroll down town all eyes were upon her. For years she surely never lived down all the accusations and rumors leveled against her.

Now, possibly, with all family and friends present, she might finally have a chance at redemption. This Son of hers, God incarnate, is in the house. This is the Son of a carpenter, the One who seemed to baffle the scholars with His unequaled wisdom and knowledge of scripture. This man is also the One who was born with a cloud of controversy and debate over His life. However, this is a new day! It is a different season, and now the stage is set for all of those who ever thought they had everything figured out about this man. Jesus, though seemingly reluctant at first, and vocal to His right at self- choice, now stands on the brink of making history. Only in scripture do we read of such miracles performed by hands like Moses, Elijah, and Elisha. However, that was years ago. No one recorded in recent years has ever worked miracles like those getting ready to happen. Again, this is a new time, a new place; a stage that is set that represents, again, a "period of time."

This setting is something new, "a Wedding," two individuals letting go of their individuality to become one. This is a time of leaving one season and rushing headlong into a new season. From this day forward their lives will never be the same again. So is true in the life of Jesus and those who would follow His life and ministry. Though Jesus looked directly at His mother and said, "Why are you asking me about what concerns you?" - He very quickly after would grant her petition. Jesus is ever present; Jesus is omnipresent, yet Mary discerned that the time was different. We, too, must take note of the time that we are in presently. Not only must we know our time, we must take note of what time we are in.

Therefore be humbled under the mighty hand of God, so that He may exalt you in due time. 1Peter 5:6

Jesus did not get ahead of his time. He stayed well within the parameters of the mission He was sent to do from the Father. Jesus stayed humble. When He was being mocked, He stayed humble.

When they tried to kill Him, He stayed humble. Jesus never let the circumstances of His mission deter His humility, and in doing so, we see how at the appointed time Jesus performed the first of many Miracles that we study to this day. The due time had come and now the Father was setting the stage for His son Jesus to be exalted. If we stay humble and follow the Spirit's leading, and even at times endure the chastisement or correcting hand from the Lord, He will raise you up and send you out.

Peering deep within this story, we stand in awe at the magnitude of the miracle. Still, lying deeper is the thirst for complete understanding of the statement concerning His time having not yet come. In one sentence He tells His mother that His time has not yet come. Then, just a few verses later; He is giving instruction to fill vessels full of water. From that, we view the miraculous taking place. It is that which lies *between* that we miss. We miss the looks on Jesus' face. We miss the want-filled expression of His mother staring at her Son as if to say, "I know You can do this. Will You please help? They have no wine. These people are important in my life. I came to help, and everyone has done the best they could possibly do, but we need help. Those who planned the wedding feast were not expecting such a turn out, so many extra people arrived. Yes, they failed to plan properly, but that is not important now. Jesus, we need Your help now. Yes, I know it is not Your time. I will not beg, force, or pull, but if there is anything You could do, please help."

I don't believe that we can accurately nail down the reason for Him making the statement, and then quickly granting her request. Also, I would not say I have the perfect explanation, nor does anyone for that case; nevertheless I believe that we are afforded some clues that we can examine. The first one we can explore is the fact of being an example or living epistle - a story lived out loud! With that being said, let's begin our exploration by asking a question of ourselves: How many times do we look at our time and make the case that we have so little of it to help another? I believe to some degree we are all guilty. Many a time we could be the miracle to someone's dilemma if we would just take the time to help. Such a fast-paced society we live in, with undue demands that we allow to be placed upon us, yet there are needs that could be met if we would reprioritize our life. Jesus is our master teacher. He always was a situational teacher. Our Savior never passed up an opportunity to teach a lesson. Jesus was never interested in doing a trick or working a sign or a wonder. He always did, and still does want us to learn, to have imparted deep within our spirit who He is, what He's like, and what will lead to Christ-likeness. Stating the previous He, at the opportune moment for sake of an object lesson, performs many a miracle so that people might believe.

At this very important wedding, the joining of two, there is a problem. The well has run dry, and quickly at that. The unthinkable has taken place - no more wine. There are many notable reasons why wine being in abundance is significant. Later in our reading we will revisit this, but for now just know that running out of wine is no trivial matter. Jesus says, "My time has not come." How many of us standing where Jesus stood have made that same statement to ourselves? I can hear the thought - *"I just walked all this way to get here, not only that I am tired, I've worked all day and I need a rest. Come back later I might be up to it, perhaps in a day or two. Let me rest awhile, then I will think about it."* Jesus had been about the Father's business walking and calling disciples to follow Him. These same men followed Him into the wedding. Sadly most if they were Jesus would take the position: *"You must know that praying and mentoring in addition to all the long conversation that has gone on these days has drained me. After all, I did just get baptized in the Jordan River. You know, there was witness that the Holy Spirit had rested upon Me like a dove. Do you have any idea what that took out of Me?"*

It never seems that the perfect time ever arises to begin our service or continue to serve. If you ever desire to launch out into ministry, you'll find the opportunities most often do not chase you down and overtake you. There is always the exception to the rule. We know this is true, but for the most part, those who step out into full-time ministry will have to do so at the most inconvenient time. It is usually at a time when it seems like Jesus can say your time has not yet come. Life does not always afford the perfect timing for ministry. You simply must step when there is a need. A need was

20

staring Jesus in the face in the form of His mother and others that had joined her in service. *Jesus, they have no wine, what are we going to do about it?* This is ministry from the heart of God, dressed in the wrong clothes with your good shoes on, but yet there is an immediate need. No, it cannot wait a moment longer. We need a remedy now! Are you willing to help now?

Jesus did not waver in his response to his mother. "My time has not come." I'm sure the air rushed out of those listening, but not his mother. She turned on her heel and boldly told the others to do as He said to do. She was confident of her Son. She knew His heart; she knew He saw a need and would not idly stand by and do nothing. How it must grieve the heart of God when in our possession, in the power of our hands, we can be the answer to another's need and yet we tell them: *No, my time has not come. No I do not have time, I've got things that I have to do. No not now, I am not even on duty, it is his responsibility. You want what now? No, I can't, I'm not even clocked in yet. OR, no I can't, I clocked out ten minutes ago.* Jesus is the best example we could ever find because throughout scripture he gives us examples of how to be a better servant to humanity. Allow me to extend an invitation to any of you that read this book. The next time you see a need that you have the slightest ability to change for the better, even if it is at the worst possible time, be the one to be a miracle worker. It may not be turning water into wine. It may not be some manifest abnormality, but know this one thing - what you do for those that cannot do for themselves will be a miracle of great significance to them.

Let us not get caught in the 'pass the buck' syndrome, always stating we don't have enough time and someone else will do it. It is possible that if you don't, no one will either.

The second possible reason why Jesus says that His time has not come yet performs this miracle, is his "perfection." As simple, yet complex, as this explanation is, God is a God of precise detail. We are living in a time when everything is rounded off at the edges. We are living in a society where "what will be, will be," a cause and effect society where if it feels good, just do it. There is no restraint, just go! Just feel good about *you*. Make yourself happy and forget

21

about others. Even if it's wrong, just be happy! I can tell you that living in Christ will not always make you feel happy! Trials and tribulations that arise from time to time in a believer's life do not always put a smile on your face and bring about feelings of happiness. Suffering is not a happy feeling. Joy and happiness are not the same. The Joy of the Lord is our strength. In the worst of times he is our strength, and our joy is knowing that this too shall pass. Many would say, "B*eing in 'this thing that I'm in' does not make me happy."*

We can be encouraged, even in bleak times, by God's words!

But do not rejoice, o my enemies, though I fall I shall arise again. Micah 7:8

That is my Joy: the Lord is on my side.

I want you to read this simple yet profound truth that we have all but forgotten in our contemporary society, a passage that has eternal implications.

But before all things, my brothers, do not swear; neither by the heaven nor by the earth, nor any other oath. But let your yes be yes, and your no, no, lest you fall into condemnation. James 5:12

Jesus does not round off the edges. His yes is yes, and His no means no. We cannot wear Him down with our coming and begging to get something that is not within His will. In the past we have heard to be careful what we pray for. I propose to you that our heavenly Father has such a love for us and has no desire to set us up for failure so we can learn lessons. I need to tell you that God wants you to succeed, and He is not going to let the enemy pillage your life for one moment. The ministry of Jesus was not a ministry of compromise. It was a ministry of perfection and precise timing. Jesus is a God of perfection and if we follow His plan we will succeed in any area of our life. Furthermore, we must make our yes be yes, and our no be no. No more rounding off the edges. Jesus was not going to be moved out of his time. Although Jesus had compassion, and though he felt for those who were attending the wedding ceremony, at that exact moment his time had not yet come.

Jesus was on a timetable from the Father and if He moved out of the time and plan he was given, the plan would not have been fulfilled. Let me speak clearly. God wants us to follow the words that He speaks to the fullest. With no implications to living under the law, I am speaking of obedience to the word, will, and voice of the Father. The father had given Jesus His plan. Remember He told us in the word that He came to do the will of the Father. If He was to deviate from that plan it was rebellion, and otherwise would have led to ultimate failure of the mission. I'm not sure how much we realize that God says what He means, and means what He says. He tells us to let our yes be yes, and our no be no. No more room for wishy-washy, double-minded thinking and talk. God wants us to get rooted in His word and walk it out. Do so under grace and mercy, but still through a life of surrendered obedience out of a love that springs from a heart for Jesus.

Jesus was not going to move one second out of time. *"No I'm not going to mess this up. All humanity rests upon my leadership. "I must stand firm for the Father, even if it means the disappointment of my mother."* He lived a precise life, one within boundaries and a timetable of obedience.

Again, I offer the second possibility being "complete obedience." How many times are you coaxed off your wall? As we see in the story that unfolds in the book of Nehemiah, he has a vision and a heartfelt passion that God has given him for the rebuilding of a once- fortified city of Jerusalem. Now it lies in ruin. He tirelessly worked with a fervor that makes modern building projects pale in comparison. Nehemiah had a plan from God, but now finds himself being pulled on by men with ulterior motives. Time and again they come to him and ask numerous things then make false accusations and threats. However, Nehemiah was determined not to be denied seeing what the Lord has placed in his heart come to completion. The Lord placed deep within Nehemiah's spirit a timetable. Although there were some who tried to stop Nehemiah's work, it ultimately came from the heart of the Lord and could not be stopped.

The word of God says that with a sword in one hand and a hammer in another he built, day after day he built, with others who caught the vision and within 52 days the walls were rebuilt.

I propose to you that "it's all about time" with the Lord. As long as we are following where the Lord leads we are neither behind nor ahead of the Lord. It is all about time, and He will see the plans that He has for us and his kingdom come to pass. Jesus operates within time. The birth of our world, as well as the first and second coming of Christ, all operate within the timing of the Lord. Jesus was disciplined, as was Nehemiah. I believe that same call to live a steadfast life, always abounding in the work of the Lord, still goes out to this day. Don't be swayed by circumstance. Don't be discouraged by the faces and the voice that try to hinder, stop, or just simply confuse the work of the Lord. Follow his plan and stay on God's time and you will see the fruit of your determination come to pass.

There has been a lot of discussion about time and its significance in our life - in our ministries and simply, in the plans for His kingdom. Time is a term that escapes our understanding. Why is it that some years creep by and others seem to have their cosmic brakes stuck on? There are years when it seems we awaken and it is spring, and sleep, then we arise, and it is winter. Still, one fact remains: God determines how much time we have to use. Our days are numbered. No one knows the day they will leave this earth, whether by way of the grave, or by way of a heavenly catching away. We must utilize each day given to us. The present season can be hindered by time in the past. If we are not careful we can lose time by holding on to time that has already passed. The past can hurt - past wounds, past offenses, and the list could go on without end. This is not the Lord's pattern for us to live by, nor is it His best for our life. The pattern the Lord sets in the second chapter of John is one of looking toward a time that **is**, and lies ahead. Jesus evaluated the time based on where He was and where He was going.

Jesus had a destiny of the cross; he had to evaluate the time based off the timetable from the Father. Jesus had to ask the question: *Would performing this miracle right here, right now, hinder me from my destiny and my mission?* Jesus was a master of evaluating the time. I believe if we could better discern the time and the season we are in, we would find there are indicators that are directly related that help to save time and better utilize our energy in our present season. We must, as children of God, evaluate every situation with the knowledge that decision-making can hinder our calling and purpose. We cannot make permanent decisions based on temporary situations. The enemy of our soul wants to make a difficult season appear permanent. This is not the case. It is a season, and they *do* change.

Lastly, after examining this miracle dealing with time, let's look at a directive that Jesus gives about this subject.

> *He answered and said to them, when it is evening, you say, fair weather; for the sky is red. And in the morning, foul weather today; for the sky is red and gloomy. Hypocrites! You can discern the face of the sky, but you cannot see the signs of the times! Matthew 16:2-3*

Jesus is drawing attention to the importance of seeing time where it is and where it is not. Our time here on earth is limited, and we must not live like we have an endless supply.

> *Who do not know of the morrow. For what is your life? For it is a vapor, which appears for a little time, and then disappears. James 4:14*

Jesus also draws our attention to the fact that not only do we have but also a short time, but all signs point to a quickening, or a wrapping up of time, as we know it. Those trying to back Jesus into a corner and trap Him that they might have Him tried on treason missed the topic of time. They knew when seasons and days changed, but they did not see what *spiritual* time it was. They missed their time. Jesus was with them in their very midst and they missed what they had been waiting for.

> *And as He drew near, He beheld the city and wept over it, saying, If you had known, even you, even at least in this*

day of yours, the things for your peace! But now they are hidden from your eyes. For the days will come on you that your enemies will raise up a rampart to you, and will surround you, and will keep you in on every side. And they will tear you down, and your children within you, and will not leave a stone on a stone because you did not know the time of your visitation. Luke 19:41-44

What a frightful thought to imagine the possibility of having among us, yet missing, the promise from the father. We had the answer to our question, and we had the fulfillment of our dreams among us, but somehow missed Him. We had all that we ever could ask for, only to miss our God given time. It is possible for us to miss our season; we can miss even what we have prayed many years for. Let us not be caught sleeping or inattentive when Jesus comes on the scene in our life.

Jesus wept when He rode into Jerusalem for He knew that they would reject Him, cast Him down, and trample His love underfoot. Great sorrow He must have felt that day at their impending loss. His grief was not based out of anger, but Love for them. How much louder could He shout it? How much longer would He have to dwell with them in order that their eyes are opened? Three and a half years of public ministry is all He was allotted to give. Any more, and familiarity would have set in. Can you hear the voices: *O that is that Jesus guy. I've seen him before; I've seen that before I've heard that before.* Jesus had a window of time to move in. Jerusalem had a window of time to accept Him and they missed their time with the King. Let us not miss our time. Let us not be asleep at the wheel.

This also, knowing the time, that it is already time to awake out of sleep; for now our salvation is nearer than when we believed. Romans 13:11

Time is quickly coming to an end and we must follow the pattern of Jesus by discerning the time and looking to Him to lead us to his perfect place in time.

"It's All about Time"

Chapter 2

Tying the Knot

I find it indicative that Jesus chose His first public miracle to be at a marriage ceremony. As previously stated, in all that happened in the life of Jesus we see how nothing He did or accomplished was by happenstance. Jesus chose the timing of His first miracle for the world to see and scribes to record. He did so in relation directly to whom He was and to what He had come to accomplish on earth. In this chapter we will examine and see the correlation of His ministry, His Father, humanity, and the church as it relates to the covenant of marriage.

The Law of Firsts:

In beginning this discussion, I would like to present some passages to establish the Law of Firsts.

> *Who has planned and done it, calling forth the generations from the beginning? I, Jehovah, am the first and the last; I am He. Isaiah 41:4*

> *I am the Alpha and the Omega, the Beginning and the Ending, the First and the Last. Revelations 22:13*

No one can lay claim to being first except Jesus the Christ. He is the Alpha and the Omega, the beginning and the end, the first and the last. Nothing was before, nor will there be anything after Him. God, who had no beginning or end, in direct relation to our first chapter, knows no time. He has no boundaries limiting him except what is worked out in His own council and will. The biblical Law of Firsts says that God originates and institutes His will for

27

mankind. We were created for worship. A desire that God had was to create man in His likeness that He might have communion or fellowship with him. God desires, still today, our worship and fellowship. Further, we see in these passages that it is deeper than surface communication; what is desired from him is an intimate relationship. This relationship is one that borders on the likeness of marriage.

Time spent and time shared, private time, which is only between two who have become one - this is a relationship that goes much deeper than dating, and further still than the limits of marriage. People marry, then a spouse dies and the other often remarries. As blessed as marriage is, there are limits. Remember, I said this relationship desired by God borders on marriage, or have some likeness and privileges of marriage. God wants a lasting, meaningful relationship that carries long into eternity with no limits of death.

> *For you shall worship no other god. For Jehovah, whose name is Jealous, is a jealous God; Exodus 34:14*

> *For Jehovah your God is a consuming fire, a jealous God. Deuteronomy 4:24*

I love this simple definition of the word Jealousy: *intolerant of unfaithfulness or rivalry.*

The Lord our God did not create us, then to compete for our affection or for us to have more meaningful unity with anything or anyone but Himself. No, the Lord chose from the Law of Firsts that we are to be loyal to Him. We are to be obedient to His will and to His kingdom first, and everything else takes a back seat. We are told to seek the kingdom of heaven first, and His righteousness, and everything else will fall into place. Through Christ's Law of Firsts, He tells us that we are His *first*, and He shares our affection with no other.

The Lord choosing to perform His first miracle at a wedding is supposed to represent a first and lasting relationship - one that is intended to be for life. We see the pattern begin to emerge in the perfection of the Lord, just how precise His miracle was and what it fulfilled, and what is accomplished on this earth. Though it was His first miracle, still today we talk and study it at great length.

Let me share with you some more passages about our Christ and how important the Law of Firsts is.

> *For whom He foreknew, He also predestinated to be conformed to the image of His Son, for Him to be the First-born among many brothers. Romans 8:29*

I will talk at length about the law of the firstborn, but let's read and examine this passage:

> *And he took Mary his betrothed wife, being with child. And while they were there, the days for her deliverance were fulfilled. And she brought forth her son, the <u>First-born</u>, and wrapped Him, and laid Him in a manger- because there was no room for them in the inn. Luke 2:5-7*

The power that came in the life of Christ was fulfilled in the Law of Firsts. The angel Gabriel came to Mary and told her what was about to take place in her life, and all that the child would accomplish. Jesus was the One of promise. The promise that was spoken over the Christ was that He would sit upon the throne of David. On the throne of the king, only the first-born son had the authority or first rights to be seated. The angel told Mary she would give birth and He would be called Son of the highest. All power and authority would rest upon the first-born son. The significance of the first was vital and important.

Woven throughout the word of God we find the theme of redemption. God is always showing His desire of redemption in spite of sin and rebellion. God desires that He provide a means of redemption. We read it was the woman who first was deceived by the serpent in the Garden of Eden. Next, we read of Eve coaxing her husband to eat the fruit that was forbidden. This seemingly simple sin would lead to the fall of mankind. Now we find Jesus' first great public miracle unfolding with a woman as a main player. A woman is now the one coming to Jesus concerning the lack of wine. Not just any ordinary woman, but one who was pure, one who was holy, one who was favored highly among women (Mary). God is allowing her to be a part of redemption by dealing in a matter of the fruit of the vine. The first time woman was mentioned dealing with fruit was from a forbidden tree, a tree that they were not allowed eating from. They had access to every tree in the garden except this one. It was because of a desire she had. This desire was for the wrong reasons, an inner lust that she had for fruit that was not good for her. This was a desire that was driven by the inner workings of carnality. The next time we read of a woman and fruit is again from desire, yet from a completely different perspective. Now, she does not desire the fruit of the vine for herself but rather for those who had come to celebrate the wedding. The first time she listened to Satan, and now a woman who was pure and determined says, "I'm not only going to listen to the Lord I am going to tell others to listen to Him as well." She tells others do what He says to do. The first time she missed it. The second, she got it right!

A chance at redemption, God is a redeeming God. Though we stumble and fall He is there to pick us up, stand us back on our feet, and provide opportunities to get it right. I rejoice in the fact that Mary is not as concerned with herself as much as she was others. I am sure people had come from near and far. What a waste it would have been to only celebrate with mere water. The wine was as much a part of the celebration as the fellowship and the food. The cost of partaking of this fruit would only come through a crushing or a bruising. We will cover wine in a later chapter, but I would like you to know that this miracle was a direct correlation to what would transpire in a supernatural way in the death of Jesus on the cross. In Jesus' death it required a bruising and a crushing, but not as in the making of wine which is a natural process. The power of death, burial, and resurrection would require a supernatural occurrence, capable only of the first and last God, the one and only God. Natural wine can be pressed out of the grape, the blood of the grape can be forced to give of its life, but Jesus had to lay down His life voluntarily. No one could take it. He had to give it. Jesus had to go through the same natural process, yet it produced a supernatural occurrence. In doing so it provided the chance at eternal life for humanity. Jesus would turn the water into wine in a supernatural occurrence that no one could deny. Never again would anyone be able to deny that the Son of the living God had come and was living among him or her.

The Law of Firsts tells us that we are to give of our first fruits. It is an important matter that you give away the first of what you have labored months to produce. Sweat, countless hours of caring, and then you're to give away the first of what it brings forth. There is power in the Law of Firsts. I believe whole-heartedly that the Lord was willing to show through this profound miracle that it would directly benefit those who would attend the wedding feast. This great and awesome miracle would bless many that had come. His first miracle, the first of many to come, would benefit no *one* person, yet it would supply above and beyond for all those present desires. The miracle was not for all; it was not for the masses. It was for those who had attended, as many were invited. Let us draw from a direct passage that mirrors the present passage.

In the gospel of Matthew, the 22nd chapter, Jesus tells yet another parable relating to the kingdom of Heaven and its likeness. The King had a wedding arranged for his son and a bride-to-be. Not just any certain one, but one that was arranged and chosen especially for his son. The thought of an arranged marriage to a complete stranger is appalling to most. An arranged marriage carries a weight of significance in our relation to the first miracle. A bride-to-be was chosen, and a knot was to be tied. This bride was chosen for her position and the addition she would make to the king's kingdom. We, the church, are the bride of Christ, a chosen generation, and a royal priesthood. We are handpicked from the Lord. Father God has arranged a wedding for His son to the bride that was chosen. Not at random or just in passing for her good looks, but more specifically, out of a deep love for us, for humanity He did choose.

For God so loved the word he gave his only begotten son. John 3:16

His only begotten Son, His first Son, He gave away to us to the world. For the redemption of all mankind he gave away His first. Those who were willing to come attended the wedding feast in Matthew 22. Invitations went out left and right, yet those who were invited did not respond to the call. They simply did not want to be a part of the wedding feast. I find it ironic that it paints the picture that they were so wrapped up with themselves that they ignored a blessing. And what were they doing to not even consider the possible benefits that were made available to them by attending the wedding feast of the King? Oh my goodness! How could they overlook the opportunity of a lifetime being a part of a dinner with the king and his royal court at the royal palace? What a missed opportunity that passed them by! The king didn't take too kindly to their lack of cordialness, nor their impropriety and lack of respect. They failed to answer a call from the king whether it was in the form of an invitation or letter of demanded presence. Shouldn't we also take note, not to overlook or disrespect an invitation from the King? What an honor to have been thought of. What a delight to know that royalty has my name, address, and number!

The word of God plainly states that many are called, but few are chosen. The chosen are those who answer the call - not only do they receive the invitation, but they act upon it and prepare to attend such a royal, festive event. Let us take notice that the call is going out all across this land - a call to arms spiritually, a call to duty, and a call to the marriage supper of the Lamb. Will we answer? Will we respond to the call and show up at the appointed hour? There were many who did not, and the king was offended. He was not willing to sit idly by and allow his name and his kingdom to be shown such disgrace. First, an invitation was sent out. Then it was rejected. Now an order is sent out for their lives to be taken. Great allegiance to the Lord of Host is required! Such privilege He offers, such an honor it is to be a part of such a Joyous event. Yet, so many refused, and being that our King is a jealous God, He requires obedience to His call and to His invitation.

Distressing, it is, to know the king had to send out his servants to pull strangers off the street so the palace halls would be filled with guests. Heartbreaking to say, this is the church of Christ at times. He has so many that know Him, yet they are nowhere to be found when needed, and when it counts. It is true... we have the faithful few. This is good. They will receive their reward, a royal crown. However, the Lord tells us in His word, He desires that none perish, but all come to the knowledge of Him and His saving grace. This Christendom that we partake in is not an exclusive club reserved for the elite, wealthy intellectuals of the day. No. To the contrary, it is an open-ended invitation to all humanity. The call trumpets piercingly. Come and dine! You may feast at Jesus' table continually without reserve. Still, we have countless no shows. How disheartening it must have been to the king. How humiliated he must have felt to go so completely out of his way, only to have those who should esteem him show absolute insolence for him and his royal family.

This was not a workday, it was not an order to police call the palace grounds. This was of great privilege to be called to such an esteemed occasion in the life of the king and his royal family. To have been a guest was a great honor. Word was sent to the king's friends and those who were on the king's books, yet they acted as if they didn't know who he was. For Pete's sake!

This is the king, and they ignore his invitation?

Read this familiar passage and notice the similarities.

He was in the world, and the world was made by him, and the world knew him not. John 1:10

We are limited in our own personal lives of the few and proud who remain faithful "through the thick and the thin." Plainly put, it is rare to have a companion (friend) that is with us, and partakes in our times of joys, down setting and disappointments. Life at its best will rarely produce more than a handful of those who come to our aid and call. I think that we look too much at what we do not have and revert to the 'grass is greener in the other field' mentality. Few can honestly say that they have no friends. At the very least, we can say with confidence that Jesus is our friend. Yes, going beyond those limitations, His word says he is a friend that sticks or stays closer than a brother.

33

What a thought - He will not only stay, but stick close to us like an adhesive - sticking close to us or on us. Jesus, speaking in not only word, but deed, says, "Hey I'm here, I'm not going anywhere; I've got your back. I know that the cards are stacked against you, but it is okay! You're not alone. I'm with you. Remember my word says that two is better than one. You don't have to go this alone. I'll be with you; I'll never leave you, Lo, even to the ends of the Earth. That's right! You and I - hand in hand. I will even lead the way. You don't have to try to figure it out. I'll be your guide, I'll be your helper, and if it gets rough along the way, I'll comfort you and hold you through life's greatest trials. Friends? Oh yes, you bet I am! I will be your life's greatest companion. Just stick with me while I stick with you."

At times, those who should show the greatest affection to the King are the ones who forget they have a personal relationship with the King. He, having been among us, having walked, talked, slept and ate, and is the same Jesus who invested His life into the fabric of our being is the One most often shunned and ignored when the call is given. "Hey, I have a royal feast Tuesday at 3pm." "Sorry I can't make it. I have a prior arrangement, maybe next time." "Hey can you meet me there at 4? I really would like to share this with you." "No, sorry, I've got to catch a flight to Seattle. You know I have an important interview and if I miss this one we could lose the account." Hear the heart of God as He asks this in reply. "Lose the account. What about you're calling? What about your soul? *For what does it prophet a man if he gains the whole world yet loses his soul.* (See Mark 8:26)

I dare say, at times, all of us, including yours truly, have taken the high road in the calling of the Lord. We look for a more appropriate time or a more suitable circumstance to simply do what we were created to do. I believe that it is a bi-situational problem - the first being *perspective*, and second being *priorities*. If perspective gets out of balance, we think that our private life must first be attended to, and then our spiritual life will happen. Truth is, the word tells us that while we were yet sinners, Christ died for us, the ungodly. If we were to change lenses and look at the word of God, we would clearly see that the number one view we should have is that of Christ's importance. Let's do an adjustment on our spiritual time, our spiritual walk, our life of devotion and fellowship with the Lord. Then when we begin to place God first, the second of the two naturally will occur.

Let me explain. Our perspective must change first, or our mind must change. Our mind is not saved - our spirit man is saved or quickened. The word of God tells us to put on the mind of Christ. Or, let me put it this way, to think the way Christ thinks. We do this by first reading, meditating, and studying the word of God. By doing so, we begin to learn the language of God. We begin to learn how He thinks, how He feels, how He loves, and basically how He desires us to see things as He does. Our second of the two cannot change until our perspective changes. When our view of God, his will, and his word change, then we begin to realign our priorities and act on the knowledge he has imparted.

Once our thinking is realigned to the God-way of thinking, we awaken to the understanding that our first priority should be to please the Lord by having a continual faith in Him. *For without faith it is impossible to please God, for those who come to him must believe that he is and he is a rewarder of those who diligently seek him. Hebrews 11:6*

Far more than just beginning in the faith, but continuing in the faith until the end is what is needed. Furthermore, not only continuing in the faith, but also ending in the faith is God's greatest desire for our life. The word of God tells us that toward the end of times, because iniquity or sin abounds, the love of many will grow cold. (*Matthew 24:12*)

There must be something that rises up within us that says, "This invitation that was sent to me is not merely to some simple event, but is a high calling from the King. It is of the highest importance! This is a glorious occasion of the King's son tying the knot and my attendance is needed and requested."

I will not take lightly the invitation sent to me. Not only will I be there, but also I will show up early in my best formal wear. I will arrive early, and upon my arrival I will ask if my services can be of use. The word of God says that Jesus did not come to be served, but to serve. *"Yes, I thank you for your offering of fine drink and hors d'oeuvres, but my gospel says it is better to give than it is to receive. Here, let me carry that tray for you, let me pour the wine, let me carry your coat and hat."*

So much planning goes into the "tying of the knot!" I am aware that some couples run off to some bordering state or some far away land and abruptly elope, but that is not the best decision for two that God has chosen to spend the rest of their lives together. To the contrary, it should be well thought out. It should be well planned. After all, the wedding ceremony is as much for the enjoyment of those attending as it is the indulgence of those exchanging vows. Give it your best! Spare nothing! It should only happen once in a lifetime. Our Christ is this way. He has been courting the church - His bride - and on a date that is well thought out, well planned, we are given an invitation to attend this glorious day. This will be a day of matchless grandeur and celebration - a wedding ceremony as never before and never after. The marriage supper of the Lamb!

> *And I heard as the sound of a great multitude, and as the sound of many waters, and as the sound of strong thunders, saying, Hallelujah! For the Lord God omnipotent reigns! Let us be glad and rejoice and we will give glory to Him. For the marriage of the Lamb has come, and His wife has prepared herself. And to her was granted that she should be arrayed in fine linen, clean and white. For the fine linen is the righteousness of the saints. And he said to me, Write, Blessed are those who have been called to the marriage supper of the Lamb. And he said to me, These are the true sayings of God. Revelations 19:6-9*

What an awesome time in the Lord to hear the sound of that great multitude of created beings. Gathered there will be Angels and humanity together alike, the rocks singing, the trees of heaven sounding with a great noise at the marriage supper of the Lamb.

Notice what is stated in verse 9 of the passage we just read. Blessed are those who have been called to the marriage supper. A central theme that runs through the word of God often overlooked, yet God allowing us to see, is the privilege of those being called to this great event. This is not a symbolic word picture or a play toward the visual of our mind; this is a literal event that will take place. We will see manifested before our eyes, this day, the ordained bride of Christ marry its groom, Jesus Christ. What a privilege we are given - an invitation to that wondrous union of Christ and the church becoming one. Blessed are those who have been called. Saints of God - we are truly blessed to have the calling that we do. We are blessed that we will do more than see it on the TV news or read it in the paper. Far greater than that, we can be there! We can be an honored guest. All we need to do is to answer the call and invoke the privilege of the written invitation.

The second chapter of the gospel of John is the heart of this book and where it was taken from. We read of Jesus performing a miracle at a wedding ceremony. I need to draw your attention to verse 2; it says '*now both Jesus and His Disciples were invited to the wedding.*' Can you begin to see the importance of the invitation? Jesus did not just stumble into this wedding. He was *invited*. An invitation was extended not only to him, but also to his disciples.

> *For the promise is to you and to your children, and to all those afar off, as many as the Lord our God shall call.*
> *Acts 2:39*

The Lord has, in His mind, a people - long before they arrive to earth through woman. He has them. He has you in His thoughts, and He extends an invitation to you long before you can hear His voice. The Lord has called. The Lord is calling even now. This is a promise of life, a promise of hope, a promise of walking, talking and simply being with Christ for all eternity. The importance of the invitation is vital, it has been *given*. "*Come to Me all you who labor and are heavy laden, and I will give you rest*". *Matthew 11:28*

Can you hear the call? Can you hear the pleading in the voice of the Living God? *"I know it has been hard. I know it has been a difficult season and a harsh winter. But come, come while there is time. Come! The table is set, and the chair has your name on it. I've reserved for you a special seat by me, come set at the finest table ever prepared, you are a part of my family. Yes it is my son's wedding and I know that it is his special day but I want you close to me, close so you can enjoy this special day with me. Please don't delay, please don't refuse me your presence, this is a once in a life time occasions, will you share it with me?"*

Jesus and His disciples where invited and they answered the call. The disciples called Him "Raboni," or master teacher. Jesus was a teacher by nature. His cousin John the Baptist was a bold communicator, preaching to the top of his lung capacity. Jesus, though passionate in His speech and delivery, was a teacher. Teachers are always on the lookout for an object lesson to administer to their students. Out the window goes the notion that He needed to be in a classroom setting: no, not this Jesus. Jesus would, at the drop of a hat, use anything and everything around Him to teach His eager students. Noting was exempt from being used as subject matter for one of Jesus' essential lessons. Jesus was using real-time teaching methods to instruct His Disciples on how to live, act, and administer His gospel. Remember, He is not just providing instruction for their leisure; He is imparting knowledge on an accelerated level. Jesus was on a timetable. I've talked about time a lot thus far, and here He is using every moment possible to teach and train his students. It was a fact that at that moment the understanding escaped them - that this masterful teacher would soon leave them, and they would have to follow what He had imparted into them and rely on the leading of the Holy Spirit.

This was more than a happy trip to a wedding ceremony. It was more than a killing of time. Far exceeding the purpose of turning water into wine, this was a lesson on service. It was a lesson about having an out of body experience (a selfless experience) and giving of one's time to another. Jesus had many reasons for attending the wedding.

Let's think of others even though we are busy; let's change the outcome of a bad day for someone if it's within our power to do so. Here Peter, James, and John... Look at how we are to be compassionate toward even the simple feelings of others. Yes, we are called to be agents of change. Look beyond me turning this water into wine, look past the awed look on the faces of the guests, look past the glimmer in the moment. Look at how their countenance was lifted when I operated in my gifting, and how it changed their whole outlook; not for a moment but for the remainder of time here. We have four more days left of this celebration. Can you see how many would have left in discouragement had we not come and intervened? Look at how doing just a simple matter, in my opinion, can change their entire outlook.

A lesson indeed, Jesus, simply by example and acting (or doing), was teaching. A lesson for us to glean from - we teach by our service. Others lives are impacted and changed for the better when we act (or do) in our God-given calling and gifting.

The call is not for us, and the gifts are not for our own consumption. They are for the whole of humanity. God calls us; God wires us so we might be a blessing to a hurting humanity. This is a humanity who has lost hope, given up, and sits by the curb of life - a People who feel like they came to a good thing, only for the good stuff to have run out and they are left with only empty vessels. The vine withered, the pitcher has run dry, and the supply of wine is spent. Let us pack our bags and grab our coats. The party is over. Unplug the music, fold up the chairs, and turn off the light. The show is over. *We have run out!*

This feeling has infested humanity. They sit with no hope, placing all their joy in the abundance of wine. When it is depleted, they feel as if they have no worth, have zero value, and can't even smile. Listen to what Jesus has to say about this very subject.

For the kingdom of God is not eating and drinking, but righteousness and peace and joy in the Holy Spirit. Romans 14:17

At times the wine does run dry. At times the well runs dry, and at times life seems to be a wilderness experience. However, one fact remains. Our trust and hope must remain in the One who turns water into wine.

> *If I have made gold my hope, or have called fine gold my trust; if I rejoiced because my wealth was great, and because my hand had gotten much; if I looked to the light when it shone, or the moon walking in brightness, and my heart has been secretly enticed, or my mouth has kissed my hand; this also would be an iniquity for the judges; for I would have denied the God above.* Job 31:24-28

Saints of God, our hope can only be in the hand of the Giver of all good things. Not in food or drink, not in riches, fame, position or power.

> *The grass withers, the flower fades; but the Word of our God shall stand forever. Isaiah 40:8*

Riches come and go, and fame comes and leaves as fast as it came. Even rivers at times dry up, but Jesus and His presence and power will sustain us for all eternity.

> *My hope is built on nothing less than Jesus' blood and righteousness. I dare not trust the sweetest frame, but wholly lean on Jesus' name. On Christ the solid rock I stand, all other ground is sinking sand; all other ground is sinking sand.*

What heartache, Jesus the Son of the living God is in the house and all that they are concerned with is wine? Rush, rush, hurry, hurry - we too get disorientated with what really matters in life. Hear the truths out of this text and I think we can apply them somewhere in our lives. Jesus was invited, but not asked, to be head of the wedding. Man is the head of woman as Christ is head of the church. Should he not also be head of our marriages, to the point of leading the ceremony and not merely being invited? Scripture still instructs us not to be unequally yoked, not marrying unbelievers.

Do not be unequally yoked together with unbelievers; for what fellowship does righteousness have with lawlessness? And what partnership does light have with darkness? 2 Corinthians 6:14

Ouch! Not my ideas or instruction, but right from the word of God, who we marry is important. Should Christ not be the center? Marrying an unbeliever allows the world to come into a perfect chemistry that the Lord has established in your life. Yoking to an unbeliever taints the pureness of the relationship God has established with you. The one who is unsaved has their own interests in mind, and the mind of Christ is nowhere to be found. The individual who is saved has the mind to please their spouse, and God takes a backseat - or in other words, is only invited to the wedding - not heading it up or leading. A rush of air expels from the heart of the one who has found themselves trapped by the attraction of flesh and a relationship has forged. The daunting question looms front and center, "What do I do now?"

As plainly as it can be asked, "Do you want a measure of pain now or immeasurable pain later by not following Gods pattern?" Yes, we know of a few success stories of a Christian marrying the unsaved, then the other coming to Christ. However, you do not know the whole story, or what transpired behind closed doors for this to happen. It simply is not worth the risk of your joy, peace, and salvation by violating God's principles. When we do, they are pain-filled reminders that He desires to be number one in our life. God does not only want to be *invited*, he wants to be in charge.

God does not want to do tricks at your wedding. He wants to cover your wedding. He wants to be Lord and to have Lordship over your wedding and marriage. Some may ask, "Okay I am now born again. What am I supposed to do, leave my spouse?" No, certainly not. The word of God says that the believer sanctifies the marriage bed. (See 1Chorinithians 7) If they will stay after your salvation, then you are to stay. The word says that a possibility remains that your Christian witness will win them to Christ. I would

41

like to once again state it is in the Law of Firsts. This very sensitive subject hinges on how your relationship or marriage started.

We see far too many victims succumbing to violating this principle in the word of God. We are living in such a free-for-all society that the notion of "have it my way" seems to reign. I pray that we will begin to step up to the plate and unapologetically proclaim that God still has standards and parameters in how we live our life. The beauty is that it is not a restrictive life, but a life of abundance and freedom in Christ. He is the one who formed and brought us into being, and He knows us better than we know ourselves. Knowing this truth - if anyone knows what is best for our lives He certainly does. The fact is, *He does*. So many times we feel that if we just had this or we just had that, we would be happier and have more joy. At times we push and pry, trying to get that which God never designed for us to have, only to find that what we were pursuing was just an illusion of happiness sent from the enemy to cloud our view of Christ and skew it out of focus. When the focus is off of our Savior and upon our wants, our desires, and us then we have lost sight of who He is and what He wants. Hear the words of the Lord that tell us that there is joy, happiness, and fulfillment in Him; that when we die to self and place Him first, He overwhelmingly makes a way for our personal desires.

Delight yourself also in Jehovah, and He shall give you the desires of your heart. Psalms 37:4

The great exchange - you give Him your life. He then gives it back to you, and with interest. Then, as an added bonus, He grants you your heart's desires. If you put Him first, which is what He wants, then he allows you to have what you want - except better and with more because *His* desires become *yours*; the two coupled is unstoppable. To the contrary, listen to what happens when we refuse the God given process:

For whoever will save his life shall lose it; but whoever shall lose his life for My sake and the gospel's, he shall save it. Mark 8:35

What a frightful thought to have been given a choice, to have known the truth and to have received an invitation, yet you wad it up and toss it in the trash, doing so as if you were throwing away an invitation sent by a troubled cousin. No, this cannot be. It should not be. When the truth is exposed and we reject knowledge, in all our efforts to grip tighter to our life we still lose it. The day is at hand and the time is set. Will you answer the call?

> *For it is impossible for those who were once enlightened, and have tasted of the heavenly gift, and were made partakers of the Holy Spirit, and have tasted the good Word of God and the powers of the world to come, and who have fallen away; it is impossible, I say, to renew them again to repentance, since they crucify the Son of God afresh to themselves and put Him to an open shame. For the earth which drinks in the rain that comes often upon it, and brings forth plants fit for those by whom it is dressed, receives blessing from God. But that which bears thorns and briers is rejected and is a curse, whose end is to be burned. Hebrews 6:4-8*

"*Having tasted of this heavenly gift.*" Oh, taste and see that the Lord is good! Yes, He is good. Jesus is our bread that has come down from heaven. In the wilderness, the children of Israel were to gather this bread from heaven (Manna) only for the present day. Anything extra that was gathered would spoil and right soon if kept overnight. The only exception to the rule was the day before the Sabbath. After all, the Lord would not have His people violate the very law He gave them. This law was of one keeping it holy and labor not on His most holy day. This gives us a glimpse of what is to transpire over and over again in the word of God.

They ran out of wine at the wedding, and then Mary came to Jesus. The Lord desires that we be reliant upon Him, coming to Him for our daily provision. When we run out, He wants us to come to Him, but before the emptying of baskets, He wants us to petition Him. Not just coming to Him in times of famine or in times of emergency, though we can confidently do this; rather He desires us to come to him *before* we run out - long before the meal barrel is depleted. *Lord give me this day my daily bread. Ask, Seek and knock. If we being earthly fathers give good gifts to our children, how be it if we go to our heavenly Father and ask for a fish, will he give us a scorpion? Or we ask for bread, will he give us a stone?* This is not the case with Jehovah Jireh. He is the Lord God that provides. The key lies in coming to Him; our God not only wants our allegiance and our faith, but He wants our complete reliance upon Him. The best example that we have in scripture, that paints all too well the mentality of carnality into the existence and self-reliance of humanity outside of Christ, is found in Luke's gospel.

And He said to them, Watch and keep yourselves from covetousness. For a man's life is not in the abundance of the things which he possesses. And He spoke a parable to them, saying, The ground of a certain rich man brought forth plentifully. And he thought within himself, saying, What shall I do, because I have no room in which to store my fruits? And he said, I will do this. I will pull down my barns and build bigger ones, and I will store all my fruits and my goods there. And I will say to my soul, Soul, you have many goods laid up for many years. Take your ease, eat drink and be merry. But God said to him, Fool! This night your soul shall be required of you, then whose shall be those things which you have prepared? So is he who lays up treasure for himself and is not rich toward God. Luke 12:15-21

Unfortunately, we see this slip into the modern teaching of today. Though I am an advocate and a teacher of the blessed life and prospering of the Lord, we must be very careful to remember just how all of our wealth arrived. Furthermore, listen to this - just how quickly it can disappear is a reminder it did not come from us.

But you shall remember Jehovah your God, for it is He who gives you power to get wealth... Deuteronomy. 8:18

Pickup any newspapers, read any headline, watch any network news, and you will see countless victims of those who put their trust in mammon or systems of the world. The fact is, we

44

cannot pinpoint a reason why it seems that some grow in wealth while others, though they work day and night, never seem to gain ground. It is a mystery to most why all their hard work never seems to pay off. We can be certain following good, sound biblical principles pertaining to wealth greatly improves ones opportunity for increase. However, it does not guarantee that we will see sizable advance in the direction of our hope in this matter. Just ask the Christian businessman who did everything right yet still lost his business due to the recession. Just ask the single mom, or single dad for that matter, and ask them if they have paid their tithes to the Lord and see if most are seeing millionaire status arrive. The paramount truth is, the Lord will bless in this manner whom He chooses to bless. We must leave this in the hands of the Lord. The blessed life is more than what a man possesses. The blessed life is more than riches, wealth, and fame. The blessed life is a wellspring of joy that rises with us each morning - thankful to be alive, for how shall the grave bless His name? Our modern western society has gotten so off track when it comes to the blessings of the Lord. Our focus is building bigger barns to store our bigger harvest of what (our) hands have made. The Lord says what I intended to be a blessing has quickly turned to Idols.

We must thank God for giving us strength to labor, and strong hands to work with. Also, we must truly recognize that God gave us all we have. This is a *heart* matter - a balance of truth in our heart that must stay in balance with the word of God. He will bless us at times beyond our wildest dreams, but when the fulfillment of a dream becomes larger than the love and the spirit of thanksgiving we have for the Fulfiller of the dream, then we have a problem bigger than our blessing. I have already stated this, but it is worth mentioning again, "God wants to be number one in our life." This seems so simple a truth, but at times we need a small adjustment to get us back in line with the Lord's Spirit.

We cannot look at what everyone else has with envy and covetousness. If we do so, it will eat away at the relationship we have with our heavenly Father. Over time you will begin to blame Him for your lack of obtaining what you feel you deserve. We must stay humble before God with a thankful heart. He has provided what we have, and He knows our ending as well as our beginning. Our Creator knows what is best for our lives.

And He said to His disciples, Therefore I say to you, Be not anxious as to your life, what you shall eat; nor for the body, what you shall put on. Life is more than food, and the body is more than clothing. Consider the ravens: for they neither sow nor reap, having neither storehouse nor barn, and God feeds them. How much more are you better than the birds? And which of you by being anxious can add one cubit to his stature? If then you are not able to do even the least, why are you anxious about the rest? Consider the lilies, how they grow; they do not toil, they do not spin. And yet I say to you that Solomon in all his glory was not arrayed like one of these. If then God so clothes the grass (which today is in the field, and tomorrow is cast into the oven) how much more will He clothe you, O little-faiths? And do not seek what you shall eat, nor what you shall drink, and stop being in anxiety. For all these things the nations of the world seek after, and your Father knows that you have need of these things. But rather seek the kingdom of God, and all these things shall be added to you. Do not fear, little flock, for it is your Father's good pleasure to give you the kingdom. Luke 12:22-32

I am hard-pressed at times to even put myself in the positions of those who are living in third-world countries. We in America live such insulated lives. Even those in the lower financial brackets of the nation are far better off than those who make their living surviving on mere dollars a week. All the social economic programs that we have here make the quality of living quite comfortable. Even those on public assistance, if careful enough, can afford luxuries that would seem out of reach to those just outside our borders. Still, we never seem to have enough, or are ever satisfied. God does not expect us to "live like a pauper" to be Holy. No, that is far from the truth and is not Christ's point in this passage. God wants us to look to Him and not put our confidence in the flesh, in mammon, in men and the financial system of this world. Neither does He want us pulling our money out of the bank nor horde. Certainly no, Jesus tells us in His word to "occupy until He returns." We need to do business, and we need more Godly leaders in the marketplace. We need those who would help fund and teach others how to be better stewards of the resources God gives.

The Lord is after some people who, if they run out of wine even at the most inconvenient of times, would be willing to serve Him without the luxuries, without the plush, posh amenities of life? These are luxuries that we have begun to expect instead of appreciate. Again, it always points back to the heart. Where is our heart, and in what do we put our faith?

Look around us. Faster, and picking up speed by the day, is a generation that is after wine and after the lavish life that they feel they need. There is nothing wrong with desiring the finer things in life, but when we begin to place a higher priority on the *things* instead of the *King*, we are in trouble. Sometimes I have been blessed above and beyond reason by these simple reminders that have been given me to these Godly principles.

At times they have come from circumstance or obstacles that I have faced. At times they have come from an obvious individual living outside the Kingdom of Christ that reminds me what is really important, as they place such priority on that which will fade, moths will eat, and rust will destroy. I've been privileged at times to receive from those who were a real friend and have dared to speak life into me - those saints who have walked before me, who learned the value of seeking the kingdom vs. trophies. We need those who love us enough to ruffle a feather or two and help direct us back on the right path. Yes, we need those who will help steer us away from a path that was only an illusion. The Devil tries to make diversions to get us off the Lord's path. Sometimes we venture off this divine path and need someone's help in redirecting us. Whether by circumstances or a leader of the Lord's choosing, either is effective if we remain sensitive to his voice and leading.

We make the mistake of thinking that when we get a little out of line God slaps us back between the lines, but this simply isn't so.

It is true there is chastening, and yes, there is correcting; true enough, at times it does not feel good. But the reality is, the pain of correction comes as a direct result of our personal sowing where we should not have sown. The Law of sowing and reaping is a painful one if lived outside of what God has blessed. God is our Shepard, He is our teacher, He is our leader, He leads us beside still waters, and He restores our soul. However, if need be, He can use a rod. Did I hear someone say Ouch? I like to say that my parents had instruments of war when it came to correction, whatever they could grab hold of, and then I was fair game to it.

I say that jokingly - they were the best! However, through it all I learned a valuable lesson. No matter what shape, color, or fashion, they *all* were effective instruments. This is God our Father. He knows what is effective, and that is why the psalmist could say with confidence, "It was good that I was afflicted." Situations or people, circumstance or the devil's attack, God can and will use issues to refine us for His purpose and His kingdom.

In Luke 12, Jesus tells His disciples to be anxious for nothing, for no one can add one cubit to his stature for this. Worry and anxiety seem to have taken captive an entire generation. Commercial after commercial has a remedy for your anxiety. Take a pill and change your mood. Depressed? Not a problem. *We've got a cure ... take this pill. Suicidal? - That's okay, take this.* So much of our society has taken the position to look to science to quell all their woes. Not to make light of those who have obvious problems that need medical intervention, but I still see room for God to come back, front and center as our Creator, and the One who knows what ails us. Jesus is still the answer, even though medicine can be very helpful and has been a great blessing to modern society. The last chapter of the book of Daniel tells us that knowledge will increase in the end times. However, society as a whole has turned to medicine as the "cure all," and this is not so. More often than not, medication masks a deeper problem. This is a spiritual problem within man.

Mary coming to Jesus telling him: *"They have no wine, can you make it happen?" Can you do something about it? Jesus can you help them to numb the hour? Can you help bring back a sedative*

48

to this wedding party? Help us hide the pain, help us just for a moment forget about what we went through to get here on this long journey. Help her over there in the corner; help her forget she is the one that wanted to get married instead of her sister. Do you know she has waited for years for a soul mate, then here he comes and now they are getting married? What about her? Can you help him forget that this wedding ceremony has brought back a flood of memories of his marriage gone sour, and she leaving him for another? He had a great wedding party; many came from all over the country to be a part of his wedding. You know they were only married eight months and she left? Jesus can make a little more wine to dull the pain of the loss of them over there. Yes, those on the portico. They lost their son three months ago and she has been in bed since. I am surprised to see them here. It is the first time she has left the house since. Jesus, can you cause a little more wine to flow for him? His nerves flare up at times. You know, a little wine takes the edge off so he can think more clearly. Hey Jesus, what about her? She does much better around a crowd if she has a glass or two.

There are so many scenarios that we could cover where many different applications of this passage apply. Perhaps you could think of one or two as you were reading this paragraph? Maybe you could place yourself in one of these situational scenarios that I just mentioned, or perhaps you know someone that cannot function without some form of chemically altering substance whether it is drink or a pill of some sort? It could possibly be a type of chemical that is not legal - an illicit drug. This type does not stereotype, it affects the rich, the poor, the educated, and those not.

Lying deep within the heart of man is the need for The God of the entire universe. The universe needs Jesus to come and place his healing hands on our life and bring restoration and transformation. Enough prescriptions have been written, enough pills have been downed, and enough drinks have been consumed. We desperately need Jesus! We need leaders to stand up and preach Christ's benefits and not help in the medication of a generation of people. We need a Jesus revolution. We need those who would be willing to reject the report of the medical doctors that says the perfect answer is in a pill, drink or a psychotic mind-altering drug to cure what only Jesus can. I have been speaking for years, as unpopular and politically incorrect, as it may be, that the flood of new diagnoses for personality, mental, and emotional problems originates from the enemy of our soul, Satan. I am baffled at the mainstream church's apathy toward spiritual oppression from the enemy. I am of the belief that a muzzle has been placed on the mouths of those who have a voice to call it what it is. We have a "pandemic of spiritual oppression" (and examining scripture we read of demonic Possession). For far too long, we as the righteousness of God have shied away from applying the full council of God's word to real world problems.

As soon as one begins to call it what it is, they are labeled as a freak and over the top. I feel Jesus longs for a people to proclaim that He came to destroy the works of the Devil. This people will join hand in hand with Christ to do the works he did. People of God, prayer works! There is power and authority in the name of Jesus!

We read through our bible and believe that Jesus is the Son of the living God. We believe that He was crucified, buried, and rose again on the third day. We believe in the gifts of the Spirit, in the institution of the church of Christ. The list could go on without end, yet we skip over the many, many accounts of the direct influence that the enemy of our soul had on people's lives. We read accounts of the man of Gadareia who, even when bound with chains, would break free. Jesus met the man who lived like an animal, was naked and growling like a dog. A word from the Lord and the man was set free. We read of the story of a man coming to Jesus asking for help because a spirit often seized his son and would often throw him in the water and fire trying to kill him. Some say – 'You mean a child was affected by demonic influence?' That sounds like a creepy horror show. Many, and few would like to believe that this could happen.

Today, rampant, we see children walking, standing, and staring into nothingness – their features appearing to be perfectly normal, but labeled with various disease. What is wrong? How can it be that these gifts of God seem to be so out of reach, and are only able to be helped through medication? We do not negate the severe state they are in, nor do we ignore or lessen the feelings of helplessness of the parents who have these children of God in their homes. Still, there lies deeper a sinister plot of the enemy to destroy and harm God's creation. Prescribed without cautions are drugs as lethal cocktails trying to help, at times, in what appears a hopeless plight. This is the same helpless feeling of the man who came to Jesus concerning his son. Many today feel this pain! What do we do? It seems we can get no help. So ready and eager is a doctor with a prescription. Here, take this three times a day. God, help us in our understanding of the frailness of humanity and the need of Your intervention.

This young boy seized and thrown in the fire was also set free by the power of Jesus. People... this same power that freed that young lad is available today. The accounts we read should give us a hint that we can count on healing even for our little ones. Jesus speaks of children often, though Jesus unwed and childless while on this earth in human flesh. Jesus had no children, but Jesus and the father being one understood what it is like being a father. Jesus was the only begotten son of the father. He understood what it was like to have sickness on the back of his son. Even to the point of when sin was placed upon the back of Jesus on the cross he had to turn for not being able to bear the sight of what it did to his son. At times we do not understand why our children go through things that we can't seem to help them with. Jesus understands the hurt and the pain.

Jesus went to great lengths in establishing how much He believed children should be protected. A charge was made that not one of His little ones be offended. If they were, it would be better for that person who committed the offense that a millstone is tied around their neck and they be cast into the sea. In other words, keep your hands off the little ones. They are cherished. Matthew 15:24-28 tells a beautiful story and informs us that healing is the children's bread. God wants his children to be healed. He desires for them to receive healing, rather than shoved in a corner medicated. Jesus then said, "Suffer the little children to come unto Me." He did not want those to push the small ones aside. He cares for our children.

51

Whether it is a physical sickness or a spiritual matter, the Lord desires that all children be whole.

Whole children will grow up to become whole adults. If the enemy can get to our children while they are young and bind them in disease of any sort, he has the greater possibility to keep them bound. Jesus clearly leads the way in praying for them while they are young. Teaching them while they are young, the bible says to train up your child in the way that they should go, and when they are old they will not depart from it. Great importance should be given to our children.

We talk about the possibilities of bodily healing, cancers being healed, tumors disappearing, the lame walking, and the blind seeing. Indeed, this is in the ministry in which God has called us. Still, why do we discount, side step, and ignore the fact that people need as much healing from spiritual sickness as they do for their physical body? God has called us to not only heal the sick in body, but to set the captives free.

I urge those in ministry, as well as laymen, to once again look at the scriptures with me and re-familiarize themselves with the knowledge that humanity is in need of those willing to confront this tough issue. A fact in the life and ministry of Jesus is He encountered this type of demonic occurrence. What makes us think that we will not today?

I like the fact that Jesus did not base His whole ministry on confronting demons as a select few do today. He simply did not skirt the issue; he hit it head on. He brought no extra attention to spiritual wickedness He simply preached the gospel. Whenever the situation did arise, or the devil showed himself, He confronted it. Jesus did not have fear, nor did He fear going to the cross or dealing with demons that impeded His steps to it. In an effort to keep balance, I would like clarify that not all bad situations are the result or cause of demonic spiritual influence. Likewise, not every "acting out" from an individual is of demonic influence; however, there are times that it is not simply the cause of a person's personality or the mood they are in. People are made sick by the enemy's oppression.

I believe God has called us to a life of moderation and balance in our thinking and approach. However, all evil originates from Satan. All evil has its origins from Satan himself, and he uses individuals. We get up in arms over doctors misdiagnosing a sickness or a disease, but the outcry of the church should be about leaders and ministers misdiagnosing problems among God's people. Have we succumbed to the pressure of popularity, bad press, and the threat of lawsuits when we shy from these tough issues affecting Gods People? God has called us to fully administer the graces given to the church for the work of the ministry.

I make these above statements not as accusations but as inquires into a much deeper problem than we realize. I feel most Christian leaders would agree that people do not need a sedative - they need healing!

The title of the chapter is Tying the Knot. We find the setting for a mighty miracle-taking place at a wedding. This is where we would say they "tie the knot." I would like for us to know God is looking for us to tie the knot in more ways than one. Far beyond simply meeting the person of your dreams, settling down and starting a family. Far more than the matter of personal marriage, even though there is nothing wrong with it. The Lord wants us to tie the knot, or simply settle things. He wants us to make a determination to believe Jesus no matter what. "I am going to follow him no matter what. I am going to have faith in him no matter what." We live much, too much, of our life with matters unsettled.

This is like someone in a personal relationship that has gone on for a number of years, and all they do is continue to date and even co-habitat, yet never commit. One party is willing to "tie the knot," but the other only wants the perks of a relationship, never willing to complete what is needed to make the relationship binding. They never "tie the knot." They want the ability to up and leave at any time. "What are you talking about? I can leave if I want. I'm not married to you. You do not own me." This party wants to retain all of the privileges of a self-filled life, but never take responsibility and dying to one's self.

On the other hand, we have the person who is committed to the relationship, but only on the surface. Yes, they are wed on paper, and yes it is legal and binding; but they are no more committed than a man in the moon. Both are dangerous, but the last one is the more dangerous of the two, for the latter of the two has eternal consequences.

Listen to the words of the Lord echoing Isaiah's Prophecy in Matthew 15:8

This people draweth nigh unto me with their mouth, and honoureth me with their lips; but their heart is far from me.

Only in word, never in deed, their words are empty - just expelled air. It is a heart matter that has never been settled. They want the miracles. They want their water turned to wine. They want their eyes opened and their limbs to work as designed; but they don't want the obligation of service to the King. They do not want the "ball and chain" that comes with an oath of covenant. They want to be able to leave at any time with no questions asked. "See you later! I have bigger fish to fry!" Solomon tells us in the book of Ecclesiastics that it is better to never vow a vow, than to vow a vow and break it.

The two uncommitted individuals stated are equally damaging. However, the one who appears to commit and even signs on the dotted line, yet has never really tied the knot, is in danger of greater eternal loss. God is looking for a people who will tie the knot for good, never to be untied. If plans fail, they will still serve Him. If dreams die, still they serve Him. If she left, if he walked out, they will still serve Christ. Through thick and thin the Lord wants people whom he can add to the "Faith Hall of Fame" found in the 11th chapter of Hebrews. You know, the people who died never having received the promise, yet they trusted the Lord. They never received the promise of the Messiah in their generation. They died in the faith of the Lord and had never seen the man called Jesus, yet they believed. What an honor to have tied the knot for their faith in the Lord. Let's take this a step further and hear these words to further instruct us on the importance of tying the knot.

> *Wherefore <u>gird</u> up the loins of your mind, be sober, and hope to the end for the grace that is to be brought unto you at the revelation of Jesus Christ;* 1 Peter 1:13

The word of God tells us to gird up the loins of our mind. This gives implication that we need to tie up, to fasten, and to encircle our mind. We need to set all the doubt aside, and, as pertaining to our faith, we need to tie the knot. We need to wrap our mind around the knowledge of the word of God, tie it up, and then tie the knot. Doing so allows us to stand in the times of circumstances without explanation. Yes, those times that can rock the faith of even the most devout believer. God gives us examples over and over in His word for the strategy to overcome during life's most trying times. Something happens within the spirit of man that quickens even our thinking to the point that makes us appear peculiar to those outside the faith of Christ. We do not react the way the world does to the same similar negative occurrence that happens to all humanity. What separates us from the world is not just our response, but rather our continued course of action or continued course of non-reaction. There is a place in the Lord we can go that allows us to simply maintain a constant, functional faith that transcends human thinking and intellect. As believers, we are subject to events just the same as those outside of Christ. However, we are afforded the ability to lean into, and even rest upon, a Rock - a solid foundation that is unmovable. Jesus the Christ is our Rock, and He is asking us to step into, to lean on, and to rest in His ability to see us through any situation that life would bring our way.

We can, as believers in Christ, get to a place where no matter what happens, we will not be moved from our faith. Though we have emotions and feelings, and to some degree are affected by them, they nevertheless do not rule us. We are consistent in our walk and journey with the Lord. Whether it is or isn't a happy day, we have the knowledge that Jesus is the same in our down setting as in our uprising. Somehow it has slipped into modern teaching that God only favors us and His blessings are resting on us if everything is going right and money is in the bank. This teaching is far from the truth. This is a false belief that God is only blessing you when your days are at their best. God is the God of the peaks and the valleys, and He is the same on top of the mountain as He was in the pit with Joseph. He is the God that was in the Lion's den with Daniel, and the fourth man in the fiery furnace with the three Hebrew boys. God is the God that brought plagues on Egypt, and still brought judgment upon a rebellious nation called Israel. He is God and He is God alone. There was no God before, nor shall there be after. God is from everlasting to everlasting. In addition, He desires that we tie the knot.

> *Wherefore the rather, brethren, give diligence to make your calling and election sure: for if ye do these things, ye shall never fall: 2 Peter 1:10*

Make your calling into Christ sure, and give due diligence to your election by grace into His marvelous light. Once and for all, tie the knot. No more questions in your mind about your faith, or about God's love for you or your place in His kingdom. Upon reading the pages of this book, I pray you feel God's overwhelming acceptance for you. He has called you; He has ransomed you with the price of the blood that he spilled on Calvary's hill. Hear Him calling this day to be transformed in the renewing of your mind. Cast down the lies that you are not good enough, or that you are not qualified enough. Pull down imaginations that you can't live this Christian life. I believe that an alarm is sounding - one that's calling the Saints of God together to strengthen the body of Christ. We can come together to build each other up in the word and spirit of the Lord.

Let it start with you. Maybe you feel like you don't have anyone that gives to you what you need. Maybe you feel like you are the one in need of someone to come to you and to your aid. You may feel like you are sinking and there is no one to throw you a lifeline. If you feel you're the one sinking further away from your first love and joy, I encourage you to tie the knot and hold on. Then when you have caught your breath, when you get your balance and are settled for just a moment, get up while you are still winded a little and do contrary to what the world would do; begin to sow.

In the middle of a famine, God instructed Isaac to sow. At His word, Isaac sowed (planted seed) and in that same year received a hundred fold. Right in the middle of famine, he did the unthinkable; he began to plant seed. Can you hear the voices? "What are you doing Isaac? You better save those seeds until things get better. You know you don't have anything to waste. You're crazy, it has not rained in years and you are going to take the only thing you have left and pour it into to a dry dusty barren ground?" Can you see the crowd gathered around in a big group watching this man drop seed into parched soil?

What separated Isaac from the crowd was his faith and obedience to a word from the Lord. The combination of the two overrides the laws of nature: and in the same year he planted he received a hundred fold in return. The same year as the planting, there was the unending famine; yet he got a return that baffles the mind today, a hundred-fold return.

We are not in, nor do we follow, the economy of the word. We are on God's time and in His economy. If He says plant in a famine, plant. If He tells you to sow into the dust, sow into the dust. Is He not the same God that formed man out of the dust? God has put within us that same creative power that says in the middle of my mess, *I am going to act upon this God given idea. In the middle of a recession, I am going to start my business. I am going to launch out into ministry. You don't have to tell me the economy is bad. I know it all too well. I've lived in this economy but I've gotten a word from the Lord and I'm choosing to believe the Lord instead of what I see. What do I have to lose? I've only just this little left. Hey, I'm going to step out in faith. The weather is not acting right and things are more difficult than they have ever been, but the Lord came to me and told me to plant now and not delay. Yes, I look crazy. Yes, it sounds crazy, but Jesus came to me and told me He would bless what I'm doing, and I choose to believe what He said.*

You may be reading this and find yourself in this position, fresh out of ideas. You might be defeated and discouraged. You gave the best you had and still found yourself coming up empty-handed. If you could block out all the voices of discouragement, you would hear the Lord with a plan, a fresh idea, a strategy, or a master plan for success. When you find yourself in a famine at the bottom, it is a good place to be - a rallying point to regroup and look to the Lord for His help and His strength. There is not a better One to have on your side in a losing season than the Lord. A mighty comeback He has for you, and for everyone around you.

Most would say, "I have nothing left and there is no one to help me. Look, everyone else is dying to." God says – sow. Begin to sow seed. Maybe it is not natural seed. Maybe it has nothing to do with sowing financial seed into the kingdom of God, or maybe it does. Either way, begin to sow or put seed into others' life or in the kingdom. Begin to serve and watch what will happen. At your lowest point, if you begin to look outside yourself and toward God first, then others, there is an exchange that takes place and God begins to cause increase into your life. When you are in a famine and at your lowest place, be determined that you are not going to sit there until you die. Get up, brush yourself off, and look around. What do you have? Use it for the glory of God. If it is a broom, begin to use it for God, sweep someone's porch for him or her. The possibilities are endless. As crazy as it sounds, God will cause blessing to come into your life, and the famine that you were in and everyone else that was with you, God turns it around for both. You stand up in your faith in the best and worst of times; God will use you to be a source and a blessing to others because you were determined to use your faith. Sow your faith into others. You are blessed by becoming a blessing, and it all started with a choice to tie the knot in your heart, your mind, and Spirit.

I implore you today to listen to the words in Hebrews, and be determined from this day forward that you are never again going to allow the enemy to wage a war of doubt and unbelief in your mind. *"From this day forward, I place a guard upon my mind, upon my thoughts, and I chose to believe God. Nothing from this day forward will move me from my faith."*

Therefore we ought to give the more earnest heed to the things which we have heard, lest at any time we should let them slip. Hebrews 2:1

Many scripture passages were written surrounding the sea and sea vessels. We can visualize a picture of masts and sails that must be securely fastened for ensuring proper use of the wind and direction of passage. They must be secured or tied off; there is safety when securement is made. Not only the use of sails and masts, but the use of ropes is of vital importance. Ropes are made to hoist up the sails and for many other purposes. Combining multiple strands of rope makes ropes. In their own individuality, their strength is limited, but woven together their strength is multiplied many times over. The same strand now has the strength of many times its original capacity. Ecclesiastes 4:12 tells of the great strength of this... *and a threefold cord is not quickly broken.* The more strands woven together, the more the strength is increased. This is good and it is encouraging. However, a single factor remains that needs our attention; if the ropes are not tied at the ends first, then the core or the strength is compromised. This happens by the fraying and unraveling of the rope. The ends must be tied up; *tie a knot in the end of the rope!*

In closing this chapter, let me encourage you to not allow all of Christ's teachings to slip through your hands. Never allow that which God has given to you be taken from you by the enemy. Don't let the best God has for you slip - cast off the lies of the enemy. Stand up in your rightful place and rest assured God cares for and loves you. God has great plans still available to you. Tying the knot in your faith, and standing back up and looking toward God, the author and finisher of your faith can overcome failure, faltering, and defeat.

"Tie the knot!"

Chapter 3

A Change for the Better

In this chapter we will look at a "change for the better." When reading of the miracle in the second chapter of John you will discover a needed change. The course was set; there was an outcome that was impending. This outcome was going to run its course with an ending that was least desired. They had run out of wine, and now it seemed the wedding ceremony was to be less the gala than had previously been thought.

Change. This seems to be the word of our generation; everyone talks about change. They have taken this word, carried it around, tossed it about, and thrown it up in the air as if it is a cute baby or an entertaining toy. A gleam in the eye of current politicians is the new buzzword - change. We find that, as with any word, if over-used and abused, it loses its punch and impact. History teaches the outcome when those using such repeated words do not follow through. The target audience is quick to remind and highlight the error. Great heavens - in plain English, what happens is the reciting of swelling, repeated speeches that only amount to volumes of hot, expelled air. They were only words and amounted to nothing more than ear candy.

There is something that lies within all of us that wants to be told what we want to hear. No one wants to hear the truth all the time. Something about our carnal nature wants things rounded off or colored in – 'spiced up' if you will. We, as humanity, lack substance, or that which can be counted on continually. That is why we look for people to tell us what we want to hear. We see things that need to change, but feel we either can't make a difference or we don't have the resources to bring about the necessary change so we remain complacent. In doing so, we often look to others to bring about change *for* us. Adding to this, we have a segment of our population that simply lacks the backbone to initiate anything. This group is always criticizing, but never willing to take appropriate measures to be the catalyst for change. It's easy to look around and notice everything that is wrong. If that is all an individual does, then they are a part of the problem. No one wants to be around someone who notices every ripple, every crack, and every discolored area in another's life.

As you read this, a name may immediately come to mind. You know, the one who always has something to say about everything and everyone - always complaining about everything. You couldn't satisfy them if it was their turn to be number one in the world 7 days a week. No, nothing makes them happy! They are not happy unless they have something to complain about. They are a miserable lot to be around. A great time is happening, everyone is having a good time at the church, house, or party and here they come. It is then everyone stops, and looks at each other as if to say, *"turn out the lights the party is over; get out the umbrellas, here comes a storm."* You know whom I am talking about. This is the person you see coming four aisles away in the store and you duck into the aisle hoping they didn't see you.

"Hey... don't act like you have not done this!"

These people never add value to anything. They're always taking and receiving, never giving, wearing you down with their continued nagging. Life is just simply a bore and bother; they would rather not try. Nothing is ever good enough. These people fight change. They do not want change. They talk as if they do; but when real change comes they fight it tooth and nail. They will be the first to complain, and the first to leave when there is work that needs to be done to implement the change.

I feel a high calling from the Lord to fight within the nature of the individual I just mentioned. Deep within all of us is a fragment that is similar to this; notice I said *fragment*. Humanity

61

hates change, if it is only the style of our hair, our dress, the city in which we live, church we attend, color of paint, or model of car we drive. It could be the restaurant or the item we get off the menu. We all have, to a degree, a part of ourselves that does not like change. Taking it a step further, we have dislikes that we voice from time to time but wait on someone else to fix. The problem is obvious and we address it at times, but then find more pressing matters that demand our time. Can you hear them say, *"After all, it's not going to change anyway?"* God is calling His people to be catalysts for change. There will always be those sitting around whining about how bad everything is. What we need are those willing to stand up and say, "If I don't, they won't."

Negative people can use the demands for change as leverage to gain control for their own personal agendas. They see a problem and rally others around them, and in doing so cause everyone to be in an uproar. They point out problems only to leave the scene with a crowd of angry people, and no direction or plan to fix anything. The only thing they were wanting was attention, center stage, and control. A desire for the change of the good of mankind never really existed; they just wanted to get a charge out of getting everyone else upset.

Not only is change needed, but deeper than that a "change for the better." However, what are needed are those who would go beyond common finger pointing and put on legs of change. We need more than horn blowers or trumpeters. The church is in need of those with hands, fingers, and feet for God. We need those who would not only move into position, but would be willing to help bring about a better change. I hear the words of James 1 as an exhortation goes forth calling us to rise to the occasion and *"be more than Hearers, be doers!"*

This is a fact we know for sure - without fail - there is a God that is not only in heaven, but is among us, and He does not change. We have a direct promise from the Lord. He promises us He will not one day suddenly, metamorphically change into something different than He was originally. *Malachi 3:6 For I am the LORD, I change not....* God let us know, He is not going to change on us. He

62

will not show up one day and us not be able to recognize whom He is. *"I will be the same as the day I introduced myself to you. Rest assured I will be there not just in the beginning but I will remain constant until the very end".*

He is the Lord thy God and He changes not! There is so much that swirls around, comes and goes, yet one fact remains: God never changes. We always speak of this first part of the passage I have shared from Malachi, yet a fact remains in the second half of this passage that needs to be noted. This is the second half; read closely . . . . *therefore ye sons of Jacob are not consumed.*

It is because of a God that changes not that we are not consumed. It is because of the faithfulness of our God that the enemy is not allowed to come into our life and rip us to shreds. I'm not sure about you, but I take great comfort knowing that I don't have to guess what kind of mood Jesus is going to be in.

Can you stop and think for just a moment? Reflect on the relationships that you have had and the ones that you've been a part of and think how many of them changed over time. Sure, there are somewhere you have knowledge and reason for the adverse change. However, for most of them you can't put your finger on what happened, or what went wrong. Everything was going great; the long lasting relationship has been a treasure. Then out of the blue, it happens. There is a change in the atmosphere, and now the relationship that you so cherished is on the brink of disaster. You stand back and ask, "What in the world just happened?" It appears to be un-repairable; that which you cherished has gone up in smoke. People change with no warning; at times they will "flip" out on you. Then you are the one left holding the pieces. You then try to realign your thoughts to make even the slightest sense out of what just happened.

Yes people do change and often we will not have a good answer as to why. We ourselves must stay true to our God ordained calling to be a Christian witness, not reacting out of the flesh. We cannot follow them down the path that would lead to our own failing. You cannot afford to get caught in their undercurrent of strife and resentment. If we keep our life pure and right in the eyes of God, we allow him to intervene, and possibly over time the relationship can be healed. Often though, we have no knowledge why they did what they did, said what they said, or acted so adversely to us. It is a good indicator that something has happened within the heart of the other person. There could be a number of reasons why this could be. I know that you could endlessly list them: offense, misunderstanding, and hurt feelings to name a few. Unfortunately, to them the relationship has become expendable. In these extreme cases there is not much you can do. However, if you value the long lasting relationship, be patient. If you allow God to work through His spirit by prayer, He can do miracles. God is the repair of the breach; He can come into the middle of a storm and change its course and outcome.

This miracle in Cana has everything to do with change. The circumstances changed back and forth almost as fast as a glance in the opposite direction. Everything had started out great; everyone was excited about the wedding. Many months of planning, the invitations went out, everyone had been buzzing for quite some time. There was an excitement about the possibility of these two getting married. They were the dream couple of the decade. These two were the kind of couple that everyone envied. It seemed like they had it all together - the education and the proper upbringing - and it were wonderfully romantic the way they met. It is widely known they had remained true to their future Spouse. Never once had they compromised their beliefs or the saving of one's self for the other. It was overheard once by attendees that their engagement was likened to a match made in heaven. The perfect colors were chosen, and the dress was long and flowing. It was the kind that many a young girl dreams about.

Many people had come from long distances, and now the day had finally arrived. These two are the center of attention without a care in the world, except to gaze in each other's eyes knowing that they will finally be together. No more restrictions, no more having to hold back the passion they shared for each other. This was a much-needed change. They had spent at least a year courting, only getting to spend brief moments together. This put a strain on the affection that each wants to express. No longer will they have to ask permission to be alone; no longer will they have to only exchange private letters sharing the depth of their love for one another. Yes, a much-needed change is coming. They have waited and waited, it seemed the day would never arrive but at last it has come, and they can spend the rest of their days together. They can now choose to be alone in private or in the company of others. The difference now is that it's their choosing; no longer will they have to obtain permission. The bonds or limits have been removed and a new day has dawned.

I hope you can sit back with me and silence your mind for a moment. Focus on the sounds of the day. Can you hear the sounds of horse hooves echoing from the distance as the guests begin to arrive? One after the other the distinguished guests stop in front of this most anticipated event. Handlers, or Equine Valets if you will, wait to lend a hand to a lady or take the reins so the guests only need to worry about straightening themselves. Laughter fills the air, as well as the clamor of hired help rushing here and there making sure all the essentials are in place. This ceremony was not to end in a day's time. This wedding would fulfill the tradition of a Jewish wedding. They will not just stand in front of a Jewish justice of the peace. A bride and groom of notoriety, they will celebrate for the full seven days as is customary. Wedding bells ring signaling the beginning of a lifetime of sharing. I can hear the sound of children running around the yard, in and out of the house, mothers calling after them to settle themselves because the wedding is soon to start. She calls for them to come down from atop the barn for fear of them falling. A father calls out to his son to retrieve the wedding gift he has forgotten from the wagon; *"Oh I hope it is not damaged from the rough ride."* His wife whispers to him, *"I pray we have done enough, there are so many wealthy guests here."* He looks back at her as if to say, *"We've done all we can do; our making it here was trying enough."*

Music begins to fill the air – harps, the flute, drums and crashing cymbals - a festive event has begun. The breeze whips through the open windows, a blending together of nature's sounds and that of man's expression of jubilant heartfelt melodies. As the day begins to draw closer to the evening, the sounds carry even further into the calm Canaan night. The neighing of the horses, the braying of the donkeys, the bleating of sheep, and the barking of dogs all join together to make a musical song of rejoicing. The bride and groom together are ready to make history; they will leave to change the world.

Can you hear with me the open conversations of family talking of the passing of years and how the children have grown? They introduce aunts and uncles to children who now are in their teens. *"Time goes by so fast; we must not wait until a wedding to get together again."* *"We cannot wait every fifteen years to gather together, let us make a pact we will not allow this to ever happen again".* *"Here let's sit down and plan this out right now".* I can hear the story being repeated about the cousin not present that just went through a horrible divorce. There's a drop in the facial expression and gasp of the one receiving such troubling news at such a happy event. Back and forth they swap stories, catching up on life and sharing life events that have transpired over the previous months and years. I can hear the swapping of jokes and the predictions of how many children these two will have. *"They will have such beautiful children with two parents as attractive as they; they are sure to have fine looking offspring."*

One says to an other: look over there in the corner. Can you see them and hear their whispers? They don't seem to fit in with the rest of the guests. It is true they were invited? They did receive an invitation, and yes it was out of courtesy. *"Well, she didn't think they would come. They simply wanted to make sure no feelings were hurt. On second thought, the least they could do was show the slightest interest in the party. They have been over there in the corner the whole time. What do you think they keep leaning into each other and whispering about?"*

The conversations go back and forth, and at times the conversation among them gets so loud that it's near deafening. One couple looks at each other, not even trying to talk over the cacophony; they nod to each other signaling to go outside to breathe. *"I cannot believe how loud it is in there! How many times you think*

66

they can play that song? Over and over, I think I will hear it in my sleep."

The sounds of a wedding ceremony fill the air signaling what must have been such a good time. What a time they must have had, with people coming and going all throughout the day. The guests arrived by the moment, some with more notoriety than others. However, a desire of the bride was to shake each and every person's hand for coming. She wanted each person to know she was thankful for his or her attendance.

Suddenly there is a change, a commotion outside, as people turn to the doorway. A silence and hush come over the party. The music softens, almost stopping. All eyes are on a tall, dark Galilean and a group of men following Him who almost seem to mimic his each and every movement. *"Who is this man, and who is the group of people that have come and changed the mood of the party? It's bad enough that we have run out of wine, now they are here. Who invited them; did they have an invitation? The tall one seems to be their leader, but why? Who is he, and why does he seem to have everyone's attention?"* There is a change in the party, and a change in the atmosphere; now Jesus has arrived. He's taken them up on their invitation and is in the house.

Word among the guests begins to spread quickly. "T*his is Jesus the son of Mary."* The questions circulate. *"Have you heard the stories that are beginning to come out about Him? Have you heard some of the things He has been saying and teaching? It's quite a stir He has been causing all around. It seems that there are many that follow Him, yet it seems there are many that want to take His life. Why do you think He came, and all the other men with Him? You mean to tell me that they follow Him wherever He goes? That is kind of creepy? You mean they left their jobs and now all they do is walk around from place to place, town to town teaching about religion? I heard some real troubling stuff the other day; someone told me that He said He was the Son of God. That is just about as radical as you get! Can you imagine how that is going to sit with the Sadducees? Well, Son of Mary or not, that kind of talk will not last long around here. It is okay if He is here; He doesn't*

67

look like a threat as long as He does not stand up and start preaching." A change has happened right before their eyes. They went from viewing life as what *might* happen, to having the One who can change lives standing in their midst.

I wonder how many times in life that we have the Son of the living God among us, and we are so caught up in what we are doing that we fail to see who has truly walked into our midst. A sad thought to say the least, but we could have been in the presence of the One who could change it all and have missed it. We call out over and over for Him to come and show up and when He does, we miss Him being in our presence.

Listen, they had run out of wine and desperately needed an intervention. They needed a change for the better and all they could do was to muster a conversation with those who were among them. They failed to see who showed up. It was Mary who came to Jesus and told Him that they were out of wine; no one else came to Him. Yes she knew Him, and yes she was his mother, but there were others there that knew who Jesus was and what He could do. I say, as men, we need to stand up and lead. I don't believe that Jesus had His men with Him for them just to stand back and look cute. I am sure they were with Him for much more than just 'hanging with the boys.' Jesus was training these men to be leaders so that when He left this earth they could continue His work. Mary was not the only one who saw there was a need when they ran out of wine. I am sure all noticed it, but it was Mary who came to Jesus. Mother or no mother, it seems all too often it is the woman who is tender hearted and steps into a bad situation. I would like to have seen one of the disciples step forward and say Jesus, *"Do you think that we can do anything about this? Do you think that there is anything that we can do to help these good folks?"*

It is true that God is looking for women to lead. We are given example after example of God using women to do a work for Him and He still does today. However, there is room for men to step up to the plate and begin to lead. A world is crying for men to stand up and step out of the shadows; men can see a need and come to Jesus to empower them to lead. If we as men always stand back and let women take the initiative, then God will continue to equip women to lead. God is looking for a yielded vessel to recognize a need and act upon it. We need more men who are gifted from God to lead those who would take their place. The Lord put strength in a man to lead and to carry out tasks that he did not equip a woman to do. But, man has all too often sat by and let the women bear the entire burden.

At the wedding in Canaan a negative change occurred, and now Mary needed this terrible thing to be reversed. What I so very much love about God is that He comes into the middle of a situation, and He doesn't just make it good by returning it to the way it was before. He comes in and makes the end better than the beginning. Remember, in the miracle we are looking at, He is paving the way for the new covenant. This covenant is a better way - a doing away with the old and ushering in with a ne and better way. Jesus' ways are better than ours. I can hear the voice of the apostles, as the need was made known. *"Well Jesus, what do we do now? We've come all this way and now it seems to have been a waste, we might as well leave. Jesus, there is nothing we can do about it now. Do you have any idea how far it is back into town? We walked all this way to get here and we're tired. I would like to sit down except there is no place to sit."*

Jesus will use anyone He desires to use. If it is a family member, He will use them. Jesus is looking for people who would come to Him. Mary came to Him, she knew she didn't like the way things were turning out and she wanted to see a change. It would have been easy for her to overlook it and write it off as a loss or say, "Well, maybe next time." However she didn't do that, she wanted a better outcome. She wanted a change for the better.

I believe at times we feel we aren't good enough or qualified. Others feel God would not listen to the likes of little them; this is so far from the truth. This is what Jesus had to say about coming to Him and asking for a change, a needed change. *John 15:7 If ye abide in me, and my words abide in you, ye shall ask what ye will, and it shall be done unto you.*

If you have a personal relationship with Jesus, regardless of gifting or talent, you can come to Him and ask what you will and it shall be done. Mary exercised this promise and she received a much-needed change. It is easy to sit back and wish something would change, but the one who gets results is the one who will come to Jesus and ask him to change it. If you are in Jesus, He is in you and abides in you. Knowing this gives you access to His miracle-working provision. Furthermore, the key that unlocks the door to the miracle is asking!

Mary did not sit idly by and let it run its course; she was looking for a change. It is my belief that she not only knew what Jesus could do; she knew He would do it. Hear the words in *Hebrews 11:6 ...for he that cometh to God must believe that He is, and that he is a rewarder of them that diligently seek Him.*

Mary came to Jesus more than hoping and knowing that he could help and change the circumstance. She came to Him believing that He **would do it** for her and the rest of the wedding party. *And all things, whatsoever ye shall ask in prayer, believing, ye shall receive. Matthew 21:22*

What moves the heart of God is when we come to Him and ask. God wants us to ask Him. When we come to Him, it shows we recognize He is supreme. Too many people won't come to Him and ask; they will wait on someone else to go before the Lord and ask. Let us not be the one who does not receive because we did not ask. Be not denied for failure to knock on the door of possibility. How are you to know that it will not come to pass? Ask Him! So what if the need or desire seems too small or too large! Is He not God who steps into people's lives and gives change for the better? At least you can be the one who made the extra effort, sought his face, and asked Him for the petition of your heart. God is a merciful God who hears and answers prayer. God wants you to come to Him, scoot close, look Him in the eyes and ask him boldly for what you need and desire.

My Children are not afraid to ask. My four girls know they can come to me and ask. If there is a way that I can make it happen for them, I will do just that. If we as earthly parents want this for our children, how much more does our heavenly Father want to change things for the better for us? Here's a power verse to stand on.

> *If you then, being evil, know how to give good gifts unto your children, how much more shall your Father who is in heaven give good things to them that ask Him? Matthew 7:11*

In our story Jesus took a negative situation and turned it into a favorable and life changing experience for the whole wedding party. All too often we are looking for everything to be favorable for us and then we feel everything is finally ok. This was not the ministry of Jesus; He came into the middle of chaos and changed everything around to bring it into order. Furthermore when He did, it was always a change for the better.

We are peering into the beginning of Jesus miracles on earth, but if we were to look at the end of His ministry we would find that He made a change for the better continually. Upon sharing the impending appointment with the cross, His resurrection, and rise back to heaven, He makes this statement:

> *Nevertheless I tell you the truth; It is expedient for you that I go away: for if I go not away, the Comforter will not come unto you; but if I depart, I will send him unto you. John 16:7*

He is telling them, *"Even though I am leaving and it will look bad, there is a change that is coming for the better. I came and I will fulfill my mission."* Part of the mission is to send one that is going to make everything better than what you see. Don't worry about the hurt, don't worry about the disappointment, I am making a change for the better. Keep a close watch and see past the natural, for it will be a change for the better. I have come and I will appear to leave, but I am sending one in my place that will bring you the comfort you desire. Jesus instructs them that it is expedient for him, (he must do it) it has to happen. *There must be a period where it looks bad and bleak, but I have told you ahead of time that it will happen. However, hold on through the rough times because it will get better, and not just better from the previous but above and beyond better.* Jesus will step into the worst-case scenarios and make changes for the better.

Jesus tells them that if He does not go away it will not happen. I need to tell you that there are some things in life **you must go through.** Even though it does not feel good, you must go through it. Even though you do not want to do it, you must. There are places you will never get to unless you go through. It is easy to look from a distance and see the beginning of a turbulent season and stop before getting there. It would be easy to bail from every undesired thing, and I also concede that it gets hard at times. However, we will never be a victor unless we have something to conquer. We will never get to the top of the mountain unless we first climb. Climbing is not always easy or fun, but to reach the top you must climb. Standing at the base looking up to the summit wishing you were up there will not yield the satisfaction of having reached a place few others have dared to venture. Sometimes in life you simply must go through. When you can't walk through the valley of the shadow of death without getting stuck, then still you must stand and it too shall pass. The worst situation that you could face, life somehow presents them. Though it would be easy to quit because of the harshness of the journey, whether or not you go through is important. You will receive a victor's crown if you go through. Hebrews 10:38 tell us that *he takes no pleasure in the one who turns back.*

Tell yourself today – "No matter what I am going through, if I come to Jesus He will change it for the better."

At times the change that Jesus brings about is not pertaining to our circumstances but within us. Something happens when we are willing to go through. The wedding party had soured and there was a need for a change. Jesus showed up and more than a bad situation changed. Here are a just a few things that changed for the better.

- Jesus went from only teaching with wisdom; He now has shown that he has power over the elements, even the working of miracles. He changed from only a teacher to miracle worker.
- Jesus vindicated his own mother and changed any previous notions about her past. He showed family and friend this was no ordinary son born out of wedlock.
- Jesus changed the outcome of certain disappointments on behalf of those who planned the wedding's amenities.
- He for certain changed H2o, (water) into wine, a more pleasing drink; a change from the bland everyday necessity to an enjoyable beverage.
- The five disciples whom He had called and joined Him, the word says: saw His glory and believed Him. These disciples have witnessed firsthand the power of His majesty.
- Forever their belief of Him has been established in their mind and heart.

With one act by the master, He changes for eternity a multiplicity of matters for the better. A change for the better is what is needed, and sadly, too many only *wish* for change. Far too many people are willing to take the needed steps to bring about change. There is a lot of talk about change, but unfortunately that is as far as most go. The kind of proactive steps needed are not just a good idea or a new year's resolution. Going much further and deeper than this is coming to Jesus our self and asking Him to bring about that which is required. Far too many people live out their whole life hoping for change and never come to the source for change. Adding to this are groups who are right beside the source, and still will not tap into, as in this story:

> Now there is a pool at the Sheep Gate at Jerusalem, which is called in Hebrew Bethesda, having five porches. In these lay a great multitude of those who were sick, of blind, lame, withered, waiting for the moving of the water. For an angel went down at a certain time into the pool and troubled the water. Then whoever first stepped in after the troubling of the water was made whole of whatever disease he had. And a certain man

73

was there, who had an infirmity thirty-eight years. When Jesus saw him lying, and knowing that he had spent much time, He said to him, do you desire to be made whole? The infirm man answered Him, Sir, when the water is troubled, I have no one to put me into the pool. But while I am coming, another steps down before me. Jesus says to him, Rise, take up your bed and walk. And immediately the man was made whole and took up his bed and walked. And it was a Sabbath on that day. John 5:2-9

In this chapter we are looking at a change for the better, and if anyone needed change for the better, this man did. This was a man whose body was wracked by sickness for 38 years. This man lay beside a healing source that most would dream to even find, yet when the time came for the stirring of the waters by the angels he said he had no one to put me into the pool. What a sad state that it is when we can look and see that what could make us whole and yet it still escapes our grasp. This should not be; we preach and teach that this man's dilemma was of his own undoing. After all, if he had someone to place him by the pool could they not also help him to get in? We as people peer over each other's fences and ask the question, *"What's wrong with them? I don't see what the issue with him is? After all, we got in the pool and came out healed. "*

Jesus and His power - Jesus and His willingness to intervene into a hopeless situation and bring about a much-needed change should be the highlight of our focus. Jesus has a desire that we not remain in our present state. He has the deepest desire to change our life for the better. As with the man by the pool of healing waters and those at the wedding feast, a common thread runs through. Jesus is full of compassion, and regardless of other's opinions Jesus is willing to help the helpless. Jesus is willing, able, and ready to walk into the midst of all our trouble and make a positive change!

Jesus, however, wanting to help and coming to this man out of compassion, asked him a tough question. *"Do you desire to be made whole?"* This was a direct question that spoke beyond the man's poor state of health. Jesus wanted to know, *"Do you want to be made whole?"* The verse reads, *"When Jesus saw him lying, and knowing that he had spent much time, He said to him, do you desire to be made whole?"* It had been 38 years that he had been stricken with the sickness that had him confined to a prone position. He obviously could not sit, he was lying down, and Jesus had to address the reality of his mindset. *"Do you want to be made whole?"* Maybe you might be reading this and find it hard to relate to the longevity of his sickness and condition. Not everyone on this earth goes through the extent of hurt and pain this man endured. If you have never been in a struggle for years without reprieve you must guard yourself to cast blame on the man for failing to do all he could. Some would say the very least he could have done was roll over into the water. We must be careful with this thinking as well as blaming the one in charge of the wine for making sure there would be enough.

The fact is there are times when life does get the best of us. All of our planning failed though we gave it our best effort. Though you tried to save the marriage they still walked out. Maybe you have been sick as long as this man and it has become a way of life. It has become all that you know. The thought of being whole and healed sounds good, but it has been this way for so long that it only seems a fantasy. This is the man's state of mind; he would like to be healed, but so many years have passed. Faithfully this man, still by the water, watches year after year as one person then the next gets their healing. Lying beside the pool he thinks, "I'll just wait on my turn and maybe someday it might happen." There is a state that people succumb to when in the battle they become hardened to the fact that the Lord still wants to do it for them regardless of time.

Jesus had to address the most difficult thing to change in this wanting man, (his mind). It is true He could change his body; He could give him new limbs and new organs or whatever his sickness was. There could be a change for the better in his body yet his mind could still be lying by the pool. Jesus had to address first this man's mind. He needs the change to begin in the mind first. We must change our thinking; God wants us to change from the inside out. It's good that we have working arms and legs, but of what use are they if we are not willing to lend them to the Lord? God wants a healing on the inside, a healing of the heart. By now after 38 years

75

this man had become battle hardened. He did not believe any longer that he had the possibility of having a better life.

Jesus asks him if he wants to be made whole, and instead of saying yes, he proceeds to tell him the reasons why he cannot. Jesus says that we can, and we give him reasons why we cannot. Moses did it when the Lord said he would be the leader of a nation delivering them out of an oppressing land, and Moses' response was, *"Lord I am slow of speech."* Gideon did it when the angel of the Lord appeared to him and wanted to commission him for a mighty task. Let's look at it. He too had suffered much for a long time and had the same thinking as the man by the pool.

> *And the Angel of Jehovah came and sat under an oak which was in Ophrah, which belonged to Joash the Abiezrite. And his son Gideon threshed wheat by the winepress, to hide it from the Midianites. And the Angel of Jehovah appeared to him, and said to him, Jehovah is with you, mighty warrior. And Gideon said to Him, O, my Lord, if Jehovah is with us, why then has all this happened to us? And where are all His miracles which our fathers told us of, saying, Did not Jehovah bring us up from Egypt? But now Jehovah has forsaken us, and delivered us into the hands of the Midianites. And Jehovah looked upon him and said, Go in your might, and you shall save Israel from the hand of the Midianites. Have I not sent you? And he said to him, O, my Lord, with what shall I save Israel? Behold, my family is poor in Manasseh, and I am the least in my father's house. Judges 6:11-15*

"God if you are telling me that, then why this?" *"God if you want me to do this then what about that?"* Gideon had seen so much adversity that he had trouble believing that it could be any different. Listen really closely to when he says, *"O, my Lord, if Jehovah is with us, why then has <u>all</u> this happened to us?"* One thing after another, then on top of that more kept coming to the point that Gideon had a hard time believing what the angel of the Lord was saying. I want us to picture this: The angel of Lord has appeared to

76

Gideon and his reaction was not to fall prostrate before the angel out of fear. Rather, he looked at him and responded in a doubtful way. Granted, we are not given the appearance or form of the angel of the Lord that appeared to him. Sometimes the angel of the Lord appeared as a man, but on most occasions, when the angel of the Lord appeared, fear fell upon those to whom he appeared. Gideon had been through so much. Gideon had witnessed so much destruction in his own family's life that God himself, or at least a direct representative (an angel), is standing in front of him and he is not moved by him. <u>Gideon had become numb by life's trials and adversities!</u>

For seven years God had given the nation of Israel over to the Midianites; complete victory He had given the Midianites over Israel. There was nothing that Israel could do that the Midianites didn't find out about, only to then come and destroy or take over.

The word of God says that Israel made dens in the caves and mountains just to escape the plunder of the invading forces.

> ....*And they left no food for Israel, neither sheep, nor ox, nor ass. For they came up with their cattle and their tents, and they came as locusts for multitude, both they and their camels were without number. And they entered into the land to destroy it. Judges 6:5*

For seven long, grueling years Gideon hid just to survive. Look at where the angel of the Lord found Gideon; he was threshing wheat by the wine press to hide it from the Midianites. He had to hide at every turn just to survive. I would again remind you, there are times in the lives of certain people when hard times just seem to linger year after year. For seven years he witnessed firsthand the harshness of trying to exist when an opposing force is trying to choke the life out of him. Many reading can relate to him.

I believe that this book has fallen into the hands of the right people, and it is not a sin issue you're dealing with. You are not bound by iniquity but there is an opposing, occupying army that has come with force that has overwhelmed you and your land. This force has set up camp over and over and is attacking, taking from you, draining you of your will to fight. The sickness has seized you for 10, 15, and 20 years or more. This sickness has not taken your life, but has been like a slow death of your will and spirit. There are times when you believe that you'd be better off if it went ahead and took your life. Some would say, *"I'm not in any shape to get into the pool even if the angel did show up and I was beside it."* This is Gideon, "If God is with us then pray tell me why all this adversity?" *"Could you tell me, if God is with me, why have the enemy's power seemed to have held on year after year?"* Gideon goes on to tell the angel that he had heard story after story about how the Lord led their fathers out of Egypt with a strong hand. He goes on to say, *"I've heard all the stories, but buddy all I've seen is hurt and pain."* I've heard all the stories of the glory days; you know how God showed miracles, signs, and wonders, but I don't see any of them around here. In fact I've never seen God do anything except allow the Midianites take everything we have. We plant a field in hopes of survival and as soon as we harvest it, they come and take everything we've worked for. Do you know how long we have worked to get that field ready for planting? As soon as we do they come and spread salt over our fields."

"The next time you come and want to tell me about how great that this God is to us, and how He wants to do great things, bring some evidence. Angel, I would like to believe you but I am having a hard time getting over the fact that we've had all these years of hardship. Come on, you can do better than that; you're going to have to show me before I'll believe this." This is we at times. Year after year can go by and when we do not see anything other than the hardship of life we can be unmoved when the Lord shows up and wants to change things for the better. I appreciate so much that God will show up even when our faith has been depleted, even when at times it looks to most as if we have lost our faith. Jesus will still show up and begin to change our life for the better. The wedding party needed a change, the children of Israel in Egypt needed a change, and Israel in the hands of Egypt needed a change for the better. Every time, Jesus showed up He changed everything.

Some go through seasons in their life as a result of the length of time they are in the struggle and nothing seems to change. It is then they are willing to forfeit most of their dreams to ease the pain of the trial. A great tactic the enemy of our souls has is to come and occupy your land, your mind, and your stuff so you cannot move forward. You are alive but you're stuck. You're breathing, but restricted. You get up in the morning, but barely, only a shadow of your previous youthful state. You came into the faith, and God birthed in you your dreams and visions. You believed he actually had you in mind. It is then, out of the blue, trials start and then they keep coming day after day, and year after year, set back after set back. You would be okay if it was just one thing. Maybe you could have handled a couple of bad reports and discouraging years, but not this many. I can hear the echo of many saying, *"This was more than I bargained for; this was more than I signed up for. If you want to know the truth, the things I wanted to do and the places I wanted to go really don't matter to me any longer. I just want the pain to end."*

The enemy of our soul is a dream stealer; he wants to come set up camp and besiege your city, dreams, and hope. Let's look for just a moment and define the word *besiege*.

Besiege: (Military) to surround (a fortified area, esp. a city) with military forces to bring about its surrender. To crowd round; hem in to overwhelm.

This was a tactic that was used in ancient military strategy; surround the city and its fortified walls and plan to stay for a long time. An army would surround a city and would, for years, whittle away at the defenses of it. Month after month they would chip away at the strong defenses, and over time they could starve out those within the walls. The opposing force could also breach the walls over time. Then the army, at just the right moment, would make one last push and break down the weakened walls, penetrating and overtaking the city. At times the enemy comes to set up camp outside of our life. The days and years click by until we find ourselves without hope and succumb to the belief that it would be better if we just surrender to him. We then say, "At least we would have food and water." However, there is a resolve that lies deep within the child of God that says, *"No not now, never will I! I may be hungry and I may feel like I will never have a cool glass of water, but this one thing I know. God gave me this dream, God gave me this vision, and He put me in the middle of it. I am not going to allow any demon or any hardships take it away from me!"*

Great stories of victories come as a result of great battles - "Without a battle you will have no victory."

Fight the good fight of faith. Lay hold on eternal life, to which you are also called and have professed a good profession before many witnesses. 1Timothy 6:12

Lay hold on eternal life; don't let the battle of your life take you under. I believe there has to be courage that flies in the face of reason. This is a faith that those around you will never understand. This stand of faith says, *"I know it has been a lot of years but I am still waiting for my breakthrough. Yes I am well aware of everything that has happened and all I've gone through, but I believe that God said He was going to make this thing right."* Adding to that, *"If I have made it this long, don't you think I should hang in there a little bit longer? I am choosing to stay with God, I am not going to get bitter, and I am not going to get hardened by this. I am going to let God bring about the much-needed change no matter how long I have to wait. I know He is going to do it because He has done it in the past, and I know that He will do it again. I don't have to throw in the towel. He said He was a way maker. I don't have to quit. He said He would give me the victory. I don't need to waste time worrying how it is going to work out. He said he would go before me, and he's got my back. For his glory shall be my rear guard."*

Life at times is a fight! There are times when the battle feels like it has finally swung your way, and then there are times when it appears the enemy has the upper hand. Either way you must not forget that Jesus is still in control. You must know this regardless of whether the battle rages hot or appears to be over only to escalate again. God is in control and He will not leave you in the fire always. God will not leave you in the heat of the battle forever; He still

80

provides peace and a calming of the storms. God shut the mouth of the lions for Daniel, He allowed Samson to gain victory in the end, even after his fall in the cutting of his hair. Samson deviated from God's plan for his life and lost the empowering strength from the Lord. It appeared his life was over and facing certain doom. However, the word of God says he slew more in his death than he did in his life. Don't ever tempt God, but also don't ever think you've failed beyond God's repair and restoration. God can change anything, even your sin and setbacks. God wants to change your world for the better, whether it is wine at a wedding party or bringing down an oppressive dictator or king. God wants to change things for the better. So much so that he does not want to just stop at matters being okay - He wants it beyond good, and a better than you ever expected.

Jesus has told us that he came to give us life and life more abundantly. He did not say he would give us life and life with more adversity. The man by the pool of Bethesda had been sick for 38 years; Gideon had seen nothing but heartache for seven years. It is all he knew, nothing more. He did not think that it could get better - *"Let's hide and continue to hide, maybe if they don't see us then we'll be okay."*

Pushed in a corner, shoved in a hole, and placed out of commission, many a great warrior intended for the Lord's service gave in to the fight and over time laid down and quit. As a Pastor I have witnessed so many unfortunate instances of people quitting in the fight. The victory was at hand and instead of outlasting the enemy they gave in to him and joined forces. This should not be. God does not want to invest so much in us for us to eventually just quit. He did not pay such a high ransom for us only to have us defect and serve the enemy. A cry goes out from the heart of God proclaiming, *"Stand in the fight! Don't retreat! Stand up and move forward!"*

The only piece of armor that the Lord didn't give was for our back; we are not to turn and run. Galatians 6:9 states, *"We should not lose heart."* The Lord has given us all we need to be victorious in the battle; whether the battle is long or short, we can win! God will see us through until the battle is won. Now is not the time to quit, retreat, or run. If we are patient and (man our post) he will send reinforcement. It is when we feel we are at our worst and feel we can't stand another day that the Lord is at hand ready to step in and come to our aid. God does not want his people destroyed; he wants them and empowers them to be the victor.

There is a brighter day regardless of how long the battle has raged. No matter how low you have sunk, the Lord is the lifter of our heads. It is then that we begin to look up and see things in a different light.

For most of this chapter we have seen how the enemy can set up strong holds in the lives of the children of God. Satan surrounds the life and mind then tries to squeeze the life out of them. He is strategically plotting over a long period of time. He pushes relentlessly to gain control. I have also shown that the Lord wants to bring Aid and deliverance to those individuals' lives by a supernatural change. I would now like us to look at the much-needed change in the life of a new couple.

When reading our story out of the 2nd chapter of John, we read that it is about a marriage ceremony. It was customary for wedding ceremonies of Jewish heritage to last seven days. Over the course of seven days many different guests would arrive and pay their respects, bring gifts, and wish their happiness to those exchanging vows. Over the course of seven days with many guest coming and going, there needed to be a great deal of supplies. It appears from our text and common knowledge that the responsibility of the supply of wine came from the bridegroom or his family. We see the ruler of the wedding party comes and directly addresses the bridegroom as to goodness of the wine. A heavy weight on the back of the man of the house, then and now, is a responsibility to provide and protect. Even in our modern culture a man carries a responsibility that cannot be overlooked. Wired into the being of man is to ensure the proper welfare of the wife and children.

Men that come from good stock want to provide for their family in ways that escape a woman's understanding. At times women can't discern men's hearts in wanting the best for the family. Sometimes she doesn't understand that this longing of this means working long hours away from home in an effort if ensure this. If only he can provide a good life for his family, if only he can give the best of what life has to offer, then he would feel as if he has accomplished something.

This nature comes from the heart of God; our heavenly Father wants to make many changes for the better in our life. He wants to infuse joy in our everyday walk. I feel there are too many teachings floating around even today that say the more broke and busted you are, the closer you are to God. This is crazy thinking at its best. *"You mean God came to earth and wants to give me life and life more abundantly, and the way He does this is to make me so miserable that I despair my own life?"* My goodness to heavens! What has happened that we think God is an Oger only wanting us in a place of despair? Where is the hope in this mindset? Where is the redemption in a thought that we have to suffer without end? Then, maybe if we have done everything just right, and maybe if we have kept all the rules, then maybe He might, after a white glove test, let us in for just a moment. And then when we are there at a place of blessing at any given time, a random inspection of all your goods can take place and be taken away for a committed foul.

Talk about restrictive and freedom-less, God has so much more and desires so much more for us. Truly He wants our life and journey to be an enjoyable one. I know that life has its twists and bends, but I have witnessed many that have chosen to live it God's way even when they were dying. I have seen many times as a pastor those who are drawing their last breath praising the Lord in their departure. It does not have to be a life of woes. It truly is a choice of how we act concerning even in the worst of circumstance. The joy of this, their joy, was in a God that was still God despite the lot they were given.

We can be the one who quits in the fight or we can be the one who will look at the fight as an opportunity to advance from the now to the future.

"Your blessing of tomorrow is birthed in the struggle of today! Don't quit in the struggle!"

The bridegroom was to take ownership of the wine for the party. The master of the ceremony came to the bridegroom and complimented him on how well he had done in saving the good wine until last. But, it could not have happened that way unless an intervention from the Lord had happened. This ceremony was the beginning of something new; a marriage was taking place and different family and friends were on hand to take part in this celebration. It was the bridegroom's responsibility to take care of the wine, and what he had prepared or bought ran out. Let's look at this and recall I said it is wired into the being of man to provide for his family. What needs to be highlighted is the very thing man provided from the start of what was supposed to be for a lifetime, failed. The wine ran out far too quickly. Without God in our life, we fail. Without God giving true provision, we fail. Without first seeing our need for God, we are doomed and destined to come up short.

First, we need to understand that what we bring to the table will fail without the Lord's intervention; He takes clay and fashions what He wills. Secondly, we see there is an attempt from the enemy to derail and bring offense from the beginning of their marriage.

We read throughout the word of God how immediately the enemy comes to steal the word (See Mark 4:15). The enemy tried to kill Jesus while he was a child, just as he did Moses. The enemy shows no mercy to that which is in infancy. The Lord will help; He will protect the young, dreams, visions, and lives of his own. God protected Jesus and Moses and will continue to lend His hands.

Changes were happening in the lives of these two lovebirds; a change from being single to engaged, a change from being engaged to being married. There were changes that were happening at a very rapid pace. There can be seasons where nothing seems to change for years, and then overnight, like dominos tumbling down, everything changes. When changes happen rapidly the enemy can slip in and bring offense if we are caught unaware. When all the attention is on the party and what the party can offer those in attendance - that is when broken focus can bring offense. The wedding party was never really for the guests, but rather for the ones getting married. They were there to partake in what something that was about two others. We as people make too many things about us, when in reality it should be about others. Jesus came to serve, not to be served. People can take offense over matters that have nothing to do with them. Surely, had Christ not intervened, those attending would have cast blame by truckloads! Can you hear the gasps of disgust? *"So you're telling me we came all this way? Hot, dry, and thirsty, and there is no wine?"*

When we read scripture, it is revealed to us as a Christ follower that God asks us to take the road least traveled. Sometimes that means letting small stuff go. How many times have you heard the voice of God prompting you; *"Just let it go?"* How many times have you heard and never heeded the prompting? Then, when you don't, moments, weeks, and even years later you wished you'd had? Words said in the heat of the moment you wish could be taken back, but cannot. I think all of us have been there at one time or another. It is when things are going crazy, when things are changing out of our control that we tend to slip.

I sense you can relate; I'm talking about the stuff we enlarge that in actuality amounts to nothing. In the heat of the moment it seemed important, but hours or days later when emotions have settled the truth shines through. The truth was that you took it the wrong way. They never meant things the way you perceived them. We can apply innumerable scenarios that could be applicable to this thought. However, we can narrow most and apply a simple principle to all; "Be slow to speak, quick to listen, and hold the actions of others lightly." We cannot see the heart of others, only God can. We are not always afforded the complete details of what people are going through. Circumstances, whether right or wrong, cause people to say, act, or do what they normally would not. I feel if we could take the teachings of Christ and apply them to our walk it would do wonders for our own peace. Give people room to not be as together as you feel you are; allow them to make mistakes without throwing them away. You've heard the adage "Don't throw the baby out with

85

the bath water." Maybe they are not as mature spiritually as you feel you are. Here is a scripture to help us.

> *Brethren, if a man be overtaken in a fault, ye which are spiritual, restore such an one in the spirit of meekness; considering thyself, lest thou also be tempted. Bear ye one another's burdens, and so fulfil the law of Christ. Galatians 6:1-2*

Clearly we see even in confirmed failure of others we are to tread lightly and have a meek spirit in going to them confronting their error. How much more should we show restraint when things are foggy? I personally like this approach: error on the side of caution when judging others' intent! Take a step back and give them room to wiggle. After all most of us are trying to wiggle through life. Life can be difficult. Just because one matter may not seem a big deal to you, it might be to others. Show love and mercy; these two coupled can triumph over most situations.

We make plans to change things and commit to a relationship. We plan for quite some time when the big day comes and all the planning comes together. Everyone is excited. Then, while everyone is watching, we run out of wine. Now what do we do? *"Hey bridegroom, why didn't you plan better? You knew all my family was going to be here and you had to go and let this happen? This was supposed to be the best day of my life and you allowed this to happen to me?"* I've seen it, and you've seen it. What was supposed to be a good day and a great time turns into a nightmare. Then everyone stands back and says, *"Stop the train and let me off. Okay, it was good to see you. I'll catch you next year. Gotta run now - take care and I'll be praying for your marriage. Hey I'll call you in a few days. Don't let this get you down, he did not mean to let this happen. Or - Hey it's okay big fellow; she did not mean to say that in front of all those people. I know it was your big day, and I am so sorry it turned out the way that it did, but it will get better just hang in there."*

Right out of the chute it explodes with heightened emotions of the two, and while all eyes are on them, they run out of wine.

What was supposed to help bring cheer now brings a lifetime of reminding the other how *he* didn't make sure wouldn't happen, or how *she* reacted to the situation.

From the beginning the enemy (Satan) wants to try to destroy or change the course of God's blessing. A tactic of Satan is to try to kill God's own while they are young. He tries to kill them before they change from being young and vulnerable, and grow and become strong. The enemy was after this marriage from the start. Satan feels if he can get them while they are young, he's got them for life. If he can bring offense early in the marriage he has a chance for the offense to grow later. This offense more times than not happens with the smallest of things; then they grow over a period of time. The enemy adds to the offense and feeds it in the mind of the other, and then it grows and begins to reproduce itself in other areas. Before you know it, he has choked the life out of what was once something beautiful and promising. God is trying to bring about a better change and the enemy wants you to revert back to where you were. The word says the one who turns back never really turns back to the way he was, but is 7 times worse than when he began. (See Matthew 12:43-45)

We cannot afford to give any ground in our life to Satan. The most needed change is to deal with tough issues in our life *now* or immediately when they happen; be quick to repent. It is true you must be wise and choose your timing to deal with and tackle tough issues. However, the problem is that we have, for far too long, let things dangle in the wind without ever really getting to the heart of the issue. We cannot continue in a life contrary to Christ's teachings and see maturity, growth and fruit. In John 15:1-10 we read that the one who bears no fruit is cut off and thrown into the fire.

The issue was not solely the lack of wine. The problem was that they were depending on the wine to bring them lasting happiness. We have to fight the temptation to look to externals to bring stimulation and relaxation. We must look to the Lord to be our portion and our source. Too much emphasis was placed on wine. Jesus was in the house. They could have looked to Him to play the main role in the beginning of their marriage, but they are troubled about running out of wine. I talked earlier in this book about the Law of Firsts, and how you start out is of great importance. The enemy wanted to derail their marriage from the beginning. Jesus wanted to be a part of the marriage or He would not have shown up; however, He wants more. Still, remaining is the knowledge that He wants to be more than just a part or minor role. He desires to be more than a miracle worker or the one who made the wine or good times to flow again. Much more importantly Jesus wants to be the head of your marriage, the very center, not the one off in the distance not knowing what role he is fulfilling. Jesus offers more than a marriage just getting by and barely functioning. He offers a marriage where He is put in his right full place as the head. When the master of the wedding party came to the bridegroom, he didn't even know where it had come from. A miracle had just happened and he had no idea that Jesus, the God of the entire universe, had just caused dirty hand water to turn to wine. Jesus was not asked to head up the wedding, he was only invited. Jesus was not asked to be the master of the ceremony; He was only the one who was called on to intervene in a crisis. Listen, Jesus wants to come to our aid and rescue, however, He desires more, and He wants to be the master of the wedding ceremony. He wants to be the head.

Jesus wants to be more than the one we turn to when we get in a jam. It seems we as humanity swing from a pendulum. We go from heartache to trouble, and from joy to sorrow. *"Help me God, I'm in a pinch. Can you come to my aid? I'm feeling kind of blue today and it seems everything is starting to unravel? Thanks God! You got me out of that one, now bring on the wine and let the good times roll."* Up and down, back and forth, we simply swing to and fro. Hot then cold, cold then hot, warm then flat-lined with no spiritual pulse to speak of. A short but crucial scripture of what the Lord desires is in

> *...be steadfast, immovable, always abounding in the work of the Lord, knowing that your labor is not without fruit in the Lord. 1 Corinthians.15:58*

Steadfast - not up and down with the flow of the wine, happy when there is a supply and depressed when it has ceased.

Immovable - I think we must arrive at a place we need to be that says I will not be moved off this wall. I've got a job that I have to finish and if I keep getting down off this wall and keep trying to get a drink of wine I'll never get this job finished. In order to produce fruit, we must remain (planted). We must have the knowledge that things might not go so well, and I might face difficulties in the process. I know this - if I remain steadfast and immovable I'm going to see some fruit. We have far too many people moving before they begin to see fruit from their labor. We start off well, but at the slightest hint of trouble we're willing to cash in the chips because the journey has gotten a little rocky. The wind begins to blow, for some individuals harder than others, and it's the ones who are willing to either speak to their storm or ride it out who will see fruit.

We cannot always judge our journey based on our neighbor's journey. You are on a personal journey, and your path may not look like someone else's. Your neighbor's journey may be smooth while yours may be rocky. You must know it is the path that the Lord has placed you on, so please keep your eyes on yours. If you begin to look at another's journey, life, or ministry, you'll veer off your course.

We are living in a pressure cooker society, pressured to do this and that, pressured to look like this or that. The pressure, like never before, has slipped into the church. Small and big churches alike feel the pressure to perform. The small church desires to change so desperately, to offer the programs that the larger ones do. The more they stretch trying to implement programs they don't have the resources to support, the more feeling of inadequacy and failure slips in. They face constant pressure trying to hang on to the few people they have, and in the process they miss the fact that Jesus is still in the house; whether the numbers are there or not. This wedding felt the same pressure. They needed a change and needed it quickly. There was a feeling of desperation. If there were not an immediate response, all would be a wash. This feeling of desperation was an important enough topic and obvious stumbling block that it was addressed in scripture. The book of Philippians the 4th chapter and 6th verse tells us to 'be anxious for nothing.' Wow, this is hard to do; yet God requires it. Scripture goes further telling us to pray and ask, but then to leave it in his hands. His mother did just that, she came to him and told him what was going on, then turned and told his servants to do whatever He said. This was a good lesson in trusting in Jesus, not getting in a heated quandary because things are up in the air and the wine has dried up. *"Jesus I have a need, I know you care and I know you are my supplier. I trust you with my petition and prayer. I know you will work this out for my good and your glory."*

Pressure from anxiety will cause you to do things you would not normally do. If you're not careful it will cause you to jeopardize your beliefs. Pressure at times will get you out of what you know is truth by trying to get you to do things that you shouldn't. Big churches are not exempt from pressure; they have set a precedent and feel they can't let the masses down. They feel pressured to perform higher than the level of last week. There is a pressure to produce more and more to keep the crowd coming and happy.

The budget has risen with the attendance and we must ensure that there remains enough coming in to cover what is going out. At times is seems it is going out faster than it's coming in. Big churches have big headaches and big overhead. The small churches want to be big, but they have no clue as to the pressure to operate at such an accelerated level. The music must be top shelf, and the staff must be highly educated and equipped. This level of proficiency is not achieved by letting anyone stand front and center to sing, teach or preach.

There is pressure at every turn; anxiety can run at high levels as it was at the wedding party. However, Jesus was not in a hurry and wasn't anxious; he simply stepped into a bad situation and made a change for the better. Whatever situation you find yourself in presently, don't think you have to go it alone. Whether its sickness, a disease-riddled body, financial collapse, loss of a spouse, failed dream, or you've simply run out of the will to fight, I encourage you to turn to Jesus and make your dilemma voiced. Jesus wants you to talk and pray to Him. Regardless of whether you've prayed a thousand times... pray again! This may be your year. This may be your turn for Him to bring about the much-needed change in your life. It's easy to say and difficult to live out, yet it is achievable. Don't be anxious and take matters into your own hands. Let Jesus work it out. Jesus is the miracle worker; He will see you through. He will work it out. Jesus will change your circumstance for the better. Hold on... don't quit! He's on the way, and He will stay and never leave.

"Jesus makes changes for the better."

Chapter 4

The Servants

In this chapter we will peer past the stereotypical role of a servant. In our subject story of the water being turned into wine there were servants at the wedding party that played a major role in the miracle. Though they were mostly unnoticed, we will find they were as much a part of the miracle scene as those attending. These servants took part in a phenomenal event and acted beyond an obscure role. They not only were serving the guests, but also by serving, helped make the miracle happen. They received no fanfare or ticker tape parade, yet they were key players that the Lord used to bring this miracle to manifestation. God wants to use those who are willing to serve. The Lord is looking for someone who will step up to the plate and be used by Him in a mighty way by serving. It is those, often over looked, that the Lord uses in such a mighty way! We, being humanity, look past the obscure, yet it seems God seeks those in obscurity to use.

When we think about servants we immediately think of a hired hand of lowly estate, close to the degree of being a slave. A picture we all can view in our mind is one of the lowest classes of people - a servant. Can you visualize the look on peoples' faces when they find out that someone they had just met was nothing more than a servant? *"You mean you serve for a living? You mean you tend to other peoples' needs?"* This is a high and lofty stance that most of our modern culture has taken. We want to be served; we want to be the one who sits in the lap of luxury and can take it easy. After all, we've earned our place of position and power. After all, we have climbed the corporate ladder and now we can take it easy for a while. *"Waiter, over here! I need more wine, my glass has run dry. Can't you see you have let me sit her for over ten minutes with an empty glass? Come at once, I will not have of this any longer! Come, hurry up, move faster, surely you can do better than that."*

It seems the church has, at times, become the one sitting in a lofty state of wanting to be served, longing and waiting for someone to come and meet their every need. *"Gimmie, gimmie, gimmie! Give me this and that! I want this, and I want that."* Listen to what Jesus had to say about service or being a servant:

For even the Son of Man did not come to be served but to serve, and to give His life as a ransom for many.
Mark 10:45

Jesus is our example, He is the light of the world, and He is the one that provides the best example of what the Father desires and wants in our life. Jesus did not come to be a King that was to sit upon a throne, calling for his many servants to come feed him grapes with fans in hand. I don't think so - not this radical leader. Jesus led from the front, not from the rear where there was no threat of danger or harm. On more than one occasion His disciples wanted to know why He would want to go to a certain area or return to a hostile area. Jesus had many foes; and not just a few, but many people were looking to take His life. They wanted more than to silence His voice; they wanted to permanently remove His presence. We find this is happening today in our culture at an alarming rate! As never before, the spirit of the anti-Christ is at work in the earth trying to remove the presence of Jesus. It's okay that you pray to Allah, or to his false Prophet Mohammad, but you dare not mention the name of Jesus. Scripture tells us that there is no other name given among men where by a man must be saved than the name of Jesus – Acts 4:112. God has exalted the name of Jesus above every other name. Though the hate mongers and blasphemers of the day continue their plot to remove the precious name of Jesus, soon every knee will bow and every tongue will confess that Jesus Christ is Lord. That is why the devil is so hard at work trying to destroy everything that Jesus stands for. Satan and his demons' time is short and they know it! The word of God tells us that Satan has gone out with great wrath for he knows his time is short. See *Revelations 12:6*

In all the danger and in all the harshness of the afflictions that he would face Jesus kept serving. He did not hide; He stayed on the front lines of the battle. Battles are not won by a loud mouthed general belching out orders. The battles of war are won by men and women who go to the frontlines in the face of enemy fire and work in service for their country or cause. Jesus was just such a leader. He went to the front day after day, serving His father on this earth. In doing so He gave us the best possible example of what service was, and what it truly means to be in the service of the King of Kings and Lord of Lords.

I was in the United States Marine Corps. I know what it is to serve, and I know what it is to face danger. I voluntarily enlisted; no one twisted my arm nor was I drafted. I knew full well that there was the possibility that one day I would have to stand and face fear, and move forward versus retreat in defeat. That possibility materialized in 1990 while stationed in Jacksonville NC. Suddam Hussein invaded Kuwait. This was a very prosperous nation but it was small. The sheer size of Iraq's army was a near free pass for complete occupation within hours of invasion. Here lies a defenseless little country in the hands of a completely demonized dictator. Iraq possessed no right to occupy, Kuwait posed no threat, they only had what Suddam wanted. Saddam wanted complete control of all the vast resources deep within Kuwait's fruitful land. It was not good enough that he had an endless supply of oil and wealth within his own borders - he wanted more. Suddam had the responsibility to protect his people and ensure their welfare, yet he only controlled and exterminated them by the thousands.

Saddam Hussein was a ruthless dictator, drunk from the cup of power! Saddam was thirsty for more and more, a bloodlust that would extend past his own borders reaching far into neighboring countries. Saddam believed that nothing was going to stand in the way of what he wanted. He believed if he had to take it to get it, he would do just that. Saddam made a fatal error! Saddam never counted on a coalition of fighting men and women who was ready to serve the nation of Kuwait by coming to their aid. We as individuals may not be an army; however, we can for certain serve others around us. A kind word, a simple note to say thanks, or a smile in a harsh situation goes a long way. We can come to others' aid by being in the room and doing nothing more than listening. At times, people are not looking for you to solve all their problems; they just need a hand up versus a hand out.

At times we as Christians quit serving and walk away. We walk away because the battle becomes too fierce, or it rages on for far too long. The Children of Israel spoke often of quitting and wanting to return to where God had delivered them. Imagine God groaning in sorrow for them - the ransomed - wanting to return to their captors in the land of Egypt. For forty years they wandered and only two of the original men made it into a promised land. Unbelief kept them out. Let us not repeat a pattern they set. Determine within yourself that you are never going back to a stronghold from which God has delivered you. Don't quit moving forward for Jesus! Resist the notion to become idle. Idleness is deadly. You must advance for the cause of Christ. We do this by refusing to quit because the battle has become hot or harsh. Keep fighting the good fight of faith. The bible tells us to endure as a good soldier! Are you enduring? If you have grown weary in your personal battle I pray for you a renewed breath from the spirit of God. Stand back up and begin moving forward!

When joining the Marine Corps I knew, beyond a doubt, that I was entering into service for my country. I knew I was joining a fighting force and it was my responsibility to learn from my instructors. They were who would train and teach me how to fight, but better yet, teach me to survive in the process. In the ensuing days and years to come, always present in the back of your mind is the thought, "Someday someone might be shooting back at me." Still, something drove you further. Something nudged you along - to train better, to listen better and to become the best you could be. After all, I was the one that made the trip to the recruiter's office. After all, I was the one who signed my name on a dotted line relinquishing control of my life. I signed a contract and was now the property of the United States Marine Corps. I was to be a tool in the hands of a great nation that needed serving. Every year thousands of our young men and women give up their rights to individuality to join our nation's military. Many do so for various personal reasons; however, whether they realize or not, they are there to serve.

The one who serves with pride is the one who knows there are honor and a cause for serving. Obviously I'm patriotic, yet I'm cautious about easily going to war putting men's lives on the line. It is a responsibility that should not be taken lightly, and should be approached with fear of making the wrong decision because "men's lives are on the line." This is a caution that should be embraced, not discarded. Embracing this caution we must not forget that Ecclesiastes says there is a time for everything under the sun, including war. Not hoped for or desired, yet required at times.

Jesus came into this world the first time as a gentle lamb; however, at the Second Advent He will be a fearless warrior. A mighty charge He shall lead, riding on a white horse called faithful and true, He will come in might and power. Jesus will arrive - still serving, except in a role few could imagine. Our Lord and Savior will be leading the way, putting down all sin and rebellion. Jesus will forever remove sin from the earth. Our Jesus is a serving God. He came to serve. He served while on this earth for 33 years, and when He went away, He went so He could still yet serve. Jesus is sitting at the right hand of the father serving, making intercession for the saints of God. Jesus left this earth so He could go serve by preparing a place for us. Right now, he is preparing a place for you and for me - a mansion like you always wanted. This grandeur palace will be just the way you had hoped for and even better. Our Lord is a serving Lord, a Lord who has all power and all might that could force us into service, yet He chose to extend an invitation rather than force hard labor and demanded service.

Saddam Hussein forced men, as did China and North Korea, to labor in their militaries. This kind of forced labor is hard and takes the spirit out of man. Jesus wants us to join in service that gives life. The world system robs the joy of service, working out of obligation or requirement. This type of service yields no return; it's an empty system that will only drag men deeper and drive them further away from the knowledge of God.

It has been said that Christianity is a mindless religion - to think you must give your life to Jesus then surrender all the things that are fun and live a life of regiment. *"No, I don't want to give my life to Christ. I still want to do this first or, I can't give this up it's just too much fun. How could what feels so good be so wrong? If I come to Jesus and enter His kingdom He will make me a slave and take all my toys."* Christ is no Saddam Hussein. He will not force you to serve Him. He will not force you to follow Him. He does not make you come to Him. He beckons and calls. There are no forced marches at gunpoint to serve or die. There is no requirement or regulation that says your church attendance should exceed all those you know. I like what scripture says about that subject, *Hebrews 10:25, Not <u>forsaking</u> the assembling of ourselves together………..*

Something is lost when we don't come to the Lord's house. In doing so, we are forsaking, or withholding something that is good and vital to our growth and walk with the Lord. Many feel it is an obligation to come to church. They feel as if it's a responsibility. This is felt, rather than from a heart for God to serve. The blessing comes from serving Christ with a willing heart - either from voluntary military service, or from a willing Christian worker serving the church in the smallest of roles. A reward is given through satisfaction of knowing no one twisted your arm; it was done because you wanted to serve. In the process of serving by giving of one's self, a fulfillment is returned that nothing can match. If we enter or begin service because we feel pressured or manipulated, it brings a forced feeling and a sense of obligation. When we have this feeling we never really put all our efforts into the cause. We act but never truly serve. We do so begrudgingly. We go through the motions; however, our heart is never really in it. This group of people will be there; show up on time every time, but there is something missing. What is missing is a conviction and passion to the cause. If these two key elements are missing in an individual, they will never rise to the level they could if a willing heart was possessed.

Take ye from among you an offering unto the LORD: whosoever is of a <u>willing heart</u>, let him bring it, an offering of the LORD; gold, and silver, and brass. Exodus 35:5

Jesus led the way. He came to us to dwell with and live among us that we might have abundant life instead of certain death. He came to us when we were bound in sin and iniquity that we might have a better life - a change for the better. With him being our teacher and our example, He wants us to emulate Him and follow a sure route. There is no better example of a selfless life of serving than Jesus Christ. The very title given to us as believers is Christians. The definition of Christian is a Christ-follower. In many and on endless occasions we are looking for what and how we are to approach a matter when we have already been given the answer. A model or mold we can pour our life into has been lived out in the life of Jesus. I remember the bumper stickers, necklaces, and bracelets that read WWJD, "What would Jesus do." This was to be a reminder to us that we were to think before reacting in any situation. This was all well and good; however, we don't have to guess what He would do. We are given what He did and how He acted. Furthermore, we are given what He told us to do. All we ever need to know as instruction pertaining to this life is recorded in the blessed Holy Scriptures.

In Exodus we just read how God spoke to Moses and gave him the institution for worship pertaining to the Tabernacle in the wilderness. Every detail was addressed. No stone was left unturned. The Lord wanted Moses to be completely aware of what He wanted and what was expected. Even through the harshness of the law given was a principal that the Lord was establishing as a foreshadowing of Jesus the Christ who would come to serve humanity. God extended an invitation for those of a willing heart to bring an offering of gold, silver, and brass. Those of a willing heart or those who loved God and wanted to be in his service would say, "All that I have is yours Lord." *God, all my gifts, my talents, and all my hope are in you. Take what I have, take my gold, take my silver, and I even have some brass. Jesus I know that you have need of them, and I know that the priests are busy. Lord my heart is willing. I want to bring them to you. I don't want you to have to travel anymore. I know it has been a rough day and I am going to bring them to you because I have a willing heart.* The word said whoever had a willing heart, let him bring them.

There is something about service that causes us to go the extra mile, gets us out of our comfort zone, and moving toward a better and higher cause. There is something about coming and bringing what we have to the Lord. Not waiting for someone to come around and collect it, but getting up and moving for the Lord. I often wonder how much of the Old Testament we discount because we think the New Testament has erased the Old. We live under the New Covenant yet there are precepts and principals included that apply to our life. If you read through Psalms and Proverbs you would find the Lord was displeased with those who were lazy. God wants us to get up and bring it to Him, to serve Him or be in His service. You can't come before a king empty handed - you must bring a gift. At the very least you can offer praise and honor unto Him who is able to save our soul. We must enter into His gates with thanksgiving in our heart and come into his courts with praise. This is the day that that Lord has made, the least we could do is rejoice and be glad.

The reason above all other reasons is to return the love He has shown us, and simply because we willing.

At times Christian leaders find themselves needing help with various projects or ministries. When approaching someone there is the feeling you have to talk people into serving. Those in ministry fight the temptation of dangling a carrot. "Hey I'll do this for you if you can help me with this." It can become frustrating for ministries who are in desperate need of a helping hand when they go to those who should serve out of love but don't have a willing heart. Too many are looking for something in return rather than out of a willing heart. I stated previously but will again, "No fulfillment can be achieved like that through kingdom service." The joy that God floods our soul with is unspeakable when we have a heart that is willing to serve Him and His cause.

In Exodus the 35th chapter, we read how an invitation was extended for those with a willing heart to bring what they had for the construction of the Tabernacle and its furnishings. We can read a little further down as to the response to the request.

And they came, every one whose <u>heart stirred him up</u>, and every one whom his spirit made <u>willing</u>, and they brought the LORD'S offering to the work of the tabernacle of the congregation, and for all his service, and for the holy garments. And they came, both men and women, as many as were <u>willing hearted</u>, and brought bracelets, and earrings, and rings, and tablets, all jewels of gold: and every man that offered an offering of gold unto the Lord. Exodus 35:21-22

They did not have to do what they did. They did not have to come and, in an act of worship, give their valuables. They brought them to Moses and then did more than dump them and leave; they began to serve him by offering their talents and gifting. They began to bring what God had given them in talents and material wealth and started serving Moses, serving God, and the Priests. God never demanded their service; it was those who had a willing heart that he desired.

"Listen, I appreciate that you showed up for the work day here at the church, but if you were going to complain about how much sleep you have lost then you might as well have stayed home. We thank you for giving your used clothes to the clothing drive but if you were going to remind us every time you come then your heart was not in the right place and you've already received your reward."

One of many offerings the people could bring to the priest so he could offer up a sacrifice on their behalf was a free will offering. This was one not required, but one that was given voluntarily. Blessed are those who, out of their own free will, bring an offering of service to the king - those who simply want to be a blessing to others on behalf of Christ.

Our knowledge of service is based more times than not on what we have heard, not seen. There is no greater fulfillment in life than to serve. Don't let anyone tell you, "It is not worth it, don't bother, others have tried, and they never made a dent in the problem." Some treaded the successful path trod in the direction from which others returned. Many give up or give in for becoming weary. In our quest to fulfill a God-given desire and leading, we will encounter along the way people who have grown weary in their service. Instead of passing quietly they wish to deter you from your intended service. These people are more than dream killers, they are saboteurs who meet you in the middle of the journey wanting you, like them, to never make it or quit in the process. They can be embittered people who have become disenchanted from failed attempts. They take on the spirit of failure and, since they never made it, don't want anyone else to make it either. They want no one to venture past them so they attempt to stop you in your tracks and get you to turn around with them.

In our story of the water turned into wine we read Mary, the mother of Jesus, was already at the wedding ceremony. She was in the house when Jesus arrived and upon Him entering the house she immediately went to Him and told Him they were out of wine. Jesus asked her, "What do I have to do with what concerns you?" After He says this, she appears to spin on her heels and address the servants that were in the house. She tells them, "Do what he says to do." The curtain closes, and in the next scene we view Jesus directly speaking to the servants. He looks at them and says, "*Fill the water pots with water.*" In this chapter we are looking at servants. I would like to propose to you that it was the servants that Jesus used to bring about the miracle of the day. Jesus never called the important guests over and filled their cups with wine as their glass was emptied and more wine was made to appear. He did not call the master of ceremony, bring him center stage and say, "*Watch this. It is going to be really cool! Now watch closely, and when you leave you can take this story to your place of position and power.*" This is not what happened at all. An exchange took place that I want us to notice. Jesus worked with those who were of low degree! That's right; through the hands of servants Jesus worked a great miracle. Jesus told them to fill the water pots and that is what they did. They obeyed the voice of the Lord and followed His instruction. Mary got their attention and told them to do what He said. They must have been gathered around when Jesus arrived at the house. Not only was it the servants' job to prepare and serve the guests wine and food, it was their duty to wash the feet of the guests. They were there in the house and in the room when Jesus showed up.

You must know they were aware they had just washed Jesus and the disciples' feet. In addition, surely they witnessed all of them wash their hands in the water of the stone pots. You must know they were fully aware they had helped muddy the waters themselves. Provided with such valuable information, we must also know they would have looked at Jesus as if He was crazy when He told them to fill the pots without first emptying them. Yes, as crazy as it sounds, we would have acted in the same manner. Servants are no less or any higher than logical thinkers, they are rich and poor, educated or just a hired hand. We were discussing whether these servants were hired, bondservants, or volunteer servants. We do not know, still we would have looked at Jesus like He was crazy. *"You want us to do what? Come on now, she just said that we are out of wine and you want us to fill up these pots?"* We as people of logic, carnality, or the flesh look for reasonable reasons for acting. Faith is something that God puts down on the inside and desires that we cultivate it. The Lord Jesus throughout scripture seemed amazed at times of the faith of people when they acted in a small measure. These were people who acted on a word or simply believed in what He said without having all the evidence in front of them, moving forward without having the tangible. It would seem that those of us in Christ could have possibly acted upon faith if we had known that this was Jesus, the son of David. Yes, those who had attended his church and heard just how great a preacher he was. But not these servants; they were busy attending to the needs of the householder. They were not afforded the luxury of having witnessed one of his great sermons. It took Mary giving them the prodding they needed. In doing so they acted on a word and faith that would put to shame most seasoned believers.

Jesus more than once acknowledged faith of this nature. In Luke the 7th chapter, we find such a story. This is a story of a centurion acting on a word from the Lord believing without seeing; Jesus turning to him, looking him dead in the eye telling him, "I say unto you, I have not found so great faith, no, not in Israel." This man was a roman Soldier who should not have had any faith in

102

Christ. The Romans had many gods they worshiped, and the Jews' God was not one of them. It was something that happened as a quickening exploded in his spirit, a happening that surpassed his intellectual mind. He believed what Jesus said, he took Him at His word, acted in faith believing, and Jesus marveled at his faith. This centurion did not need a picture in advance. He knew by faith that this was no ordinary man. The servants at this wedding party did what Jesus said to do. Two points I'd like to make. The first is they listened to Mary, and the second is they obeyed the word of Jesus.

At times we, in the body of Christ, forget we are called to be a servant. Servants are not only called to serve but they are also called to follow orders given by someone in a position of authority. Mary stepped up to the plate, took charge, and gave a directive. The beauty of it all is that the servants did what was instructed. We as servants must listen to those whom the Lord has placed over our life.

Concerning those whom God has placed in a position of authority over us spiritually... *Obey them that have the rule over you, and submit yourselves: for they watch for your souls, as they that must give account, that they may do it with joy, and not with grief: for that is unprofitable for you. Hebrews 13.7*

I have witnessed as a pastor the extremes to which individuals take freedoms in the church. At times there is a belief that it should be a free for all - anyone doing anything they desire at anytime. *After all, Jesus is love, right?* It is completely the opposite. Although we are under the new and better covenant, we are still following a pattern. Temple worship and the tabernacle in the wilderness were patterns that were to be followed. There was an established way that they were to approach God. Not one thing was overlooked when it came to their approach to the Lord. This was done in order. God's house is a house of order and He gave directions on how we are to come to Him, even in the New Testament church. I truly wonder how far out of order we have gotten as the church in our attempt to draw the masses. I wonder how many principles we have overstepped and overlooked in our feeble attempt to be more seeker-sensitive. I can find nowhere in the word of God where Jesus compromised any of His values to attempt to get people to like Him so they would follow Him. Jesus said He is the way the truth and the life; without truth there is no life. Jesus never told us what we wanted to hear to make us feel good about ourselves; He always met the truth head on. Never once did Jesus skirt the issue of our heart. Though we are not to follow regimented religion as ordinances have been done away with in the name of Jesus, there still must be order in God's house.

At times we must be willing to follow some type of order or, better put, direction. You don't have to obey anyone if you so choose. However, we are given instruction by scripture that the Lord places every authority that is in place there. The Lord is after our heart, so He places people and situations in our life and we either submit to authority or rebel. The Lord will test our heart concerning authority. Even the most corrupt Politician, unsubmitted to Christ Christian leader with unresolved issues in their personal life. The word of God says that if they made it into position, He put them there. Hard at times to understand, yet it is true that God would put into a position one that goes against his word, but in the full council of our savior he has a purpose for their being there. There is a blessing that comes from submitting to authority. God blesses the one who would be willing to follow the orders of, as in our story, a woman. Mary gave the command to do what He says and the blessing of wine came through them doing what she said. How many times have you personally seen or known of someone leaving or quitting because they did not want to do what was instructed to do? If one has a problem with authority it will show up time and again in a person's life. As a result, a continued pattern develops that shows they have a problem with authority and continually blame everyone else for their problems on the job, at home, in church, and in marriage. These individuals will blame everyone else and believe they have been done wrong everywhere they have worked or attempted to serve. However, the truth is they have a problem submitting.

Submitting yourselves one to another in the fear of God.
Ephesians 5:21

The servants in our story helped bring about the miracle through their obedience and their obvious faith in this man whom they had never met. What a lethal combination against darkness - "faith and obedience." These two powerful virtues and characteristics of these servants caused an explosion of the manifested glory of God. I propose to you whether it comes through authority in our life or directly through the mouth of Jesus, when we act upon a word from the Lord there is a miracle that is waiting in the wings. A miracle that's all ready formed and fashioned, ready to be given if only we would have faith and obedience to His word.

We always look for the heavy hitting individual in our church to bring about the blessing. I believe it to be our nature; however, God uses those of lowly estate to bring about the mightiest of his miracles. The most obscure people are the ones that God enlists for His service, and when they submit to His will and allow them self to be used, a miracle takes place time and time again. We find in scripture that God uses people like you and me, but rarely do you find where God went to someone who was high and lofty to do a great work. Rightfully so, as they would take ownership and those onlookers would attribute the miracle to their position and power. God says he resists the proud but gives grace to the humble, the humble of heart and mind. Listen to the words of Isaiah whom the Lord says He will look to and enlist in his service.

So says Jehovah, Heaven is My throne, and earth My footstool. Where, then, is the house that you build for Me? And where is the place of My rest? For all those My hand has made, and all those exist, says Jehovah. But to this one I will look, to the afflicted and contrite spirit, and the one who trembles at My Word. Isaiah 66:1-2

God is not saying He can't use someone who is talented and gifted. He is not saying He can't use one who is in a prominent position of power and prestige. That is not what He is saying at all. What He is saying is that He will use the one who simply will do what He says, when He says it. One who will tremble at His word; or, in other words, has a spirit that is useable and employable toward His service. He tells us that He can use servants that he can retool,

105

reshape, and fit into the mold that He has, and that not of their own. God tells us, "I'm not interested in the house that you can build Me. I am interested in the house I can build in you." God can use a servant that has an unbendable will and an un-yielding spirit, but they will only fulfill His purpose and never individually be fulfilled within. God is looking for a servant who will follow directions and directives. God uses people to "work out in us His will." He will put people in our life that will help knock off rough areas. These are areas that God can't use, or that which is not profitable. He puts people in our lives that "rub us the wrong way" to help bring impurities to the surface. One way that God works out His will in us is to put us in no win situations with people in position of authority directly over us. Often time we feel like they are singling us out and picking on us for no apparent reason. We will sometimes get discouraged and angry at the harsh treatment we feel we are receiving when all along the way it was God that divinely placed us in that position. There was a lesson we needed to learn. It was a lesson He will use later in our life and ministry. This type of instruction cannot come from a school; it must come through a person. It is in dealing with people that we get refined. Dealing with life we learn to be servants. Jesus prayed to the Father that He not take us out of the world but keep us in the world.

The most effective way the Lord will train us to be obedient servants is to put us in difficult, real life situations. It's kind of like Christian Soldier 101, or on-the-job training module 15. God puts us in these circumstances to grow and mature us. Remember, He is looking for servants - ones who will be in service for His kingdom. Good servants are properly trained and equipped; this is why He will call people of lowly estate versus people who are in a high and lofty position. Many who are above are not willing to come down from the perch they rest on to serve. On the other hand, there are those who are on the bottom looking to climb. Those already on the bottom have nowhere to go but up. This is why the Lord said in His word that it is easier for a camel to fit through the eye of a needle than a rich man to make it to heaven. It is hard to give up what you feel you have earned and are entitled to. Jesus also tells us in *Mark 10:31, "But many that are first shall be last; and the last shall be first.*

God is looking for servants who are willing to "give up to go up." God is looking for willing servants who would follow paths least traveled - a forerunner, if you will, that wants to work for the Lord and receive any wage that He would give. Whether it is a lot or little, they just want to serve His kingdom at all costs, and for as long as He asks.

There is always the exception to every rule regarding people. A fact must be noted; God reserves the right to touch the heart of one in a place of position and power. We cannot, nor will we, limit God to touch the heart of the wealthy and wise! God can and will use who He wants and who He wills. We as humanity continue in cycles and patterns; our nature and attributes mimic those who have gone before us. This is why the world needed and still needs a savior. All mankind is bankrupt without Jesus!

At times we can have a grandeur vision of serving in a great capacity as a servant of the Lord. Although this is good, we need to be aware that even if the Lord puts this in our heart, we need to allow God to hold the timetable for it. Sometimes service in the kingdom at a low degree will extend past our liking. In other words, following the will of God will, at times, keep you in a place longer than you want to be there. We want to climb and climb and feel that we deserve the mountaintop versus digging in the valley. Not that there is anything wrong with aspirations of bigger and better, but we must not forget that the Lord wants us to be in the place that He designed for us. At times the assignment is in an obscure place. At times the calling on our life will conflict with the flesh or what we want to do. God will never override our will. He leads and guides the way. Our Savior and Teacher will never push and rule you with an iron fist. He will allow circumstance to help persuade us, but He will never impose His will upon us. This is the beauty of serving Him. Servants do so because they have a heart after their Master. They do so out of love for the one they are serving - not out of obligation, but rather out of the goodness of their heart. It will be one who is willing to accept the assignment of the Lord, and one who is willing to lay down their life and let God have his in theirs.

Jonah was one who did not want to use his gift in the way God wanted him to use it. He did not like the people of Nineveh; he despised everything they stood for. The nation had no idea of what it was to serve the true and living God. It was a pagan city, a city that was flourishing. Scripture calls it "that great city." From the outside it would appear that they had it all together, so why would they need salvation? God thought otherwise and desired that they be spared from destruction. Jonah did not like it. Though he was called and anointed to be a prophet, he wanted to choose where and when he would use his gifts. This is just not acceptable with the Lord. He wants more than a yielded vessel. This is not enough. He wants a *willing* vessel. He wants more than just saying, "Lord use me," but rather, "Use me where and how you want me." It's an easy thing to say, but hard at times to lay down your will and submit to being used in a bad place at a bad time.

Jonah did not want to go. He had better things in mind. He wanted to stay right where he was in his comfort zone preaching to those he knew and liked. He was angry that God would even want to save a people like the Ninevites. Can we establish a fact right now? God reserves the right to save anyone He wants to save. Maybe it is an ex-spouse who needs the Lord? Maybe God wants to save a father who molested you while you were a child and you have never gotten over the hurt of it? God wants to save humanity, and at times He wants to save people we dislike. It's not uncommon to dislike someone, and that doesn't make you a heathen. Jesus really showed anger and dislike for the religious right of the day. Sadducees and Pharisees he called a 'brood of vipers.' Not sure if that sounds like dislike in your book, but where I'm from that sounds a little bit like it. However, Jesus himself desired that not one of them should perish. No, this is the message of the gospel - "to all who would believe." God wants us to conform to His image, not Him to ours.

Repentance is what he is after. A war that is waging in the flesh is to be in control of what we possess. Even if God has given it to us, we are nothing more than stewards of the gift. God tells us freely that we have received, so shall we freely give. Jonah did not want to give; he wanted to choose how he and the gifts he possessed were going to be used. I've seen it so many times that it saddens me as a pastor, and I'm sure coaches and employers can attest as well. It's saddening when people who possess great talents and gifting have gotten out of the area of their gifting and talents - squandering away what God has so generously given. *No, I'm not going to do it. I'm not going there. I'm not going to talk to them.* Heartbreak for God is for Him to have invested so much into His people, only for them to waste what He has given. God has made an investment in your life. With this fact I must state, He wants to use you where He planted you.

Jonah did not want to be used the way God wanted to use him. God subsequently used adverse circumstances to get Jonah to conform. Either by circumstance or willing, God's will is going to be accomplished. We are more than pawns in the hand of a heartless God, we are chosen to take part in His master plan and remember it is *His* plan. It is not that God does not care for what we desire. We can rest assured that His word tells us to delight in Him and He will grant the desires of our heart. The one fact that is paramount is this - God will continue to establish His kingdom and bring it into full view, but he doesn't want to do it alone. He requests our participation. He extends an outstretched arm offering partnership, with Christ as the head. We will reap all the benefits as the king and owner except that Jesus must lead and we follow.

My father always made the comment that anything that that had two heads is a monster. The longer I live, and the more I manage and God gives me to govern, I have found this to be true. Whether it is in business or in the corporate church, there must be one single head, one that has the final say. It is not as if others' opinions don't count. It is not as if what others have to say is not of value. God cares what we think.

God was going to destroy Sodom and Gomorrah, and declared it to Abraham. When receiving this disturbing news, Abraham began to dialogue with God through a series of questions. Abraham first asked God that if he found 50 righteous people there, would He spare the city, and the Lord's response was yes. Abraham reduced that number and repeats it all the way down to 10 people -

the number of his nephew Lot and his family - who had made their home there. God again said yes, He would spare the city. However, He already knew that it was not going to happen. Only Lot, his two daughters, and his wife would heed the warning. What I would like for us to see is that God cares what we think and feel, but ultimately it is His will that will be accomplished in the earth.

The greatest blessing of the Lord is to find His will and get in it. Like a mighty river of Joy and fulfillment is one who is in the will of the Father. Jonah, as you have heard, was the prophet who never really got it. He could not get past the haze of humanity or carnal thinking. When we look past our religious blinding, we can see that God wants to save those whom we don't like or care for. It is then when we see an all-loving and all-caring God that came to earth to save, yes, but even more than just us. For God so loved the world that he "gave," and to this day He keeps giving and giving. Reaching and reaching out to those who are lost and inviting them to take part in the harvest of this end time.

Will we be used for His glory even if it means staying in a job that we don't like because God has asked us to be a light where we are the only one "saved"? Will we stay in a marriage that is "trying" to say the least? You've given your heart to the Lord and yet your spouse riles you and mocks the Lord you serve. They stay with you, but make life hard at best. Still, God asks you to stay for His sake and glory. Will you stay and obey the Lord? Will you stay on the job? Will you answer the call to be in an undesired circumstance for the Lord? Will you be willing to be used by God to be a lamp for Him, shining in a very dark world? Will you be used by the Lord to stay in a bad location? Will you be used by God to go into a bad location, if only for the reasons he has asked you to go? This is the high calling of God; many will serve God in the good life and easy surroundings where it is safe, with little chance of harm or discomfort. Yet, there is a high calling for those that submit themselves to be used as a vessel of Lord.

You may never be a martyr where they extinguish your life, but you may martyr your chances of being in their group or clique by taking a stand for God and the cause of the cross. You may forever mark yourself as one who does not compromise your faith and relationship with Christ. You have made a stance to say you are not ashamed of the gospel, and you are not ashamed to be counted among the brethren.

Maybe God *will* call you to physical martyrdom. All over the globe everyday there are people who have to choose to confess Jesus or give their life. Everyday there are people who choose Jesus over the fear of losing their life and they choose to confess that Jesus is Lord. We in the west are so insulated from knowing that this still happens. If you dig just a little past the message of wealth and prosperity you would see that people are still laying down their life for Jesus.

What will you do if asked to deny Jesus or give our neck to the executioner?

What will you do if Jesus asks you to lay down our life?

Will you say, "Is there an easier way? Is there another place versus Nineveh?"

It is happening at such a quickening rate - men and women of the cloth abandoning their posts and choosing to give in to sin and rebellion. In all the discouraging news of the day, still there is a light. This light and glimmer of hope is a people who have a made up minds. There are many people that never get news coverage for their work, yet carry the torch of Christ, willing to go and do whatever is asked of them as the Spirit of God dictates. News travels fast in the media-inundated society we live in. It seems daily we hear of ministries or ministers who have fallen or made the wrong choice at the apex of their calling. This is sad and disheartening. Nevertheless, a call goes out for those willing to pick up the torch, or pick up the baton that has either been dropped or thrown away. In light of all the negative news that is appearing on the national headlines as I type these words, we must not forget this: For every one of these fallen, self-serving individuals, there is an abundance of willing vessels that are looking for a chance to spread their wings for Christ.

Out of every heartbreaking story of leaders gone astray there is a positive side of the coin if looked for. It seems when one of these scenarios happens, like the one this week as I'm writing concerning a 'Mega Church Pastor coming out of the closet as gay' takes place, an awakening out of sleep happens among those who hold true to a literal interpretation of scripture. When we see ministers come out as gay, abusing children sexually, or getting caught in a scandal, we have the opportunity as never before to preach truth to a dying world. Jesus did it in His day with a people who carried titles as servants, but in reality were wolves in disguise. Jesus used the likes of these as subject matter. Far surpassing holding men, servants, or everyone to the Levitical law, Jesus addressed the condition of the heart. Though we are no longer under the Mosaic Law through ordnances, Jesus tells us to be circumcised in our heart. It is a "heart matter." Men have, as 2Timmothy 3 says, *become lovers of themselves and of pleasure rather than of God.* I confidently am of the knowledge that the Lord knows right where they are and what they are doing. In the wake of those hirelings who have left the sheep to be devoured by wolves, God has remaining those who are servants after His own heart. We cannot lose sight that God is sovereign and He knew what they were going to do when they did it. Nothing is out of the sight and knowledge of God. God is looking for someone to see a problem and step in to fix it. If you see bad example after bad example, then you be the one who makes it a point to be the opposite! Be the one who chooses to set the bar high and live a consecrated life.

At times we give so much attention to all the problems swirling around us that we forget that there is a God who has earth as his footstool and has heaven as his throne. God is still in control and though we can't do anything about what others are doing, we can answer the call and be available to what God is asking us to do. I have chosen to highlight this subject because we have a choice and an opportunity to serve no matter what others do or don't do. We must keep our eyes upon the risen Savior and follow His leading and leave all the questions to Him. We must not lean on our own understanding, but in all our ways acknowledge Him, and He will be the one to direct our path. There will be times that we will not understand why the examples we have been given failed, but this I know; a trumpet is sounding for you to gird on your spiritual sword for there is a battle that still needs to be fought, a good fight of faith! A call goes out that asks a profound question; whom shall I send? Will you say, "Send me Lord, and let me be one of your chosen servants?"

In our story of Jesus' first miracle we find the servants did what they were asked and instructed to do. We read of the master of the wedding party coming to the bridegroom about the goodness of the wine that came through the water. We then hear something, which interests you and hopefully me; a scripture says that the governor did not know where the wine came from, only the servants knew. Oh my, what a privilege we have as servants of the Lord to be in such close proximity to the King of King and the Lord of Lords! The servants knew where the wine came from because they took part in what the Lord did. They could have refused, but they submitted and they received the blessing of not just knowing where the fine wine came from, but having had a part in it. These servants who had no outward appearance of greatness, which had to work for their keep, witnessed something first hand that people of high stature desired to see. This was an opportunity that forever changed their lives and the lives of others. This was only possible because they were serving.

There are things we will never see, there are places we will never go, and things we will never take part of in the Lord if we are not serving in some capacity. The Priest saw the glory of God because he was serving. The servants at the wedding ceremony were able to partake in the glory of the miracle because they were serving. I thank God for those willing to serve, taking the gospel of Christ places I'll never be able to go. Around the world there are many nameless servants doing a work for Jesus simply because they love the Lord and want to serve. Many are in it for the wrong reason, this is true, but following the example of Jesus when the disciples came to him upset about others preaching in the name of Jesus. He tells them whether in pretense or not, the name of Jesus is preached. The name of Jesus will be spread, whether as a willing servant, or at times a self-serving servant. Jesus name will be proclaimed.

In closing this chapter, I would like to look at the life of one notable servant by the name of Elisha. This was a man that had to give up to go up. He had to lay down his agenda and follow for an extended period of time. He served longer than most would even think about. He served a cause that was bigger than he was. He followed a servant who was following God. There are times that God asks us to serve Him by serving others, and sometimes there is a servant he has chosen for a time period.

God spoke to Elijah that he was to anoint Elisha to be a prophet in his departure. Elijah found Elisha plowing in a field with twelve yoke of Oxen and as Elijah cast his mantel upon him, a request was made.

And he left the oxen, and ran after Elijah, and said, Let me, I pray thee, kiss my father and my mother, and then I will follow thee. And he said unto him, Go back again: for what have I done to thee? 1Kings 19:20

He was making a statement of commitment. He was telling Elijah, "If you let me go, I will be back and forever be your servant and follow you." Two things he did; one, he took the oxen and boiled them with the instruments of plowing, and two, he kissed his father and mother goodbye. He forever said goodbye to the life he once lived. By this act he was saying, "My life is no longer my own, I have nothing to come back to. I have destroyed my way to make a living. I've killed the oxen and burnt the implements. Even further, I said my goodbyes for life, told my mom and dad I loved them, then kissed them goodbye. I wonder how many have left thinking they would be gone for a long time only to return quickly to their trade, or the comfort of mom and dad.

A great lesson in servant hood is that how we start greatly effects our commitment during the difficult years of service. If we leave ourselves an out, then when times get tough we will be tempted to return to where there is familiarity and the comfort of a hot meal and warm bed. Not Elisha, he told Elijah, "I must do this. I will close the door to the possibility of return to the past. If I leave a way of return I will surely be lured back to the past." This is not God's best, nor His will for your life. God wants us to enter servant hood so we can train to train. Yes, when we serve we are in training for the future. God never intended for us to enter service and never grow out of entry-level service. When we enter service, we take part in a great exchange; God gives as we give. We give our self and He gives grace to endure hardship along the way. We give of our time, and He gives the talents as tools for the job at hand. We give our heart and He floods it with joy and fulfillment. Never do we give without God giving more. Service is always rewarded. Rewards may not come in the form of money, however it could. Nevertheless, God gives and then keeps giving when we enter service.

Elisha burnt the bridge to the past for a life of service to the one that held the keys to his future. He understood there was a mantle that the Lord had for him and he saw that Elijah was a man of God. Elijah cast his mantle upon Elisha and he was willing and ready to follow and serve Elijah. Scripture tells us that he went and did what he said he would do, then returned and ministered to Elijah and began to serve him. I wonder how many men of God who are called have left an escape route back to a trade or career. *Okay, if this whole God thing does not work out I have hidden this or that.* Not Elisha, he killed the oxen, burned the instruments of plowing, and then invited friends and family to show them, "Hey I won't be back." He stated, "The Elisha you know is now as good as dead. I have pledged my life to serve Elijah and his God."

It is true that the vast majority of Christians will not serve on this level, though are often asked by God. There are many who reject such allegiance to his request of enlistment. The word of God says, "many are called but few are chosen." (Matthew 22:14) Few will answer such a high calling as to walk away from all they know and become a soldier in the army of the Lord. Just as in Elijah's day when God told him he had seven thousand who had never bent their knee to Baal, today He has reserved for Himself those who will follow the pattern of Elisha. What an honor to follow such a man of God. What a privilege to be called into such a selfless calling. It is commonly believed that he served Elijah for 10 years, past the point of most willing to serve an organization, yet he served an individual.

We read that near the end of Elijah's ministry he instructed Elisha to stay behind as he went on. Three times Elisha said, "No, I don't think so. I started off with you, and you told me the only way I would get this double portion and anointing is to stay with you. I not only believe in you, I believe in the One who has anointed you. If it takes following you into some uncertain times, then I'll do what it takes and go where you go." Unlike the masses leaving when times get tough, Elisha refused to abstain from danger. Remember that Jezebel is still after the life of Elijah during this time. He had become a father to Elisha and was surely concerned for his safety, yet Elisha would not stay behind. Three times he would reject the plea to stay behind. In doing so, Elisha was able to see the chariot of the Lord come and take Elijah up in a whirlwind. Elijah's mantle came down; Elisha picked it up, and received from his faithfulness a double portion of his anointing. We read in scripture of Elisha performing twice the miracles that Elijah performed, validating a fulfillment of a promise made.

There is a supernatural transfer that takes place when we are in service to the King and while in His presence He works wonders. Once you have been in the presence of the King and have taken part in His work and see how it changes lives, it is then that strength is gained through serving.

In no other way can you receive this powerful impartation than through entering into service of the King. I can only imagine what the servants thought when they were to serve the guests and they drew out the wine that they knew they had been water just moments before.

If ever this miracle was engraved in the heart of anyone, it surely was in the hearts and minds of the servants. It was good that the Governor of the feast tasted of the goodness of the wine. Still I believe the greater reward of the blessing was to the ones who had taken part in the miracle. The servants knew firsthand what happened and how it happened. Their mind was forever changed about the power of this Prophet. What a joy it must have been to be able to know that what they were giving others was not of a natural occurrence, but had happened at the instruction of this Nazarene guest. When you begin to serve with and for the Lord, He uses your hands to bring about miracles for others. Very easily He could have just spoken, and the vessels could have filled themselves with fresh flowing wine. This was not what He wanted. He wants our service, and He wants us to take part and use our hands.

I am confident in saying that when the servants arose from their sleep that morning they had no clue they would be used in such a manner. As far as they were concerned, the day of labor could not pass soon enough. Jesus had far more in store for them that life-changing day. I'm confident if they were here today to recount the unfolding of the events of that day there would still be an excitement in their voice and a smile on their face.

At times God still uses this process of recruitment. He shows up when you are going about your day and invites you into a miracle. He doesn't send you to or through some miracle training school to launch you out into the world with your backpack full of miracle tricks. No, Jesus shows up right where you are and gives instruction on what to do and how to do it.

When there was a great need to feed the multitudes because of a lack of food, He told the disciples to feed them. God was training them to use the power He had given them. God wants that same participation from us, a willing set of hands that can be used in His service. God will give the provision and the direction, but He wants us to be an extension of his glory.

I'm not sure where or at what season this book finds you in your life. It's possible this finds you already in His service, which is a good thing. Strengthen yourself, for even greater assignments lie ahead. Maybe you find yourself depleted from service and feel disenchanted from not seeing any benefit of your labor. If this is you, take comfort knowing the Lord has said your labor (service) is not in vain. God will remember your labor of love. It could be that you want to serve the kingdom of God but don't know where to begin. I would like to share with you that there are needs all around us. All the Lord is looking for is someone to step into the middle of a need. Regardless of your talent and experience, the Lord wants to use you in ways that you never thought he would. I will take this a step further and say, "God wants to use you to be someone else's miracle."

Whom shall I send? - God

Chapter 5

Just Do It

His mother saith unto the servants, "Whatsoever He saith unto you, do it." John 2:5

The Shoe Company Nike made multiple millions through a slogan campaign that was short but effective - "Just do it." Two thousand years earlier there was a woman named Mary, the mother of Jesus, who was concerned for guests at a wedding party. Mary gave a directive to servants who were working this festive event that still rings true today. "Just do it." This was a short but profound instruction given to the previous chapter's subject matter, the servants. Immediately we see the connection of being a servant, having a person in authority above you, and then submitting and following through with the command. Clearly we see Jesus is painting a picture and laying out a pattern that we can follow. This pattern is one that yielded a supernatural outcome. Mary told the servant to do whatever Jesus told them to do. She knew He was going to do something, though she obviously did not know how He was going to do it. What she did know is, He would somehow fix the problem and meet the need of the hour. How He was going to accomplish this she didn't know, so she simply told them to do whatever He says.

She didn't care how He was going to do it, she only knew He would, or she would never have told them to follow His instructions to the letter. "Whatever He tells you to do, do it, regardless of how crazy it seems. Regardless of how silly it will look or feel, go ahead and do what he says." There is a great blessing that comes from following the leading of the Holy Spirit.

Many go through life wondering what God wants, and where God wants them to go. God wants more for us than wandering around with no clue of His will. I acknowledge at times that the Lord can be silent, with no whispers in the ear or a loud profound pronouncement for your life. To carry this further, the silence can be for extended lengths of time. But always if we ask, He answers. Furthermore, when he does, it will be in a way that is real and relevant to you. God wants to speak to you; He desires a people, whom He created, to communicate with Him.

At times you must go back to the beginning of something to find a reference point pertaining to the original intent and purpose. We will do just that. Read with me and see. In the first book of Moses, otherwise called Genesis, we find God stepping down from heaven and walking with Adam in the cool of the day in the Garden of Eden. There was a bond that God and Adam shared; however, God reserved headship over Adam. Still, they shared a personal relationship that seems to eclipse our understanding of the quality fellowship God desires between Himself and humanity. We read that God walked with Adam, so we certainly can ascertain there was an agreement between the two. The book of Amos the third chapter states that, "two can't walk together except they are agreed." There was an agreement and harmony between the two. The only voice that Adam heard was the Lord's. The voice that God intended him to hear perpetually was His. It was along the way through rebellion that Adam stepped out of agreement with God and began to listen to a voice that previously had no place.

In Genesis 3:17, the Lord made a judgment over man's life for this reason - "*Because thou hast hearkened unto the voice of thy wife.*" Adam cast off his authority and gave it to his wife. Adam hearkened, listened, or followed the voice of his wife over the voice of God. The number one voice we are to listen to is the voice of God. Hands down, there is no other way. In no other path is there more safety than in following the voice of God. I do not imply that as husbands you are not to listen to the ideas, feelings, or suggestions of your wife. Nor do I imply that as wives you are not to listen to the voice of, or be in subjection to your husband. Many times God will speak to the wife in a God-centered marriage and help to bring direction and wisdom. We see that Adam's relationship with his wife was to be modeled after the relationship of his and God's. God and Adam walked together, they communed, and fellowshipped. However God had headship over Adam, and as long as Adam was in submission to the headship, harmony and blessings flowed.

We are to listen to the voice of the Lord. Some may say, "How do I do this? Are you telling me that God is going to speak to me in a voice I can hear?" I would say it is possible that He would, and you cannot count that out. We are living in a day that even among the brethren they limit the God who has no limits. God is not limited by space, time, or any form of boundaries. God can choose to speak audibly to you if He wishes. I must admit, I cannot say I have heard an audible voice. I have heard a voice that was loud enough that I would like to think others could hear but in actuality, probably not. Still, to me it is all I needed to hear. God makes Himself known to me, as He will to you. Whether it is through his written word, which is His primary way of speaking, or by a nudging or prompting in your spirit, He will speak to His people. God wants a people who will listen for His voice. The inner witness of the Holy Spirit will not lead you astray. God wanted Adam's affection and adoration but something happened along the way. Adam's downfall was not in eating the forbidden fruit; no, it was much deeper than sinking his teeth into a lush piece of ripe fruit. It was not in the juice running down his chin, smiling as he committed sin in eating what was forbidden. God himself provides damning evidence his sin started before the act manifested. Adam gave ear to his wife; the one who should be led was now leading.

God wants to be number one!

God told Adam, "Because you have hearkened to the voice of your wife" (Gen. 3:17). Eve's sin was one and the same - she listened to a voice that she should never have given ear to. Eve gave her ear to a subtle serpent and when she gave him her ear he took both her and Adam down at the same time. There are times we must watch and protect each other as husband and wife. When married to a believing spouse, for reasons known or unknown, they start to drift and listen to a voice that is not of God. It is then we must be a help to each other. We, when married, are called to be one, coming into agreement of the covenant of marriage ordained by God. What we are not called to do is to openly disobey the direct laws or principles of God. Yes, it is true that we don't live under the law, but we are under grace. God still has laws that He has instructed us not to break. We can't get to heaven by keeping laws, but there is a separation or loss of rewards that occurs when we violate them. The law of sowing and reaping is still in effect today. (See Galatians 6:7) When out of even subtle rebellion we don't follow God's voice, there is a negative outcome that takes place. I do praise God and live in and under the umbrella of Grace, but I too must acknowledge that I know all too well the negative harvest received from not doing things God's way. Whether it was through ignorance or refusing to heed to the gentle urgings of the Holy Spirit, a less desirable outcome was received. God wants the best for us in every area of our life. His Holy Spirit leads us.

We are living in a time that few want to hold up the banner of the Lord and truly proclaim that sin separates. No longer is it popular to hear a message on repentance and confession of one's sins. I know we could have endless debates as to the extent to which sin separates us from God, but that is neither my purpose nor my axe to grind. Rather I would hope that we, as the body of Christ, would again begin to fall on our knees and ask a Holy God to forgive our iniquity. A cry going out from the heart of God is a pleading for His people to follow the voice that has already spoken. We get bored with the voice from the past; we want a fresh and new Prophecy to play with. The Lord has already spoken concerning what He wants, what He expects pertaining to your life. I am the biggest defender and advocate of the Gifts of the Spirit, yet I hold true to the teachings of Christ that say a perverse generation seeks a sign and wonder. Profound as it might be, God wants trust. He wants us to trust Him on what He has already spoken. Believe in Him in what he has already said (His written word).

I must ask the question - have you ever told your children you and them were going somewhere, and without fail as you're getting things ready they keep asking, "Are we still going?" For those of you who have experienced this, I believe you can relate.

After the fifth or sixth time of having to reassure them that what you said is true and it's going to happen, it is then that there can be slight heartache on your part. Either they don't believe you, or it is not happening fast enough for them. In the same way as parents wanting their children to simply trust them, God, too, wants our trust in knowing what He has said He will also do.

> *God is not a man, that He should lie; neither the son of man, that He should repent: hath He said, and shall He not do it? or hath He spoken, and shall He not make it good? Numbers 23:19*

The Lord will fulfill His word! Rest assured that what He has said will most assuredly happen. So when He gives instruction to not eat from the tree of the knowledge of good and evil, don't do it. For if you do, when you do, you will surely die. Fully know it will happen. When God says something He means it. We as humanity begin to justify and reason it out in our mind on how we can get what we want, even when the Lord said that we couldn't have it. Goodness, this is such a powerful truth. We will come up with all kinds of reasons and excuses as to why we didn't follow what the Lord has already said. God is not a man that He should lie; men at times stretch matters to fit their circumstances. The God we serve is not that way. Our God does not lie, nor does He allow men to justify lying to fit their life. God has asked His people to live a life above reproach. Nothing will cloud a man's character in another's eye quicker than to find out he has handled the truth recklessly. When someone lies to get what he or she want or to get out of something, it forever marks his or her life. It is hard to place trust in one that is known to be less than honest. Truth at times stings; but truth is a healer and must be heralded at all times.

Satan twisted the word of God to get the attention of Eve. She lent her ear to Satan and that was all that was needed to topple, like dominos, the blessings that were pillars in her and Adams life. It wouldn't seem that God would be so harsh and banish them from the Garden of Eden for one act of disobedience. God means what He says and says what He means! We must remember that the Lord told them, "If you do it, you shall surely die." That is what He said.

Satan lied and told Eve, "You shall not surely die." I propose to you that the first voice is the Lord's and the second is a false, cheap imitation. You cannot afford to second-guess God; He means what He says. The Lord works within His will determining if you will or will not get a second chance at getting it right. Adam and Eve were not afforded a second chance in the Garden of Eden. They were forever expelled. Then to top it off, God made sure that they did not try to sneak back in. God stationed angels with flaming swords to guard the entrance to the garden. Though I do not believe myself to be old, I'm aware that I have lived more than half my life. I don't have the time to make mistakes any longer. As I look back over my life I am keenly aware of the decisions I've made whether good or bad that have affected my life.

In both instances, I see how both set the course for years to come. When we are young we weigh ramifications of our decisions far less, but as we age, we learn from a master teacher called the past. Then we see we can't afford to make more mistakes. Unfortunately there are those who are more advanced in years who should know better by now, but refuse to learn. Year after year they keep repeating the same mistakes, caught in a cycle they have the power to break, yet they don't. They become a slave to their own poor choices and decisions. If you would, bear with me for a moment. Look over your shoulder and be honest with yourself. I want you to reflect and think about the decisions you've made more times than not – whether they helped you or brought harm to your life. I can hear the case being made that there is always the unexpected and the uncontrollable. It is true; life has a way of socking it to us at times. There are occasions when you did everything within your power to do it right and it still crashed down around you.

You did your homework and it checked out great. You jumped in only for the water to drain out in the middle of your jump. There is nowhere to go. Expect to brace for the impending impact. Yes I am aware and have suffered these things too. These monstrous, ugly, and painful experiences are not what I am talking about. I am talking about the outcomes that we could have prevented - the outcomes that could have been better. In all truth, they were meant to promote you. You know the ones - those in which we had the power to change, but did nothing. I believe we can help or hurt our destiny. This was Eve; she had already given way to the lust of the eye and saw the fruit higher than her relationship with God. Adam had not yet done so. When he found Eve's evidence in hand, she could have repented. Instead she helped to further her sin by involving her husband.

Adam could have made a good decision in spite of Eve's poor choice and defiant decision. He had the power to help rectify a life-altering choice made by his wife. Adam was the head and was responsible for the spiritual direction of his home. He could have covered his wife and her sin by leading and being a Godly example, but he did not. The result was banishment from the perfect garden. He saw it was sin, he knew it was wrong, yet he followed his wife off the edge of emptiness. What a heartbreaking story, knowing that he could have saved his own wife's hide, but instead gave in as well. It was possible that God through Adam could redeem his own wife and pay her ransom, but instead he became a slave with her. Easily stated: "Two wrongs don't make a right." It is said that love blinds the eyes of the beholder. But I propose to you that for the sake of loving the Lord above all, we should be willing to listen to the voice of the Lord versus a wayward spouse. We can take this even further and apply this to any relationship, whether it is friends, siblings, or a boss asking us to do something that is either sinful or illegal.

Compromising God's principals does not pay the profitable wage that is portrayed. It has a payday, but it maybe not the one we would like. There is pleasure in sin for a season; but seasons change and you may not like the next one that follows. I want God's best for my life even if it means being unpopular with ones that should support me. I want to live a life above reproach and be blameless in the eyes of God. If we choose this route, then, even though others make false accusation, we still have an advocate that stands in our stead - an advocate that comes to our aid defending us. There is power in our Christian life when we choose to do it God's way and not our own. I think of Abraham who was in a hard press, when on his journey he and Sara found themselves in the middle of a famine.

Not knowing what to do he sent his wife ahead into Egypt, and told her to say she was his sister.

Right from the start it was a no win situation. He could not win by perpetuating a lie. He sent her in under false pretense; he lied and also asked her to lie. It is one thing for us to lie but when we enlist the help of others especially those who are close to us, we do more damage than we bargain for. We find in Genesis Twelve that there was a famine in the land and he told her to tell them she is his sister and she did. Pharaoh heard of her beauty and being told she was his sister desired her to be his new beautiful wife. God plagued Pharaoh and he soon caught on that his troubling came from having another man's wife so he sent Sarah and Abraham away. To make matters worse, as if he had not learned the first time, he again in Genesis 20:2 repeated the same mistake. *And Abraham said of Sarah his wife, She is my sister: and Abimelech king of Gerar sent, and took Sarah.*

Had God not given King Abimelech a dream and told him "if you keep that woman you're as good as dead," Abraham would have forever lost his wife. Talk about not learning from past mistakes. It's true that God bailed him out twice, but what about the strain that it put on their relationship? It would not take much thought to realize he placed more value on his life then he did on hers and the covenant of marriage. He was willing to save his own skin in exchange for his bride. Abraham was supposed to cover her and protect her; instead he was willing twice to give her away. This is not what God has said marriage was supposed to be. We, as the husband, are supposed to follow the pattern given to us in

1 Peter 3:7 that tells us, "...*dwell with them according to knowledge, giving honour unto the wife, as unto the weaker vessel.*

Abraham balked twice at being the husband he was called to be. The passage you just read told you the woman is the weaker vessel and the man is to cover and protect her. I know we are living in a postmodern society that says women can do it all alone and they don't need a man to help with anything. In no way will I, or can we, diminish the progress that women have made. Yet there is a pattern that was established from the beginning as scripture outlines. In the days of Abraham, women were completely reliant upon the man for their survival. He twice sent her into another man's house out of fear they would kill him. To make matters worse, he followed the pattern of all mankind (Adam) by repeating the same mistake twice.

We find an account of Sarah, his wife, coming to him and insisting he take her servant and lay with her in order to bear a child for them that was promised, but had yet to arrive. We are aware there was no law yet in place that forbade him from this almost criminal act, yet surely there was a moral law written upon his heart that said it was wrong. The age-old adage that says," *How can it be wrong if it feels so good*" is not applicable in this case. Sorry, in no way was that a wise thing to do. Surely the leading of the Lord hadn't prompted him to make such a foolish decision? We plainly see a pattern that responsibility rests on the man to make Godly, timely, scriptural decisions. Abraham was given the ball, and time after time he fumbled.

Not only did his poor decisions affect his wife, they affected his entire family. They were decisions that were not reversible. Sarah came to Abraham after the fact, not being able to stand one more day. "Abraham, *I don t care that I gave her to you, and I don't care if that boy came from your loins. I want them gone by sundown!"*

Mary whirled and looked the servants square in the eye and said, "Do what he says to do." Previously, we found a less favorable situation with an embittered Sarah who was at the end of her own rope, giving an order that seemed unimaginable to anyone. We read the account in Genesis 21 of Sarah being angered over her own poor choice of coming to Abraham and telling him to send his son and the bondwoman away.

I can hear the exasperation in Abrahams voice, "You want me to do what?" *Sarah that is my son and you want me to send them away. Where will they go, and how will they survive, what shall they eat and whom shall protect them?* As hard as it is to understand,

God comes down to Abraham and tells him two things pertaining to his present dilemma. First, He tells him the same thing Mary told the servants that most blessed day, "Just do it." God told Abraham to do as the woman has said. I can only imagine the look on his face to know that God Himself has just told him to give away his son. Abraham did as God said, and would again face the same circumstance when God told him to take his now only son Isaac and offer him up as a sacrifice on top of Mt. Moriah. Twice Abraham is asked to do the unthinkable. Many of us face difficult tests in life, stretching our faith beyond the limits of our intellect. Few ever face the same indescribable pain of having been told to give away your son twice by The Lord God almighty.

I have thought many times about God telling Abraham to send his son Ishmael away, and not only his child, but also his wife Hagar. Sarah must have forgotten she not only asked her husband and slave girl to hook up, but she gave her to him as a wife. Now Abraham is faced with the choice of disobeying God or sending away part of his family. I want you to know, though it was a mistake, a bad choice, and though he made the blunder of a lifetime, it was still his son. How many of us have made such mistakes? Maybe you did not descend to the level of depravity that they did. This, in those days, was not so uncommon to do - marrying multiple wives. However, a child by a wife other than Sarah was not what God said He would do. The society we live in is far different than previous generations, changing and morally eroding by the day. With that being said, you don't give your man to another woman. There is just something wrong with that! No woman I've ever known would share her husband with any other woman. Not to mention that she gave away that which she had relations with to be her husband. She gave away and divided what was solely hers, and now legally she had to divide and share all his possessions.

It was doubly aggravating for Sarah to know it was of her own doing that she was in the mess she was in. She gave her servant to her husband in haste, and now wants an easy way out of her poor decision. There are some decisions made that turn out to be less than wise; these poor decisions cannot be so easily undone. I know we all would like to blink and change some of those poor choices. We would prefer to lie down and arise wishing it were only a dream. I'm sorry, but this is not possible. God is a forgiving God; God is a God of love, and wants to help us through our blunders. However, some things we will have to live with for life. It is not that God does not want to come to our rescue. It is not that he doesn't want to wash away all our mistakes. Sometimes we tie God's hands due to choices that we make. Through the governing hand of God and the eternal laws that he set in place by his will, we reap what we sow. We, at best, could pray for a crop failure on many seeds that we have sown!

Something was at work behind the scenes that we cannot see upon first reading this story. Hidden just out of sight, God had a plan far bigger than Sarah's mistake and Abraham's failure. I am sure as you have read these passages you possibly thought to yourself "Wait a minute. I have done far less than what Sarah did and look how she got off so easy when my simple mistake cost me everything. Look how Abraham failed miserably as a husband and father yet he seemed to be blessed in the end."

Sarah came to Abraham and said, "Send her away," and then God spoke directly to Abraham backing her up with a command. *Just do it; "Abraham, In all that Sarah has said to you, listen to her voice" (Genesis 21:12).*
For many, when first reading this, they can be appalled and bewildered that God would tell Abraham to do such a thing. It is only when you begin to understand the nature of God; you see His directives are to fulfill His purpose on earth - in us, and what is already decreed in Heaven. God takes our mistakes and turns them into potential.

I don't believe that most set out to make the blunder of the century. Only a fraction of individuals have a careless attitude. It is true that not everyone's priorities are in the right place, but most people, Christian or not, don't intentionally make decisions that will destroy their life. This is why we need the ministry of the Holy Spirit. There are times in our life that every indicator points towards us making a right choice. But, lying just beneath the surface or out of sight is that one thing that will keep it from being a wise decision.

There is a way that seemeth right unto a man, but the end thereof are the ways of death. Proverbs 16:25

It is in these situations of difficulty the Holy Spirit can and will lead us around, through, or over these pitfalls. I'm sure that all who are reading this book could take ownership of a not so wise choice that we committed everything toward. We sold the farm, all on the chance of a lifetime hoping never again to worry about jockeying and positioning our self in life. "This one is it; it has to be God. There's no way this could be a mistake." "She looks so good and is intelligent; surely God sent her my way. It's okay, don't worry about me... I'll lead her to the Lord." "Don't worry about me, her divorce will be over in five weeks." "She said she loves me." "He has it all going for him - a good job, great family, and plans for the future." "I know you're concerned for me, but it's going to work out. He said he's tried to cut down a little on his drinking; he's working on it."

A business deal we have an opportunity to invest in and looks so good and is almost a done deal. "I should dig just a little deeper, but I have so much to do. After all, they come with a great reputation." A year later you find yourself in a mess up to your eyeballs. You tell yourself things could have been different if you had just made the decision to slow your rushed pace and prioritize. Had you sought God, then you would have understood that this decision could cost you all your dreams. The list of scenarios and examples from all those who share in this inexhaustible list all have one thing in common. Every last one, if afforded the opportunity, would have thought it through better, and, if they are a Christian, prayed about it first. Many wish they had the chance to return and pray more before having made such a pivotal decision. All of this is true; however, a fact is erected in front. What's done is done! We all too often are enrolled in the school of hard knocks and its instructors are past failures and bad decisions.

I cherish what I once heard, and although I'm not sure from whom this truth was spoken, let me share it with you. It reads like this - "The best teacher is not mistakes, rather the best teacher is the

Holy Spirit." Wow, what a relief to know that there is a God ordained path to good decision-making and the one who can make all the difference in our choices is the Holy Spirit! I'm not sure about you, but I want to make good, timely, wise, and Holy Spirit directed decisions. Okay, the question of the day, what do you do now that you've made the decision and it did not turn out like you had thought and had hoped? We are living in a time in which life's pace has quickened and the reality of one bad decision can set you back for years. This knowledge lets us understand that not only do we need the Holy Spirit to lead us, but we also need his ministry to help us once we have committed to one of these life-altering decisions.

It would be easy to point fingers and say, "I told you so, I tried to warn you." The world is full of people who would like to highlight all of your blunders and mistakes. We don't need anyone to remind us that we are in the middle of suffering. We know all too well that had we done this or had we done that, we wouldn't be in the middle of what we're in now. I feel God has allowed me to speak directly to you, to those whom this applies, follow again the title of this chapter. "Just do it." Do whatever the Holy Spirit tells you to do. Get in God's word and let Him illuminate the path out of trouble. I cannot guarantee the exit will be immediate. What I do know is that God provides a way of escape. Through good Godly council and following Scriptural principals, He will lead you out and back on the path to the abundant life.

Many get in these tough, tight places feeling as if it's no use - "It will never get better. I've made too many mistakes," and instead of leaning on the Lord, they give up. They feel like too much has happened, too much has gone wrong. Why try now then slip further away and separate themselves from the lifeline? They leave the Church; they quit praying and cut off all contact with those who are in the faith. I know at times those who should be a help to us shun and condemn us because of our bad choices. This is true, yet there are still countless others that will help you back onto your feet and point you back toward Christ.

Once it's done, it's done. There are times that you can't change what has happened even if you tried until you dropped. Folks, it's done! In some things there will be no do over's. What is needed is a remedy for your dilemma, redemption from your past, and a God of the present. God is always the answer - this will never change!

This is the God that we serve, if we would simply do what He says to do, today. I'm not sure where this reading finds you in life, but whether on top of the world or feeling like you're beneath, one fact towering above all is, "Jesus is Lord of all." Hear this - He is Lord of the good choices *and* the bad! God does not condone open sin and poor choices; however, what he does provide is an unobstructed path to his throne. If a humble and contrite spirit abides in you, then there is nothing that God can't redeem in your life. There is no promise that things will go back to the way they were before your poor choice was made. The promise He does give is He is Lord of the Harvest, the good harvest and the bad; He is Lord over them both. God will not cast you away; God will not throw you away regardless of how badly you've blown it. He still makes a way for you to come back to him. Jesus will never leave you nor will He ever forsake you. We needed a savior before the mistakes, and we still need one during and after.

It grieves the heart of God knowing that men close the door to His presence. Men who are but flesh themselves all too often cast judgment and mortally wound God's children. In doing so, they forever erect a fence to keep God's children out. These judgmental men suppose they have knowledge of the limits of God's mercy and grace. This should not be. I believe that God reserves the right to be God. If God chooses to extend His grace and mercy beyond our comprehension, then it is His own choosing and we should be okay with God's decisions. The scripture of God addressing the potter and the clay applies here as well. "Shall the clay say to the potter what it shall become?" We can assuredly apply it to this as well. Shall the clay say to the potter what he shall do with another lump of clay?" It is all in the Lord's choosing. Let us not condemn our self and bring condemnation on our own life because of elevating our self as God and judge. There is but one God, and we must follow the pattern of Christ, preaching and teaching that all men should repent for the kingdom of heaven is at hand. Not out of a self-righteous heart, but out of a serving heart that allows God to remain God.

I am reminded of a parable that Jesus taught his disciples that relates to this topic. In Luke the 12th chapter, we read a very startling account that applies to this day. We can become just like these men we will read about if we don't guard our self from feeling we have a right to more, or a bigger stake in the kingdom, based off our tenure in it. We will read that although God blesses faithfulness, He still reserves the right to be the Master of the house. We cannot arrive at the place that says, "I have paid my dues and I deserve more because I have worked hard and longer." Before we read this passage, I would like to remind us of a scripture in 1 Corinthians 3:7-8 So *then neither is he who plants anything, nor he who waters, but God who gives the increase. So he planting, and he watering, are one, and each one shall receive his own reward according to his own labor.*

The Lord is not implying that they are not important or cherished, but rather they are only equal with each other. No super Apostles or Holy Spirit Prodigy - we need to understand that when people rise in the Kingdom in a place of authority or prominence, it was God's plan for their life. Jealousy sets in when we feel God and life have cheated us, and we should have gotten more out of the deal for all of our service. Let's read about some jealous workers that levied a complaint against their employer, and then the business owner's response. You cannot glean the required understanding except we read the whole passage. When reading this, think of yourself and inwardly ask a personal question: Have I done this? Am I doing it now, and do I feel like I have earned or deserve better, more and all of what is due me? Remember God has told us that He will give us our portion in due time; see Luke 12:42.

Let's read a parable pertaining to this matter.

For the kingdom of Heaven is like a man, a housemaster, who went out early in the morning to hire laborers into his vineyard. And when he had agreed with the laborers for a denarius a day, he sent them into his vineyard. And he went out about the third hour and saw others standing idle in the marketplace. And he said to them, you also go into the vineyard, and whatever is right I will give you. And they went. And he went out about the sixth and ninth hour and did likewise. And about the eleventh hour he went out and found others standing idle, and said to them, why do you stand here all day idle? They said to him, Because no one has hired us. He said to them, You also go into the vineyard, and you shall receive whatever is right. So when evening had come, the lord of the vineyard said to his steward, Call the laborers and pay them their wage, beginning from the last to the first. And when they who were hired about the eleventh hour came, they each one received a denarius. But when the first came, they supposed that they would received more; and they also each one received a denarius. And receiving it they murmured against the master of the house, saying, These last have worked only one hour, and you have made them equal to us who have borne the burden and heat of the day. But he answered one of them and said, Friend, I do you no wrong. Did you not agree with me for a denarius? Take yours, and go; I will give to this last one the same as to you. Is it not lawful for me to do what I want with my own? Is your eye evil because I am good? So the last shall be first, and the first last, for many are called, but few are chosen. Matthew 20:1-16

These men entered into service in the beginning just like those at the end, agreeing to work for a wage. This was a wage that was predetermined by the lord of the vineyard. They willingly engaged in labor that they were promised, a wage they would receive in exchange for their labor. But when the end of the day had come and they gathered to receive payment for their service, it was then

134

they were not happy to find that those who had come at the end of the day received the same payment as them. I believe that an appropriate word here would be "ouch"! I am sure all of us have been in situations in where it seemed we had been short-changed, and in some cases it might be factual. In those cases, God says that He will deal with the employer who cheats his hired help and judge the one with an unbalanced scale; see Proverbs 11.

However, to those who simply enter into service into the Kingdom and become embittered with the lot they receive, God reminds us that He says a servant is worthy of His hire. Still, it is God that gives out or distributes gifts and rewards. Because we as a society have taken on a demanding state of mind, we look toward God in the same way. We feel as if we have a right to what is owed to us. In the season I am writing this chapter, I am reminded that it is in this month that we as a nation celebrate our thanksgiving for the Provisions that God gave our forefathers in settling this great nation we comfortably occupy. The notion of bigger and better has seemed to always be in our sight and thought. What is needed is a thankful heart for what He has already given us. I believe God wants us to grow and increase, but not at the expense of outgrowing our boundaries that keep us coming to God in a needing way. God said it is hard for a rich man to get into heaven. However, it is not impossible for the rich to enter into heaven, for many the Lord chooses to bless financially. The overwhelming evidence is - the more we have, the more we tend to lean on our own strength. Jesus is referring to the importance of having a thankful heart and spirit. Tell God often how thankful you are for His many provisions. I'm not sure about you but when my children express thankfulness for what was given to them, large or small, it makes me want to give even more.

We can move the heart of God toward us by doing what He has said to do in his word. Again, the simple phrase "just do it" has power. I believe that we need not put yokes up on others' necks with regulations. Nonetheless, we cannot ignore that God gives us a clear path that we are to come to, or approach, a Holy God. Keeping with this thought, see how the Lord assures us we can come to Him and then illuminates the way into His presence.

Do not be anxious about anything, but in everything by prayer and supplication, with thanksgiving, let your requests be made known to God. Philippians 4:6

Mary told the servants at the wedding feast, "Whatever He says to do, do it." In other words, however He says to do it, do it that way, or adhere to the way He has said to do it. Be anxious for nothing. You can rest assured He will hear you and His ear is attentive to your prayer. Don't worry how it's going to work out, or if it will. God tells us not to be anxious because He is on His job as Lord of all, and you are His responsibility. "He loves and cares about you". Knowing this, He tells us in (everything) big or small, important or insignificant, by prayer and supplication, and with thanksgiving let your request be made known to God. God knows we have needs and can, unlike Satan, read our mind. He knows our prayerful thoughts, but He wants us to make them known to Him. We might ask, "If an all knowing God can know even my thoughts then why should I take time to tell Him?"

Let me help you here - "He wants time with us." Let me make a statement and then ask a question. You can at times look at a silent look on the face of a child, spouse, or friend and you know what they want to ask, even though you can't read their mind. If this is true of you and me, then don't you want them to go ahead and ask? There is an exchange that takes place when we verbalize our thoughts, questions, and requests that can't be fulfilled in any other way except to verbalize them. God wants a one on one exchange to take place. When we purposely move ahead, set time aside to follow His pattern and get alone with Him and pray, make requests, and petition Him. It is then we fulfill the fellowship that He had with mankind in the Garden of Eden walking and talking with Adam. God is a personal God who wants fellowship with His creation. God wants us to come to Him and ask. Not only ask and petition, but also go one step further, expressing with thanksgiving. When we ask and ask and never acknowledge His faithfulness already proven in your life, then it gives the impression that He is only our God in times of trouble. We should give thanks to the Lord for He is good and His mercy endures forever. Through the good, the bad, and the ugly He is worthy to be thanked. We can thank Him that it is because of Jesus' shed blood on the cross that we are not consumed. We can thank Him that He has given us life; thank Him that we have breath in our bodies. We can thank Him for far more than what most give Him credit for. If our spiritual eyes were opened and we were to see what He has saved us from, I'm sure you couldn't contain yourself from loudly offering up your gratitude and thanksgiving for covering, protecting, and ordering your steps. Just do It!

Even when it makes no sense… do whatever Jesus says!

We read a story in the book of 2 Kings that fulfills the title of this chapter. It was a horrible situation the commander of the army of the King of Syria was in. He was a mighty warrior and leader, but he had a major problem that would, without a doubt, be the ruin of him if something were not done. Naaman was a leper, a mighty fighting man, but he was fighting an opponent he could not defeat. The King of Syria heard from an Israeli girl they had kidnapped that there was power to heal in Samaria with the Prophet. The King of Syria sent a letter to the king of Israel and requested he heal his servant Naaman. The King of Israel tears his clothing in utter disbelief and begins to believe it is a plot to plan an attack. Elisha gets word of it and steps in.

> And it happened when Elisha the man of God heard that the king of Israel had torn his clothes, he sent to the king, saying, Why have you torn your clothes? Let him now come to me, and he shall know that there is a prophet in Israel. And Naaman came with his horses and with his chariot, and stood at the door of the house of Elisha. And Elisha sent a messenger to him, saying, Go and wash in Jordan seven times, and your flesh shall come to you, and you shall be clean. But Naaman was angry, and went away. And he said, Behold, I said within myself, He will surely come out to me and stand and call on the name of Jehovah his God, and strike his hand over the place and recover the leper. Are not Abana and Pharpar, rivers of Damascus, better than all the waters

of Israel? May I not wash in them, and be clean? And he turned and went away in a rage. And his servants came near and spoke to him and said, My father, if the prophet had told you to do a great thing, would you not have done it? How much rather then, when he says to you, Wash and be clean? And he went down and dipped seven times in Jordan, according to the saying of the man of God. And his flesh came again like the flesh of a little boy, and he was clean. 2 Kings 5:8-14

We can see from this that God not only cares for us, but cares for humanity. This was a captain in the army of Syria; the Syrians were enemies of the nation of Israel. At times we cannot grasp why God would extend mercy and grace to those we don't share a like faith with. A story is told of a people who God brought out of bondage who refused to follow Him or do what He said; yet He still shows grace. God not only loves the saved, He also loves the unsaved!

And they refused to obey, neither were they mindful of Your wonders which You did among them. But they hardened their necks, and in their rebellion appointed a captain to return to their bondage. But You are a God ready to pardon, gracious and merciful, slow to anger, and of great kindness, and did not forsake them. Nehemiah 9:17

At times, we want God to come and set everyone straight - rain down fire and brimstone. Contrary to our wayward wishes, more times than not we see God waiting and being patient with them. We feel that God deals harshly and immediately with us, and those who are in open rebellion to His word He lets go about their business. The primary principal that we cannot escape is that God is God, and He tells us that He is slow to anger. He repeats this again in Psalms 145:8, "Jehovah *is gracious and full of pity; slow to anger, and of great mercy.*"

Can we say that about ourselves? Probably, to a degree we can say we believe God should have stepped in long ago; after all, they are in sin. There is an attribute of God that we as humanity lack; it is a true compassion that escapes our understanding. Noted, we all strive to embody God's finest qualities, but yet we fall short much too often - God does not. His nature is fulfilled on this earth, it is easy to look at our surroundings and be troubled by what we see - God does not. He is always in control, and at any moment in time He can correct the mess, command order, or have judgment commence in an instant. It was true in our life (pre-salvation), and is true in those in the world and world system. God is slow to anger and He shows compassion even to those we don't like and who embody all evil.

Christianity is not an exclusive club where we can decide who is allowed in and who is not. God desires that none perish but all come to the saving knowledge of Jesus Christ. So if it takes someone countless years to come into the kingdom, praise God they made it into the marvelous light! Making reference again, let's not be Jonah the Prophet who never really got it.

Elisha said, "Send him to me that he may know that there is a prophet in Israel." Elisha understood that God was at work and he was hearing from God. Within himself Elisha was saying, "I know that he is not one of us, I know that he is our arch enemy and has meant us harm. But the God I serve is not limited to my private use, and He can use this situation and turn it into a great work. My God can bless an enemy and, in turn, my enemy can bless me." When the favor of the Lord is on your life he can even make your enemies to be at peace with you, see Proverbs 16:7.

Naaman, not truly knowing the God of Israel, came to the house of the prophet out of desperation. This man had Leprosy and would eventually die from it. However, he went on a word from his king, and as vile as he was, he came to the right place, to the right man. Elisha knew God; this was the same servant that we looked at in our previous chapter. Elisha had a relationship with God and was willing to administer grace to one who should receive death. In the end of this story we read that even Elisha's servant mentions how

Elisha spared Naaman's life. Not only did Elisha have the power of God to heal, he had the power of God to call down fire from heaven. Remember his teacher was Elijah the Great. He did not act in haste, and in doing so fulfilled the teachings of Christ long before Christ came to earth as a man. Elisha never returned evil for evil, nor did he take revenge and snuff this man's life out, though the power to do so was at his disposal. He prayed for the one who spitefully used others and blessed the one who cursed them. Elisha was willing to send a word to him, and then pray for him as well.

Naaman came desperate but full of pride. After all, he was a pagan; he worshiped many gods. Not only was he a Pagan, he was commander in Chief of the Army of Syria. The only one higher than him was the King. What a position of power! I hope you can see the irony of the situation - here is a man of position and stature who is an enemy of the One who holds the key to his future. Leprosy was a slow death sentence, eating at one's body until it consumes all that is useable. What good is it to posses the scepter of power if you have no hands to hold it? What good is it to have Chariots as swift as lightening if you have no fingers to hold the reins? What good is it to have strong stallions if you have no legs to swing over to mount? Yes, Naaman was in a dire strait fighting for far more than to keep his position as the Armies top general; he was fighting for his life. Isn't it a sobering fact that when faced with death we will do things that we were not willing to do previous.

We go through life trying to climb and climb wishing we could just reach this level or that level. "If I get this job or that job then everything will be okay and I will have finally arrived." Then you get to the top and find out it's lonely and the air is thin, making it hard to breathe. Many make it to the top only to find that life is more stressful at the top than at the bottom. Naaman found himself at this juncture in life. He did not know God; all he knew was serving false gods had not helped, and had left him leprous with no change in his condition. His power and position had gotten him no return. Now he was desperate, and he was standing at the door in a foreign land humbling himself to a preacher man. A mighty man of war who was skilled in the art of warfare is now standing at the house of a weak defenseless holy man. What a sense of disgust he felt. He wanted healing and was willing to travel, but that was all he was willing to do. Look at how there are reserved times God will humble even the most prideful of men.

God's number one purpose for man on this earth is for them to humble themselves before a holy King (King Jesus). God will put down rebellion and sin, this is true, but God does not want to beat someone down. He desires a free will offering of our self. God does not want us to be squashed under His mighty powerful right hand. To the contrary - He wants us to come to Him as a child and simply honor that He is God. Regardless of this truth, God reserves the right to demand submission to those whom He calls. We can focus on the fact that Naaman is from a Pagan land worshiping thousands of gods. However we can't forget that the word of God says He will provide salvation to as many as the Father calls. God calls out to those whom we never think He would, even to a Pagan Army leader; see John 6:44.

Though we know that this is an Old Testament account, we still see indicators and signs that point toward the redemptive work of the cross. We can clearly see that there was a drawing or calling of this man out of his present nation, rank, family, and personal beliefs. This is God when He calls. Whether in a state of desperation or rearranging of one's life, God has a way of getting the people He calls in the right place at the right time. I would like to propose to you that God knows how to bring men to salvation, even if it means allowing desperate means in order to bring it about. God is not the author of confusion or of sickness, but He can use all means to bring us to repentance - even when it looks like all means are exhausted. A note to you who have family and friends that you see year after year living a life of destruction. Their lifestyle makes it appear all hope is lost for their salvation; God has means and ways to bring about a miraculous miracle of salvation. Staying with the thread of God doing the impossible and working a miracle, I wish to convey the knowledge that God is supreme and will secure the salvation to as many as He will call. A call went out to Naaman, "There is healing in Samaria." He acted on that word and followed it to its source. Standing in front of the door of the Prophet Elisha's house,

he was expecting Elisha to show up upon his knock.   After a,
Naaman was a man of authority.

Much to Naaman's surprise Elisha never came to the door,
but only sent a word through a messenger. Naaman had a problem
and Elisha had a solution. "Go and wash in the Jordan River seven
times." Naaman was furious with this directive, but why? Though
he went on a word to Elijah's house and humbled himself by doing
so, he still was full of pride and worldly arrogance. He could have
gotten his healing, but God, through the prophet, was after far more
than a healing of the flesh. God wanted this man to know who He
was; God wanted salvation of a soul. Naaman, at this disrespect
from Elisha, was beyond angered to the point of leaving, raging mad,
speaking out loud saying, "He will surely come out to me. Stand
and call on the name of the Lord his God, and wave his hand over
the place and heal this Leprosy!"

Naaman was offended; first, that Elisha did not have the
courtesy to come to the door, but only send a word. Secondly, he
was offended at the solution; the thought of him washing in the
Jordan was repulsive and ignorant. God tells us that He takes the
foolish things of the world to confound the wise.   This was
foolishness to him. He had come all that way only to be disrespected
and humiliated by being told to go wash in the muddy Jordan River.
He was told what to do but, instead of (just doing it), he went away
furious.   I wonder how many times we come to God looking for a
solution only to have been given an answer that we didn't approve
of? We want this or that and wonder why we don't see the result we
believe we should receive when the answer has already been given.
Forgive, be kind, show meekness, have long-suffering, be gentle; the
list could go on and on. More times than not our answer has nothing
to do with our faith. We simply "just don't want to do It!"

We're looking for a mountain moving, and rightfully so, He
has told us it is ours; yet He continues instructing that it is the small
foxes that spoil the vine. Our vine that bears fruit of much kind is
spoiled by a lack of, or total disregard for, the small yet vital matters
of our life. *"But God, I came all this way; I had faith but You want
me to do what?   But God, I paid my tithe and was faithful in my*

attendance and still you want me to do what? God, you don't know how bad they hurt me. They were the ones that were wrong and you want me to call them and tell them I'm sorry? God it's not okay - I still am hurting over what they said." Naaman went away mad over the word sent by Elisha. Look at this, Elisha told him what to do. He never sent him away empty-handed. Naaman was angry at what Elisha told him to do. Instead of (just doing it) he stormed off. He did not like what he was told to do. His life hung in the balance and he was willing to let his pride stand in the way of his divine healing, so he went away mad.

> *Pride goes before destruction, and a haughty spirit before a fall. Proverbs 16:18*

Pride nearly cost this man his chance at a new beginning. Certain doom loomed over the head of this man, and because he did not like what he heard, he was willing to walk away and give it all up. This should not be; we should not give up so easily on our miracle. We let offense stand in the way of true liberation and freedom. Naaman stumbled at a word from the Lord; he became offended and walked away from a chance of divine healing. We too are given such words and follow this same unfortunate pattern. Read the words of this passage and see Naaman, and at times, see us.

> *And a Stone-of-stumbling and a Rock-of-offense to those disobeying, who stumble at the Word, to which they also were appointed. 1 Peter 2:8*

Not all of us stumble to the point of rejecting salvation, or stumble with the end result of dying in our sin. However, when we fail to follow the simplest statutes from the word, we hinder that which will bring about an abundant life. Naaman had a word that was appointed to him, given by the prophet he was to go wash seven times in the Jordan River. This word was an offense to him and he stumbled at the very simplistic nature of the word. It was too simple and made no sense to him. He simply could not act on faith with the word given him. I feel we at times are this way. We try and reason out what we have been told to do, and then we stumble and never fully do, go, or accomplish all that God has spoken. A case is made

143

from the Lord to (just do It) - a complete abandonment of logical reasoning acting on a word from the Lord.

I must tell you that if and when you ever do decide to take God at his word and step out, it can be a lonely journey in the beginning. Not many want to follow you to places that no one else has gone before. Jesus' own family, the ones you would expect to support Him, lived in unbelief of His power. One thing we know for certain is that after the miracle of turning water into wine, they no longer were in disbelief.

When stepping out on a word and away from the crowd, and walking in the power of that dream, you might have to lean only on God because of a lack of support. This serves as proof, if you will that God will use to strengthen our resolve and tighten the reliance upon Him, His strength, and provision. In the beginning it will appear you are all-alone and are walking a path only wide enough for one. On the outside this feeling and appearance is true; but in actuality there are many who are walking closely behind with eyes on your footsteps. They are watching to see if you are going to make it, to see if you are going to stumble and fall. They may not be walking beside at the present but many are not far behind. Not everyone has the strength you do, not many have the grit and fortitude you do. Not many have a reckless faith that you possess, which is why you, my friend, are assigned a word. Walk; God tells us to step, the Spirit nudges us to move up and move out, and God is calling higher.

There does come a time when our faith pays off. I boldly proclaim that faith does pay! His word tells us there is a 30, 60, 100-fold return on God invested seeds. It is true that we don't serve God to gain monetarily. I whole-heartedly agree, though His word does not lie. God does choose to reward and bless at times with financial rewards, whether it is here on this earth or in heaven with jewels in your crown. Faith has a payoff – if not through monetary blessings then surely through spiritual blessings. God is a giver. I am not making a case for a payout through service, but rather that God honors the faithful. I thank the Lord that I serve a God that rewards his servants, blessing them with many good gifts of his choosing!

The God of Second Chances

Right out of the chute I need you to know that God reserves the right to extend the offer of a second, third, fourth and........... Chance if he so chooses. I praise Him that He did just that for me. I do wish I had a Samuel testimony, serving God from his youth. I cannot stake claim to that; I am a product of God's never ending mercy and grace. I am a child of the second chance, knowing the word and choosing a different path for any number of reasons. Many can say they had a word assigned to them and unfortunately chose an alternate route that led to disaster. Yes, I proclaim loudly that God gives second chances and much beyond. Altering our understanding is a God who chooses to administer Grace in times when we as humanity have given up many times before. God chooses to reserve the right to remain God. Digging much deeper and searching far more we see the heart and intent of man is an all knowing and seeing God. God gives His only begotten son to a world that rejected His word sent through the Prophets and the Law. God looked down on Humanity and said, 'I have a better way; I will send my Son and redeem them from the curse of the law of sin and death."

A second, third, and fourth chance He gives humanity that does not exclude anyone regardless of race, creed, or tongue. God's grace and mercy is limitless and reaches far beyond our understanding, a fondness that reaches beyond any individual group of people. Read this and hear the God of second chances.

> *And I have other sheep who are not of this fold. I must also lead those, and they shall hear My voice, and there shall be one flock, one Shepherd. John 10:16*

Flying in the face of religious hierarchy Jesus came to save more than just one, our church and Christian denomination. In my encounters with people from many different backgrounds, denominations, and belief system I have found far too many feel they have the one true path to heaven. Though possessing the belief in Christ and his work on the cross, they rebut any others doctrine except the one they cleave to. This is not evil unto itself until finally and fatally they've elevated themselves to a greater revelation, which has afforded them an open view of salvation and eternity. They no longer believe possible the salvation of others except those whom they convert. Through professing Christ they have lost view of the finished work of the cross, and it's far reaching call. Extending far beyond the requirement of faith in Christ and repentance they administer regulations, ordinances, and at times liberties, Christ never gave. Jesus came that the world through Him might be saved regardless of where and who they came from. Jesus has sheep that were not of the fold of Israel. Jesus had sheep that were gentiles and he intended them to be brought into His fold. I see a possible error in elevating our self beyond the limitless grace of Christ. By Grace through faith we are saved! God is God all by Himself and reserves the right to save those He desires by placing a call in their direction and over their life.

This same calling is at work today; God is calling many people from Islam, Buddhism and many different walks of life to the saving knowledge of Jesus Christ. This high calling of God requires them to walk away from false religions and false gods to serve a living Christ. Remember the mandate to "go ye into all the world," not just those to our liking. This foreshadow of Christ's grace was given in the life of Naaman. God gives second chances to people who will go and do a great work for Him and the power of the second chance will propel them to greatness. Instead of failure holding them back, God uses it as a catalyst that launches them into their calling for Christ. Naaman heard the word from God but walked away. If it had not been for an unnamed servant, Naaman would have forever lost his chance at salvation and healing. I shared with you in our last chapter the power in being a servant; here, once again, we see how God uses the life of a servant.

We read that after Naaman turned away in a rage that his servants came near to him and gave an insightful observation. His servants brought a powerful word that would offer Naaman a second chance.

And his servants came near and spoke to him and said,
My father, if the prophet had told you to do a great
thing, would you not have done it? How much rather
then, when he says to you, Wash and be clean?
2 Kings 5:13

Again I must state that a servant represents one of low degree, as is a child. We are told that we must have faith like a child to come to Jesus. The servant was of low degree but had a simple understanding that escaped Naaman. *"Master, if the Prophet had told you to do great thing you would have done it, but because he has told you to do something so simple you are willing to walk away from it all."* All because he was offended, he was willing to let it all go and give up on his chance at healing. I can hear the pleading in the voice of the servants saying, "Master, do this. Master, you have come all this way. Please, I beg you just do it - just do what he has said to do." Praise God for people who will stand in the gap for us when we have missed it. Praise God that He'll send a word again that will get our attention.

It is easy for us to look at the mistake Naaman made. We could focus on Naaman's pride and unwillingness to humble himself at such a simple directive. But I would like to draw your attention to the fact that he did do it. In the end, what God is looking for are a people who would "just do it!" Yes, God wants an immediate submission and acting upon the word of the Lord. It is true; nevertheless, Naaman, better late than never, did do what he was instructed to do! In doing so his skin was made clean like that of a child. This was great! He got his healing but it did not stop there. Listen to his remarks to the man of God once he received his healing. Notice now he is talking directly to the man of God, he's not talking through a messenger or servant as was done previously.

And he returned to the man of God, he and all his company.
And he came and stood before him. And he said, Behold, now I know
that there is no God in all the earth, but in Israel. And now please
take a blessing from your servant 2 Kings 5:15

147

Naaman had encounter with a living God to the point of salvation, understanding, and enlightenment. "There is no God in all the earth except in Israel." He was saying he now knows whom the one true and living God was. He goes on to tell the Prophet that even when he returns home to his own land and goes into the temple of Rammon - that if by force of the leaning on his hand his master makes him kneel down - that he will be truly worshiping the God of Israel. What an encounter he had with the Lord, this man had his whole life changed by acting on a work from the Lord. Many would have discounted him long before he ever reached Samaria where Elisha was. Many would have said he is not worthy, after all the violence he has brought. Far too many would have said he blew it when he walked away angry. However, let us look at the end result; an influential man with a position of authority in a pagan land was saved by the God of Israel! I'm not sure how that speaks to you, but to me that is very profound and powerful.

This man's salvation was strategic of the Lord. God wants others saved that they might be used to save others. If we as the body of Christ could be kingdom minded verses condemnation minded then we could rapidly advance the kingdom of God.

Many people have blown it in the Christian faith, fallen in the Christian way. Many a soul is in need of grace and mercy. Furthermore, God is looking for people who would humble themselves and look at their need verses what they have done. When we see our brother or sister in sin, we are to go to them humbly lest we be caught and ensnared. If they repent we have snatched them out of the fire. All too often we are not willing to allow people to be restored, they trip and fall and instead of a helping hand we keep a hand on them holding them down. Somehow, if only it would start with us. We could be the one to echo that God is the God of the second chance. A hurting humanity is looking for a chance at redemption, only to be shoved to the side and left for dead, this must change! Many a wounded soldier lies on the battlefield of life as result of a self-inflicted wound. Mortally wounded with no medic in sight, as the battle of life rages hotter and hotter, and in the chaos of war there is friendly fire. Sadly, it is

148

friend shooting friend. What a tragedy this is. Let us pray that God steps into our lives and bring order out of disorder.

A cry is rising from the heart of God, "Pharaoh Let my people go!" A defiant enemy tries harder by the day to keep in his clutches a people destined to reign. God told Moses that he was going to be the savior of children of Israel in spite of their flaws and insufficiencies. This was a God given assignment that went beyond any physical and spiritual limitation. God equips the one whom He calls, and sends the one he equips. I'm not sure of your life, where you're at, or what you're faced with. Maybe God has given what seems to be an impossible assignment. It is possible you have tried and it failed. You attempted reconciliation and they refused. You might be reading this and have an incurable disease raging through your body that has brought you near to death. Let me encourage you to cling to the word He has given you.

If you don't feel God has given you a word, let me speak to you where you are at now. Don't quit, fight to the end, cleave to life, hold on to the promises of God and His hand will sustain you. In the season of the writing of this book the economic woes have engulfed much of our society. It has not discriminated against anyone; it could be you that has fallen on hard times. Job loss, failed business, loss of one's retirement, and bankruptcy and foreclosures are at an all time high. I plead with you, don't cast off your faith, and don't go back, look back, or give up. God is closer than you think. The answer is closer than you believe and better than what you'd hoped for. In every dilemma God will give a directive, if it is only to stand and wait…

Whatever He says to do, do it!!!

A profound truth and directive was uttered at a wedding feast that reverberates to this day. It was uttered at a wedding feast in Cana. Whatever God has already spoken, whatever He will speak to you in the days to come, you cannot go wrong by hearing and obeying His voice. Let me encourage you, whatever you know to do that is right…

Just do it!

149

Chapter 6

The Water

    A central theme since the formation of the world and the creation of all things, we learn that water has been essential for the sustaining of life. The human body was created to live and thrive through the consumption of water. We learn from a young age that you can live an extended period of time without food, but you can only live a few days without water. We find the subject of water is more than merely woven through the word of God; it is one of central importance. In the King James translation we find the word 'water' being used 363 times and the word 'waters' 258 times. Adding the two, we find there are 621 times that the subject of water is addressed and mentioned. This should be a clue that God is directing our attention to the subject of water. Through many different applications and many different subjects, water is ether used or addressed. Regardless of how it is used, the subject of water is an important topic as far as the bible is concerned. I was born and raised in the USA, the land of the free and the home of the brave, and all the luxuries that it has to offer; but at the top of the list of luxuries is clean, fresh, drinkable water. I found some basic facts on water that I thought would be interesting and would set the stage for covering water as it pertains to our miracle.

1.   Approximately 66% of the human body consists of water.
2.   The total amount of water in the body of an average adult is 37 liters' (or aprx.10 gallons).
3.   Human brains are 75% water.
4.   Human bones are 25% water.
5.   Human blood is 83% water.

Water is, without a doubt, the single most important source of life on the planet. We watch as scientists and astrologers search and investigate for life on other planets. Their primary argument for the possibility of life on other planets is to find evidence of water. They argue over and again about having found water to prove their theory that life exists outside of our atmosphere. Just when you think you know your friend or family member, out of the blue the discussion of life outside planet earth arises and you find that most have differing opinions. This is not a topic of debate; rather an observation that what separates earth from other planets is its abundance of water. I am a great advocate of being the very best steward of what God has given us. However, Satan has a hidden agenda, as subtle as it might be, to spread fear that we will run out of water. Yes, an often over-looked tool that the Antichrist will use as leverage is the supply of fresh drinkable water.

As I write these words, wars are being waged across the globe, and deliberation is occurring over the rights to water. Not just the fight for food, but over water. The very thing that most of us can walk a few steps, turn on the faucet and instantly receive is an endless supply of fresh drinking water. It is those things, which are most abundant that average people think least about. Yet, there are a growing number of radical environmentalists, whose agenda is for their own purposes that have waged a public war on society. A plan brewing that is gaining steam by the day is the worship of water. What we give our time to, what has our heart, what we look to is our God. We are seeing scripture come alive and manifest before our eyes. Listen to the words of this passage and see if it sounds anything like our investigation.

For the wrath of God is revealed from Heaven against all ungodliness and unrighteousness of men, who suppress the truth in unrighteousness, because the thing which may be known of God is clearly revealed within them, for God revealed it to them. For the unseen things of Him from the creation of the world are clearly seen, being realized by the things that are made, even His eternal power and Godhead, for them to be without excuse. Because, knowing God, they did not glorify Him as God, neither were thankful. But they became vain in their imaginations, and their foolish heart was darkened. Professing to be wise, they became fools and changed the glory of the incorruptible God into an image made like corruptible man, and birds, and four-footed animals, and creeping things. Therefore God also gave them up to uncleanness through the lusts of their hearts, to dishonor their own bodies between themselves. For they changed the truth of God into a lie, and they worshiped and served the created thing more than the Creator, who is blessed forever. Amen. Romans 1:18-25

It's happening at such a quickening pace; with the help of the media this propaganda that originates from the heart of Satan is spreading rampantly. The enemy of our soul wants to spread fear. Scripture tells us that fear originates from Satan and that fear brings torment, but perfect Love casts out fear. Satan wants us to have fear, a tactic he is using to try to drive people covertly to him. Get them to fear and they will look for someone to come to their aid. This tactic is driven through placing fear in the hearts of men, and through deception he forges a false relationship for the sole purpose of gaining their allegiance and ultimately controlling their thinking.

Most assuredly, Satan is subtle and has many tricks, many which are in operation today and many that are working in the minds of those who have rejected the message of Christ. *Look to creation; don't look at me (Satan). No, not yet, that will come in due time. Just look to the trees, water, oceans, lakes, streams, and stars. Oh yes, just look at how great all this creation is and how you must hold on to and protect it. Hurry, scurry and gather into your barns! Faster now, you must get it while the getting is good! Yes, that is good; see how the earth takes good care of you?*

The worship of creation (pantheism) is a metaphysical and religious position. Broadly defined, it is the view that (1) "God is everything and everything is God ... the world is either identical to God or in some way a self-expression of his nature" (Owen 1971: 74). Similarly, it is the view that (2) everything that exists constitutes a "unity" and this all-inclusive unity is in some sense divine.

What?? I can hear even the most elementary of bible students ask this! Flying in the face of the knowledge of creation and the creator is the belief that the trees are God, the sun is God and the Moon is divine. Wow, a people that are educated with a worldview, yet biblically ignorant, are a growing segment of society. This is a root in the worship of all things nature and all things cosmic with shoots that have sprung up all over the world. If we don't take care of mother earth, she will this or she will that? The news flash for the day is the earth is not our mother - neither is she our provider. The word of God says that as long as the earth remains there shall be seed time and harvest.

While the earth remains, seedtime and harvest, cold and heat, summer and winter, and day and night shall not cease. Genesis 8:22

The Lord has promised us that He would provide for us. Not once has He cut off a people who He created. God is in the business of preserving humanity. That's the message of the cross - *For God so Loved the World.* Even dealing with a fallen world and people in the days of Noah, God desired to preserve humanity through the saving of Noah and his family. He along the way made provision to accomplish this astonishing task. Humanity believes itself to be self-reliant, and God, time and again, proves that without Him we would have not life or existence.

All the new regulations that spring up through various treaties, regulations and policies nationally and internationally all hinge on a race of people that desperately desires to be in control of their own destiny. Self-reliance and creation worship - *if I don't protect the environment it will collapse.* How arrogant this must be in the mind of God a generation of people so caught up in the fantasy of their mind that they feel they have the power not only to worship creation, but to preserve it. Men over the course of time have looked to everything except the one true living God for their existence. It seems too simple and too mundane. *Why worship a God I cannot see? That's not exciting enough. Look at the sun and all its power; see how that star over there glistens just right? This forest has been*

153

so faithful over time; see how it give us oxygen? This is the age-old thinking that it is impossible for one God who has no beginning or end to have created everything in and out of our world.

We get a portion of the title of this book from this chapter, and it is my hope to highlight the importance of very often over-looked subjects in the bible. This first miracle of Jesus gives us a glimpse of just how important water is to our understanding of God, and what He desires to reveal of himself. The Lord could have very easily made wine appear in the vessels, but this was not His choice. He told them to fill the six water pots. Jesus is not a counterfeit, nor does He counterfeit. Satan is the imitator and counterfeit; this is the very thing that drove him to sin and subsequent expulsion from heaven - he wanted to be like God. He wanted the worship, and he wanted the fame and glory that the Father receives. Jesus performed His first miracle by turning the water in to wine, not magically making it appear. Even though it is well within His power, it was not His choosing. The new King James Interpretation says that there were twenty to thirty gallons of water already in each vessel. If the conversion from Firskin's to gallons is correct we see now that was a lot of water to begin with, not counting what was added to them.

I can see highlighted instruction that the Lord wants us to glean from. The Lord has the power to change anything He desires to change. The Lord is in the business of change; He wants to change our outlook on life, He want to change our direction, He wants to change our heart. He wants to transform or change our mind. We are the clay and he is the potter. He wants to change that lump of clay into a vessel he can pour into, and use to pour out into others. The word of God says He "changes not." He is the one thing that does not change. We can count on Him to be there and never leave or ever change. What He does desire is for us to change, or be conformed, into His image. The Lord wants to change things in our life. Jesus wanted them to see more than just watching things appear and disappear; the magicians of the day worked their witchcraft.

Jesus always goes deeper than the surface. He is after our heart. He wanted more than the excitement of their emotions. He desired the change of their heart, to turn hearts toward Him as their provider. God has called us to work, God has called us to manage and steward all that He has given to us, and yet deeper is the desire for complete reliance on Him. The desperation in Mary's statement clearly shows that had Jesus not made provision, the party would have been over. They had no wine, but they did have water. They were never *completely* without provision. Isn't it an awesome thing to know that God will never leave you completely empty? There were six water pots for the customary washing according to Levitical law with extra enfaces given by men. A big to do was made by the religious right of the day over the washing before eating. Indeed, they always made a big deal over washing the outside.

These six stone pots carry a great weight of importance in our understanding of how Jesus, to this day, wants us to look inwardly vs. outwardly. Great importance was given in this time and day to appearance, or that which appeared to be the right way of doing it. *Do it this way, and do it that way. No you're not doing it right. Here, hold it this way. No, you are not standing the right way. No, you don't wear that to church, you should wear this.* So much regulation and so much importance were given on the appearance and rituals of the day. It is worth noting this practice is still coveted today - long flowing robes, ridiculously high collars, emblems worn around the neck, and carrying incense burners. Their appearance seems to be so holy. Wow, didn't that feel Holy? Jesus addressed this repeatedly in His teachings, over riding the tradition and addition of man's regulations to God's original. Forgive me, I've stated this a lot in this book already, but here goes again, "God is after the heart..." We can wash the outside and clean up the habits, but still be defiled on the inside; so God goes to the heart. (Mind, will, and emotions) The word of God says that evil originates in the heart. We can appear Holy, yet still be a monster in the inside.

Having a form of godliness, but denying the power thereof...2 Timothy 3:5

It is true; people can fool even the best of us. "You mean they did what? No, that is impossible, I know him. She used to teach Sunday school? It's simply not possible that they could have done what is accused." At times we are fooled by the package and are blown away that the contents are not what was labeled on the outside. Listen to what the Lord has to say about this matter.

> *But the LORD said unto Samuel, Look not on his countenance, or on the height of his stature; because I have refused him: for the Lord seeth not as man seeth; for man looketh on the outward appearance, but the LORD looketh on the heart.* I Samuel 16:7

A problem in that day and a problem still, is the thought we can look at an individual and tell whether they are Holy. The bible tells us to *abstain from the very appearance of evil;* this is true. However, we cannot judge a book by its cover because we can be fooled. Giving no glory to the enemy, yet for instructional purposes, I would like us to think on the headlines of the day. We hear scandal after scandal of Catholic and Protestant Priests being found guilty of molesting young children. Furthermore, these wolves 's in sheep's clothing is not limited to mainline traditional denominations. This problem is also in the country Christian church and the famous TV ministries of the day. The community/civic program involved Sunday school teacher from KS who was found to be one of America's notorious serial killers – yes, it is true that no segment of the professing Christian community can be judged by appearance.

Going further still, the head of the evangelical association (name withheld) preaching a strong biblical anti-gay message is found to frequent male prostitutes. We stand back and ask the question, "What is going on and how did we miss that?"

If we go back to the source, or bible, we rediscover it is not in the ceremonial washing of hands, it is not in the long robes and ten-pound bibles we carry, it is the submitted heart we possess. Look with me and see the first miracle Jesus does, turning the water into wine, from within the very stone pots that were meant for washing. The Lord took the religious institutions of that day and turned them on their head. There were six stone water pots used for washing men's hands; six is the number of man. Jesus, being so precise in everything that He does, uses a number that is assigned to man and astounds a crowd by performing that which man can never do. *For with men things are impossible but with God all things are possible Mattew 19:26.* The very vessels that He uses are symbolic in and of themselves.

Stone vessels are a picture of man's heart – rough, callous, and insensitive to the Love of God. We are in scripture called vessels, or a particular item that is meant to contain substance. In this case it's water. Earlier I gave a few facts that pertained to the human body and how much of its makeup is water. We are vessels, we are vessels for blood and we are vessels for water. The flesh is unyielding, and so are these stone water pots. Unbendable but not unbreakable, they are not indestructible. However, their very nature is that of rigidity, stiffness, and inflexibility. This is a perfect picture of the human heart. The Lord did a work with these water pots and uses them as an object lesson and worked a miracle with them. Just like these water pots, the Lord wants to use us; he desires to work through us. Just like these stone pots with all of our hang-ups, all our faults, and all our failures - He wants to use us. These stone water pots were cold and lacked natural beauty, yet He would work a wonder through them.

Maybe you have felt you're not polished. Maybe you have felt you have two left feet and God can never use you. Possibly you have felt it is over and all that you've went through and everything that has happened has taken from you. All you have left is just a stony reminder of what could have been. This is not the case; the Lord can work miracles through your places of stone. The Lord does His best work through impossible situations. Your places of stone, those that never seem to soften, can become useable. Even the worst of the worst the Lord can turn around for His glory and for His purpose. These pots were not just sitting and taking up space, they were in use. However, the Lord had a better use for them. You may already find yourself well into life with no thought that God has a use for you to do a work for Him. These stone water pots were not meant to hold wine; they were molded to contain water for the washing of dirty hands. Now the Lord takes them and changes their man-made purpose.

The Lord can take your man-made purposes and change them and make better use of them. You know the ones I'm talking about. They are the ones that you thought was of no use. God can take your talents and your gifts - even the ones over looked by the world - and work a miracle through them. Your life should not be a life of stone cold uselessness, or one of old washed up dreams and dead hopes. No, this is not the case. The Lord can change the outcome of your life. Jesus stepped into the middle of a dilemma and changed the outcome.

There was a course that was set. They failed to plan properly, and ran out. They didn't know what to do, but there was someone who knew Jesus. So they went to the Source and everyone was blessed by it. At times we're the one who didn't properly prepare and it looks like all of our life will be a wash. Sometimes we're the ones who simply came to the wedding party, and through no count of our own we run into a snag in life and are suffering right along with everyone else. Life at times throws us curve balls when we were expecting a soft underhanded pitch. Nevertheless, the Lord is the one who can change the outcome. Regardless of how bleak it looks, regardless of how bad the situation is, as long as we go to Jesus, He can change the outcome. Look at this; we can be the one to bless others by going to Jesus for another. Mary came to Jesus and told Him "They have no wine." She was interceding for others, He granted her request, and the rest was blessed. We can go to Jesus on others' behalf and help change the outcome of a bad situation. There is power in interceding for others. We have the right to come before Jesus and make our requests and petitions made known to Him. We don't go to Him sheepishly or shyly; humble yes, but according to Hebrews 4:16 *we can come boldly before the throne of grace.* In other words, we can come before Him confidently. We can be confident that He hears us and confident that we have access to the Father.

What an honor to know that the Lord allows those who, even through life's worst of the worst, still have an advocate (someone on your side). If I could speak out of the pages of this book I would tell you that you're not alone. You are closer than you ever thought. Don't let life allow that heart of yours to turn to stone. Don't let

Satan sell you the lie that it's all over and your life is just stone cold. Hey, look up! The best is yet to come. God allowed you to pick up this book so I could encourage you to get back in the race. Stand back up, get a cool drink of water from the spirit of God, and know for sure that you are on a winning team. You might say: *that is good and well, I've heard it before, and I've tried it numerous times. You just don't know all that has happened. It's too late, I can't Love again, and I can't live again. Man, I just don't feel anything anymore.* Listen to the words that Jesus has for us whether we have succumbed to sin or life has just beaten the stuffing out of us.

> *And I will put a new spirit within you; and I will take the stony heart out of their flesh, and will give them an heart of flesh: Ezekiel 11:19*

I like in this passage that the Lord said He would do it! No self-help books, no finding the winner within. Jesus can do what we cannot do on our own. We need him to take the rough places and the areas of our heart that resemble a boulder and remove them for good. God wants to put into us a heart of flesh. A heart of flesh is pliable, something that can be worked with. A heart of stone has no ability to be shaped into a usable vessel. God can take our shortcomings and make them change into a work from the Master. God can use anyone and anything He desires. On this occasion He did something that had never been done before; it was a <u>first</u>. He also used these stone water pots for something they had never been used for - again, a first.

There is a possibility that the Lord wants to use you for something that you have never done before. It is possible that the Lord wants to use you for a task that you have never even dreamed of. It could be that you have not over-looked the potential; the truth is, you have never thought of it before. God wants to do a first in your life. God used stone hand washing water pots to work his miracle of wine making. The very same pots that they previously had washed their hands in now held a miraculous miracle, wine. Crazy to think that He used something we would have never chosen. The Lord used dirty washing water. I use this with a hint of humor, and I pray you not only see, but think, about it being washing water.

Let's look at this verse again - *And there were set there six waterpots of stone, after the manner of the purifying of the Jews, containing two or three firkins apiece. John 2:6*

There was already water in the pots, the same water that they had washed with. Nowhere do we find where they dumped out the water and started over. The following verse tells us that He told them to fill them; they filled them to the brim. They never dumped out the original water; this is so enlightening. Jesus takes that which is not meant for consumption and adds to it. His glory does a miracle and now, not only is it useable; he then transforms it supernaturally. Wow! What a wonderful thought. Jesus does not wait until we are all cleaned up and polished before He makes use of us. If Jesus so chooses He will put us to good use. This miracle validates, Romans 5:6, *"For when we were yet without strength, in due time Christ died for the ungodly."*

Jesus does not strip us of everything and then say, "Okay let me look at you and see if I can do anything with you." If that were the case we would not need grace. Jesus takes a filthy mess and changes it right before our eyes. We need Him exactly the way we are, and He fulfills our need and meets us right there. The word of God says we have no righteousness of our own; nothing that we can do is going to earn that grace. He comes to us full of dirty human hand-washed water and begins to transform us. Jesus begins to work a miracle, and that which was dirty He makes new. Jesus transforms and purifies our life into a new work. We become a new creature. We become new; everything in us becomes new. Something in us that was broken now becomes something that He has made. We can't take credit; the world can't take credit - only Jesus by His miracle-working hand can take credit for it.

They never emptied the vessels before filling them; there was water that was already in them. They filled the stone pots the rest of the way up to the brim and Jesus changed the water to wine. We are afforded a glance into this concept in the book of 2 Kings in the fourth chapter. Upon Elisha's return to Gilgal there was a great famine in the land. It came about dinnertime and the sons of the prophets were sitting before him and he told his servant to put on a large pot of stew on to boil so they might be fed. His servant went out into a field and gathered gourds from a wild vine. He was obviously unaware that it was poisonous fruit from this vine. He was not sure what they were, only that it appeared to be something that could be eaten. They sliced the fruit in the pot, cooked it, and served the men. Then a cry went out to Elisha, "Man of God there is death in the pot!" In only a way that faith could invoke, Elisha knew there was a need to be met, so he acted in faith and had a supernatural outcome. The same concept as Jesus used, Elisha instructed his servant to bring him some meal. Instead of dumping out the pot and going hungry, Elisha adds to the pot. They added what I would like to call "Holy Ghost meal" to the pot. The word says they ate and nothing was harmful in the pot.

In that same fashion, Jesus instructed that the six stone water pots be filled with water in addition to what was already in the pots. The same as in the story of the hungry prophets, Jesus adds to what is in place and there is a supernatural transformation that happens. The bacteria and germs from hand washing water are not just purified, but transformed into something that is useable not only for us, but for others as well. In each story we see similarities, and in each it is not for the benefit of a single individual. When the Lord desires to bless, He desires to bless a wedding party, a city, a nation, and a planet that He loves. Yes, Jesus is the loving provider and the caring supplier. Jesus can pour His love into our lives, and though there is poison in our vessel, He can add His spirit. That which would have killed us and is not fit for consumption can be changed.

Think on the life of Joseph, despised by his brothers for the favor shown to him by their father. They took him and threw him in a pit. Once in the pit, he is then sold as a slave to a passing band of marauders. He is then taken to Egypt where he is once again sold, now working in Potiphar's house. He excels in spite of it all and is put in charge of everything in the house, except for one thing - the only thing off limits is Potiphar's wife. She, looking to make Joseph a trophy in a lust driven rage, wrongly accuses him and gets him thrown in prison. Just when you think it can't get any worse, he is forgotten after he did a favor of interpreting a dream and for two more years he is left to rot. Talk about "how low can you go?"

Joseph sank as low into adversity as any one person can sink. Joseph had the opportunity to let all the poison of hurt, pain, discouragement, and any other thing you can think of get into him. If anyone could have carried that poison in the pot he could have; but he desired to follow the God he knew and not stay full of poison. His father heard that there was grain in Egypt and sent his sons, Joseph's brothers, to procure grain so that the family would not starve.

I love this story because it depicts so well us not pouring out or trying to get cleaned up to come to God, but letting God use who we are and what we have. His brothers came to him, and after ensuring all of them were present he released them from their shame, bondage, and of their actions. Joseph could have told them, "I'm the second in command of all Egypt and you're going to pay for what you did to me. I am going to do twice to you what you did me." Yet Joseph let the Love of God add to all that was done to him; and get this - his whole family was fed and kept alive. The Love of God made the poison in the pot, the filthy water in the pot, pure. God sent him ahead of them so that a great deliverance might be wrought through his hands. Joseph told his brothers, "You meant it for harm, but God meant it for good that many people might be saved."

We are given example after example of people just like Joseph that should be bitter and full of poison - the kind of poison that would kill everyone that comes in contact with it. However, they chose to let the Love of God turn all the poison into something that was of use. I think of Steven, when the Jews, looking up to heaven and asking God to forgive them as he is breathing his last breath, are stoning him. I think of the Apostle Paul and Silas in a Philippian jail casting off anger and resentment for the beatings and harsh treatment. These were two men who were arrested and scourged for their casting out of a demon from a young girl (the Lord's work). They find themselves in grotesque, deplorable conditions. Instead of singing the blues they began in the midnight hour to sing praises to God. These men were in jail, but they refused to allow the jail to get in them.

As complicated as this may seem they made a choice to praise God. If anyone had a right to give up and die, these two men did. I am sure that at our best we have an idea of what a first century prison was like, but I am positive that we fall far short of seeing the filth and death of one; they were beyond bad. Somehow, through it all, they lifted praises instead of angry fists at God. They refused to allow that which was on the outside to get on the inside.

I don't negate the severity of your storm or the pain of your trial. I simply believe we have a choice as to how we act during and after the fact. I also do not believe that this is something that we can naturally do; like the many instances that I have reminded us where an exchange happened. In every instance they exchanged the poison for the Love of God. It was not of their own doing, but God in the middle of the pot, in the middle of the circumstance, and changed what was dangerous and turned it into a glorious thing. Because of all that these men went through, we can be spiritually fed by men who dared to follow it Gods way versus men's.

Maybe you are like all these men who have a reason, and possibly a right, to let a root of poison into your life. It could be you who have felt the anguish of any number of life altering circumstances. Many of these circumstances have brought people to their knees. Ones now that you and I are faced with and what I've walked through has left something in me that I don't like. This is something that gets up with me every morning and follows me throughout the day. It could be that on the outside you appear to be whole, but on the inside you're half of who you once were. It could be you appear on the outside to function and have a smile on your face, yet on the inside there is that something that nags and eats away at your being. There are so many in life that have poison in their pot - partially filled, germ infested waters in the pot of their soul. It is not seen on the exterior but when the party is over and everyone has gone home, it is struggling to gain control of you. There are days that are better than others, and then there are days when it wins completely, rendering you helpless and a slave to its hand.

Maybe you have never walked through a trying struggle or faced afflictions to the magnitude we've discussed. It is true that not all go through difficulties that extreme; but I dare to say you do not have to look far to find someone who has, and may *still* be in the middle of it. Friends and family members, no one is immune to this problem. It is easy to laugh or discount their suffering. Still, I believe we as blood-bought Christians should stand up for those who cannot find their way out of the gloom and haze that surrounds their life. We can be like Jesus who shows compassion and intervenes in the middle of a wedding party disaster. We can be Elijah who doesn't blame his servant, but helps to bring healing to the pot. We can be Joseph who had every right to be bitter, yet showed compassion to those who did him the greatest harm, and his brothers at that. We can be Steven who dared to look to heaven versus those who were stoning him. Hard to say at the least – yes, I know all too well, yet it is not impossible.

Maybe not always, but I feel at times we forget the high calling of being a Christian or a follower of Christ. Christ came and paved the way. He walked the road for us; He marked out the pitfalls and then gave us the map around, over, and through. The gospel we live by, the message we preach, is not one of complete isolation from a fallen world but of being saved through it. We are not going to have a bubble that surrounds us; Jesus didn't and we won't either. It is not in the plush life of the palace; Moses showed us how to leave it for the cause of the higher calling. It is not in the stabbing away at the American dream of fine cars and luxury homes. This is well and good; however a deeper issue is demanding our attention and requiring our affection. It is one of being not only a hearer of the word, but a doer. This flies in the face of popular teaching and culture, yet on a daily basis we are given opportunities to fulfill this kind of faith walk.

Each day we are given opportunities to bear fruits of the Spirit. Every day we have the choice to give peace away or keep it. We can be gentile or we can be a sledgehammer. We can be mean spirited or kind hearted. The list is compelling and a good barometer of our spiritual maturity. *You mean there is more than my positive confession, my sowing of financial seeds and my attendance to church? You mean the Lord really expects me to forgive? I thought God said He would avenge His very elect and put down all evil. Do you have any idea what they did to my family and me? Have you any idea what they said?* Principles are part of the package, those we don't like nor want to adhere to, are closest to the Lord's heart. There is more that is required than believing in Christ, for the word says the demons in hell believe and tremble. There is more than simply believing we must live out the full council His will. Listen to *Psalms 40:7 Then said I, Lo, I come: in the volume of the book it is written of me.*

Jesus is not coming in part of the book; He is coming in the fullness of his book. Without doubt we're not going to receive rewards in heaven for collecting the most toys here on earth. *Boy... he and she really had faith for that Bentley and Beverly Hills estate.* Children of God I want you to know it's an honor that we can live a financially blessed life; however, Jesus is coming back after saved souls and He has given us instruction to pray that laborers be sent into the harvest, to save those from the poison of sin and filth of iniquity. He's coming back to save us from a fallen world, not a crashing stock market.

The water is such a miraculous part of Jesus first miracle. The Lord is always looking to purify his people. As the stew and water in the pot we as people in world become tainted and it takes God to wash away the residue of this sin nature.

And I will sanctify my great name, which was profaned among the heathen, which ye have profaned in the midst of them; and the heathen shall know that I am the LORD, saith the Lord GOD, when I shall be sanctified in you before their eyes. For I will take you from among the heathen, and gather you out of all countries, and will bring you into your own land. Then will I sprinkle clean water upon you, and ye shall be clean: from all your filthiness, and from all your idols, will I cleanse you. Ezekiel 36:23-25

We as people have a tendency to drift or wander. Matthew 7:14 tell us that. *Straight is the gate, and narrow is the way, which leadeth unto life…* This path is narrow, and being that it is narrow we tend to take our eyes off of it and drift. The nation of Israel drifted as we do from the pureness of God's best. We tend to get off track and, without notice, look up only to see we've gotten far off course. The children of Israel had been dispersed from their homeland.

All the sin and iniquity has finally caught up with them and they find themselves in a foreign land mingling among the people of the land, marring and worshiping foreign gods. This is a people who once knew God but has now grown cold to His holiness. A prophecy was given and yet stands that the Lord shall gather His people back unto Him. He shall call them home from the lands of the heathen and with His redeeming hand cleanse them from all filthiness. The word of God repeatedly shows us the relevance of God using water to cleanse us from sin.

In the days of Noah, God cleansed the entire world with a baptism of water (the Flood). Moses' life was spared and saved through water; he was placed in a basket in the Nile River. The children of Israel were saved from the Egyptian army through water as they crossed the Red Sea on dry ground. Some forty years later they again passed into their inheritance and received their promise on dry ground through the waters of the Jordan River. At the command of the Lord to Joshua the Priest stepped into the Jordan and the Lord stood the water on end with an invisible hand. John is afforded the privilege of baptizing Jesus in this same Jordan, and when Jesus comes up out of the water the Holy Spirit is seen resting on Him as a Dove. Not a chance remains that Jesus randomly chose His first miracle to be turning the water into wine.

The book of Ecclesiastes tells us that in all we get, get understanding. Though we may never completely understand everything that happens in our life, God has meaning in them and Romans 8:28 tell us that He works all things out for our good. At times we overlook and discount small things that have happened and are happening even now; yet the Lord had and has meaning in them.

He wants us to seek him to look deep and search out Him and His purpose.

It is the glory of God to conceal a thing: but the honours of kings is to search out a matter. Proverbs 25:2

It is in the searching and the seeking that we grow close to God. He tells us to seek Him while He may be found. We learn so much in our searching and seeking of him. Jesus, though his ways are higher than ours, is not elusive. He wants us to seek Him, and when we do He reveals Himself to us. God tells us to grow in grace and the knowledge of Him. When we search Him out He reveals Himself more and more to us. God cherishes the quality time we spend with Him- learning about Him, praying to Him, and simply being in His presence. What an awesome privilege we have that we can enter the Holy of Holies, which was once only the privilege of the High Priest. Now we too can come in and see, learn, and hear things once only dreamed about. Draw near unto Him, pull your chair up to His table, and relax on His breast as John did. Let Him begin to tell you who He really is. In the closeness, all the voices of the world are drowned out by His.

God said He was going to gather His people back unto Himself and wash their filth with water. There are places that we go that only God can bring us back from. He is the only one who can rescue us out of foreign lands. I like the fact that in all my struggles fighting to get out and back home, He comes, rescues, and redeems. In all my efforts that fail He still cares and comes to my aid. The children of Israel disobeyed God time after time and still He continually called them home. When they get there they are given the king's treatment. He washes them from the past and present and changes their clothes. Jesus is the refiner's fire and the launderer's soap. Just when we think things have gone too far, He comes to the rescue. Just when it looks like all hope is lost and we've messed up too much; Jesus comes with an army of angels to fight the battle on our behalf. He comes to free us; He comes to liberate us from an opposing force. The enemy wants to hold us hostage and to carry us away to a foreign land and hold us captive. Jesus has come to set the captives free.

Water is something that washes away, carries away all the unpleasant things that life dishes out. Jesus says that He will not always do it alone, that He invites and empowers us to operate in the authority He has given us. We must use what He has given us, the word of God, which through faith is able to save our souls. Paul speaking about the treatment of the wife by the husband gives a startling revelation that we all should follow. There is an importance of the application of applying the word of God to our lives, not just looking at it but to be covered over by its flow.

That he might sanctify and cleanse it with the washing of
water by the word. Ephesians 5:26

To be immersed in the word of God, to be washed over and over again like stepping into a bath to be cleansed from the dirt of a hard day's work, we can be fully immersed in the word of God that washes over our whole being, mind, body and spirit. The word of God is like water that flows into a dry place. It is a fountain that springs up like water out of the Rock for the children of Israel to drink in the desert land. The word of God will wash away all the dross of life and sins slag. The water of God's word if applied can purify the most defiled life, marriage and circumstance. Man is head of the wife as Christ is head of the church; we are given instruction how we are to conduct our self and the leading of the home. Wash with the water of the word, the home the marriage the children, the water of the word is that which will lead to life and purify an otherwise stagnant home.

From the beginning, as with Jesus' first miracle, water was a key player. Going back to the very beginning we find the account of water.

In the beginning God created the heaven and the earth.
And the earth was without form, and void; and darkness
was upon the face of the deep. And the Spirit of God
moved upon the face of the waters. And God said, Let
there be light: and there was light. And God saw the
light, that it was good: and God divided the light from

the darkness. And God called the light Day, and the darkness he called Night. And the evening and the morning were the first day. And God said, Let there be a (firmament in the midst) of the waters, and let it divide the waters from the waters. And God made the firmament, and divided the waters which were under the firmament from the waters which were above the firmament: and it was so. And God called the firmament Heaven. And the evening and the morning were the second day. And God said, let the waters (under the heaven be gathered together) unto one place, and let the dry land appear: and it was so. Genesis 1:1-9

When we read the word of God there are times we read right through important facts that we inadvertently over look. If you were to read the account of creation again and possibly a third time, you would see it is like the earth being formed in the midst of the water. Almost like a child in the womb of a mother being formed in an embryonic sack that is made up of primarily water. Evolutionists miss so much the perfection and the preciseness from which everything was created, not evolved. I receive much comfort and get very excited to know that this same God who created the entire universe had me in mind and my eternal existence. I am eager to see my heavenly home.

We have such a short period of time on this earth; we are just passing through, Sojourners in a foreign land. Our citizenship is in heaven and this same God who fashioned and formed this world has a place that He has prepared for you and me.

In our story in the second chapter of John, the miracle came through the water. Wine did not simply appear into empty pots. Jesus told them to fill the six water pots and it was through the water that that the wine appeared. Very easily Jesus could have made wine appear, but He chose to do it a different way. It is good that we look to the Lord to fulfill our desires and to work a wonder in our life and in our midst. The greater work is to allow the Lord to do it in a way that *He* chooses to do it. Herein lies the possibility for Him to show up and answer a prayer, but it happens in an entirely different way than we thought. We as humanity being creatures of habit get used to God doing something a certain way. We, then, are always looking for it to happen the way it did in the past. While we stand waiting on that previous form, Jesus shows up and shows us that He cannot be defined by the past except through His faithfulness. This is why so many people feel let down at times. They have seen God do this or do that in another's life and when He does not manifest His glory in the same way to them, they feel cheated or short changed. I am the first to say, the extent of God's sovereignty escapes my understanding at times but this I know - through years of serving and walking with Him, He has shown me He is faithful to His promises. God reserves the right to be God and choose the way He shows His glory and answers petitions and prayers.

I would like to pause and say "make your petition and prayers made known unto God with thanksgiving", go ahead and do that it is good and honorable he desires that we come to him but let him remain the chief decider of the means".

In knowing that He chose the water to use is why we must investigate possibilities He had for choosing this root verse, the miraculous appearance of wine.

Let us first look at who Jesus is and what the word says about Him.

If we were to turn just two chapters over from our story of the wedding ceremony we would find Jesus going to great lengths intervening in one's life. We read a story of Jesus in the 4th chapter of John being tired from his journey, sitting down upon a well - not beside a well but on the well. Jacob being tired from his run from Pharaoh sat down beside a well; not so with this Jesus, though He was tired He did not sit on the ground. He sat on the well. Jesus is the source. I like the fact He gives the visual in part to His instruction of no one coming to the Father except through Him. Here He sits on the well, as a gate to the well itself. *There is life in the well, but you must come through Me. I am the door, I am the path, I am the way unto eternal life.*

In this actual account of a recorded event we are given a glimpse into the miracle exchange of life being given through water. This gift went beyond just quenching one's thirst, but an eternal remedy to a lifetime of hurt, grief, and moral failure. A woman comes to the well to draw water, as was her daily duty, and on her arrival she is confronted by the Living Christ. A stranger to her, yet she recognized He was a Jew. She, for any number of reasons, could have arrived at this knowledge. Clothes, speech - the list could be added to as reason to her conclusion but one fact stands - she knew He was a Jew and she also knew Jews had no dealing with the likes of her (a Samaritan woman). This was no ordinary Samaritan woman; this possibly middle-aged woman was well worn from life's ups and downs. Jesus confronts her circumstance straightforward, refusing to skirt the issues that not only have plagued her but also still persist even to the present. This woman had been married five times and now is living or co-habiting in the same house. Living outside the covenant of marriage, she has given up on ever living in happiness. She has settled for far less than the best God has to offer.

She came to the well and Jesus, sitting on the well, asks her to give Him a drink. I find her response interesting.

> *Then saith the woman of Samaria unto him, How is it that thou, being a Jew, askest drink of me, which am a woman of Samaria? for the Jews have no dealings with the Samaritans. Jesus answered and said unto her, If thou knewest the gift of God, and who it is that saith to thee, Give me to drink; thou wouldest have asked of him, and he would have given thee living water. The woman saith unto him, Sir, thou hast nothing to draw with, and the well is deep: from whence then hast thou that living water?* John 4:9-11

She told Him, "Sir you have nothing to draw with." She came to the well empty-handed herself. Very interesting that she came to draw water and she herself had a lack of it. Isn't that our way, always coming before God empty-handed? All of us have big plans, big Ideas, and great dreams but when standing in front of the Living God we appear empty-handed. With this peek, Jesus allows us into his providing nature, which is incredibly reassuring, and allows us to draw from this same well, a spiritual well that we have no means of our own. We need Jesus, we need His help, and we need His intervention into our lives. She, as we do, looked at the natural and saw no way of drawing out of the well for the well was deep. She had no means and she saw no means that Jesus had (Sir you have nothing to draw with). The well was deep. So are the things of God. They are deep. We must be willing to go deep within the well of Christ for our thirst and deep spiritual need. To be met, we must be willing to go deep in and with the Lord.

Jesus response to her was one that was not only situational, but also eternal. The matter far exceeded the present need of physical thirst. His directive to her was, "I have a way that you cannot see, but if you believe you will see." If you knew who was asking you would have asked of me living water. I cleave to the position that, as of yet, Jesus had not revealed Himself to her. Now the stage is set and all the pillars are erected that might hold up the truth past the experience of the encounter. Once He addresses her lack and her past against the truth of the present, He opens her eyes and Christ is revealed unto her. I bring your attention to the fact that Jesus allows for situations to arise and arrive in your life that corner us so we have nowhere else to run. Once in place Jesus, as He does so often over the course of our life, reveals Himself to us. Through this process He solidifies Himself in our hearts, mind, and spirit. God wants us to not run any longer from the core message of the cross. We need Jesus in our life, we need Him in our life and we have nothing - only our self that we can bring to Him. We can give of our self, and in our giving He gives back to us living water. This water changes forever the thirst we once had. This embattled Samaritan woman came thirsting for that which the natural could never quench. Five husbands and now a live-in boyfriend - all the thirst for the world and Jesus is on the scene to change her cravings.

Blessed are they which do hunger and thirst after righteousness: for they shall be filled. Matthew 5:6

Not only is there a desire for us to go deeper, and not only is there a thirst that needs quenched, but we are given the promise of

Jesus fulfilling this very deep and divine need. Jesus said that He would fill us if only we would thirst after this living water. This is a wellspring that can spring up from deep within our being - a joy unspeakable and full of glory.

Jesus tells her that there is water that she could draw from that would give her eternal life. He carries this same theme and truth into chapter 7 of this same book of John.

In the last day, that great day of the feast, Jesus stood and cried, saying, if any man thirst, let him come unto me, and drink. He that believeth on me, as the scripture hath said, out of his belly shall flow rivers of living water. John 7:37-38

Verse 39 goes on to say that this He spoke of the Holy Ghost, which had not yet been given because He had not yet been glorified. A promise that Jesus fulfilled upon his ascension to heaven and the giving in full on the day of Pentecost, the Holy Ghost came in power.

He tells us that if anyone thirsts, they can come to Him and He will give them this gift of the Holy Spirit. This Holy Spirit cannot only appease our thirst, we can factually let this same living water flow from our own bellies. I stated in the beginning of this chapter that in the creation of the earth we live in, it was as if the earth was given through water as a woman gives birth to a child through water. Out of her belly she gives birth to a living breathing form of life, so shall the one who drinks of this living water of life. We too shall flow out of ourselves, rivers of living water; we can, through the Holy Spirit's empowerment, be a source of life to others that are around us. The great invitation that Jesus extends to us is that one of being a laborer and co-laborer with Christ. Scripture goes on to call us ambassadors for Christ. A spokesman for Him, we can take part and serve verses only receiving. Out of your bellies shall flow rivers of living water. Water that takes you somewhere, a river is something that will carry you to a place.

Scripture is so complete that it never fails but fulfills each lesson Jesus wants us to learn and informs us of His nature. We find many times over that He wants the living water He spoke about to be a vital part of our life. All accounts point towards our needing Him, and without having received this vital part of the ministry of God we surely will not succeed in any of our efforts that need to have lasting results. For a moment they will progress, but without them having begun in the spirit of God we put out hands to need's constant inflow from this same source; but there must first be a beginning.

Jesus answered, Verily, verily, I say unto thee, Except a man be born of water and of the Spirit, he cannot enter into the kingdom of God. John 3:5

"Except a man be born of the water and of the spirit…" Here we see that there must be that first initial requirement to be born again which allows entrance into not just the heavenly kingdom, but His Kingdom that is now at hand. Being born of the spirit of and of water affords us the ability to partake in this heavenly privilege here and now. All that God has for us and all He has made available to us must first be received after being born again. *Ye must be born again.* The baptism of his spirit and of fire burns away all the impurities of sin's effects, but the washing of regeneration that Titus 3:5 speaks of washes away from us; it carries away far from us the filth of sin and iniquity.

The water of the spirit of the Lord can and will do that which we cannot do. It is an awesome thing to know that Jesus has not just dropped clues to follow as if we are on a never-ending quest to find the all-elusive God. To the contrary, He provides us clear instruction on how to succeed. The first miracle of Jesus was through water; it is by no accident that He purposely arranged the circumstance for the unveiling and the revelation of the Son of God who came in power, not only in word but deed (power). When Jesus begins a work in us He not only starts it but also finishes that which He started without fail. You can rest assured that as a blood bought child of God He knows how to accomplish what He began in you and on your behalf. We tend to, at times, lie down in the middle, *it is too hard, too many distractions, too difficult.* We as people start a vast array of projects and too often we never finish what we start. Not so with Jesus, He doesn't have to find a way. He *is* the way the truth and the life.

I feel like the Lord would have us to know that the water by which this miracle was preformed is still available to us today. This water is life changing and has healing properties that no earthly purification can reproduce. This water can run into the driest places of our life and renew even the driest of places. I think of the picture of the desert before with its wasteland appearance and then the miraculous transformation that takes place after a great season of rain. Almost appearing overnight we see beauty that is unequaled in appearance. I have often thought, "You mean that was in there?" All that was needed was water and the seed that lay dormant springs forth to life. Be encouraged with the words of the Prophet Isaiah.

For I will pour water upon him that is thirsty, and floods upon the dry ground: I will pour my spirit upon thy seed, and my blessing upon thine offspring: And they shall spring up as among the grass, as willows by the water courses. Isaiah 44:3-4

What a thought that our God will not leave us in a barren state; He comes to our aid and meets beyond our expectation the desires of our heart. – This is our God. At times we feel like if we just had a sip or just a small drink then we would be okay. This is not God's best; He has more than a drink or sip he has a fountain that springs forth out a rock. Jesus is a fountain of life that can give and keep on giving. I cannot wait to see that river that flows from that rock.

There is a river, the streams whereof shall make glad the city of God, the holy place of the tabernacles of the most High. Psalms 46:4

I am not sure what you might be facing as you read this book. There are so many of you that I would love to have the chance to meet, yet will not. I pray that if you find yourself in that place of want. Maybe it is in the beginning of your dreams as those at the wedding party. Maybe you are in the middle of, possibly the end of your journey and the road has come to a near impasse. Hear Jesus' words, that's He is the living water - a source that will never fail. Streams run dry and clouds withhold the waters in their bowels. But this Jesus will never fail. He does not run dry, always caring, always giving; He is a source of life. We can come to him in our lack and need and He changes, He transforms, and He washes away all life's impurities.

Jesus is the water in the miracle of the wine!

Jesus is the essence of life!

Chapter 7

The Woman

The woman recorded in John the second chapter played a pivotal role that no other could have. Mary was the mother of Jesus the Messiah. She was the one who knew better than any, this man called Jesus. It is this Jesus, the center of the entire universe that has been invited to a wedding feast. No other at this event knew Jesus' unique nature better. Mary was the one who had given birth to this man, the One whom the Father had sent down from heaven. Jesus, the only begotten of the father, came to earth not as a roaring Lion, but as a lamb - an innocent Baby Boy. Mary had a visitation from an angel named Gabriel that forever changed her life. Let's focus on this life-changing encounter and read just how the event unfolds.

And in the sixth month the angel Gabriel was sent from God unto a city of Galilee, named Nazareth, To a virgin espoused to a man whose name was Joseph, of the house of David; and the virgin's name was Mary. And the angel came in unto her, and said, Hail, thou that art highly favoured, the Lord is with thee: blessed art thou among women. And when she saw him, she was troubled at his saying, and cast in her mind what manner of salutation this should be. And the angel said unto her, Fear not, Mary: for thou hast found favour with God. And, behold, thou shalt conceive in thy womb, and bring forth a son, and shalt call his name JESUS. He shall be great, and shall be called the Son of the Highest: and the Lord God shall give unto him the throne of his father David: And he shall reign over the house of Jacob for ever; and of his kingdom there shall be no end. Then said Mary unto the angel, How shall this be, seeing I

*know not a man? And the angel answered and said unto
her, The Holy Ghost shall come upon thee, and the
power of the Highest shall overshadow thee: therefore
also that holy thing which shall be born of thee shall be
called the Son of God. And, behold, thy cousin Elisabeth,
she hath also conceived a son in her old age: and this is
the sixth month with her, who was called barren. For
with God nothing shall be impossible. And Mary said,
Behold the handmaid of the Lord; be it unto me
according to thy word. And the angel departed from her.
Luke 1:26-38*

Reading this statement more thoroughly, we see Gabriel's
announcement to Mary: *"Thou art highly favored, the Lord is with
thee: blessed art thou among women."* He tells her two things: she
not only has favor on her life, but *she* is highly favored. Secondly,
he tells her, *"Blessed is she among women."* What was it that made
this woman stand out from the crowd? We almost certainly can
stake the claim she was beyond the age of youth that some say she
was, for the angel called her a woman. However, we also know she
was still in the very early period of life. Not to argue or to hold
personal knowledge of her exact age, but we know common belief
places her age still well within her teens. Though I do not have
complete understanding why this young woman was so highly
favored and blessed, I do feel I have a good Idea. With that being
said, I pray I can reveal to you through the reading of scripture
reasons for the favor bestowed on her. We will see that God didn't
randomly pick Mary out of a crowd. We know from the Word in
Acts 10:34, that God is no respecter of person. However, we also
glean from *2 Chronicles 16:9,* that the eyes of the LORD run to and
fro throughout the whole earth, to show himself strong on the behalf
of *them* whose heart *is* perfect toward him.

Also we read in *1Peter 3:12* that, *the eyes of the
Lord are over the righteous, and his ears are open unto
their prayers... again* in *Proverbs 5:21 For the ways of
man are before the eyes of the LORD, and he pondereth
all his goings.*

178

All Scriptures align and are in complete agreement with the other, regardless of those who try to detract from its perfectness. By this we see a pattern begin to emerge, that gives us indication that many have been chosen for a specific reason, rather than random selection. God did not choose this young woman by happenstance. Mary was chosen for a purpose that surpassed the exterior of her girlish looks and nature. God was looking to show Himself strong in a vessel, a vessel of honor. God looked to bring redemption to mankind, and He desired to use the vessel of a woman, and not just an ordinary vessel, rather a vessel of honor. Mary was no ordinary girl. Mary's heart was already turned to the Lord. We see by reading her Oblation to the Lord that she knew God; she was no stranger to His goodness and mercy. God's eyes went to and fro throughout the entire earth looking for the one in whom He could pour out his glory.

God in his scheme of time had found the chosen vessel and was ready to overshadow a little girl from Nazareth.

Mary, so highly blessed and favored, what made you move the heart of God? What placed you in the center of God's attention? Was it your charm? Was it your beauty? Was it the way you had hoped and dreamed to one day grow up and change the world? Maybe you had some special talent and gift. Maybe you were a prodigy and did everything a little better than all other women. Could it be that you made some special vow to God, that if He made you the most favored woman alive you would do some great task for Him? The list is endless, and we could ask or ponder all the reasons as to why it was that God had chosen this woman. Many could attest to her Jewish heritage that made her so special in the eyes of God. Many more could point to her soon to be marriage to Joseph who was in the lineage of King David. It is true we could make the case for all the above, yet one fact remains - she knew God. Far more than a superficial, ritualistic relationship, she knew God deeply and intimately!

God is looking for a vessel that he can move mightily through. In this chapter we will see how God not only redeemed mankind in a masculine sense, but He, in the process, brought women back in right standing with his order. I have referenced many times throughout this book that God is after our heart (the mind, will, and emotions). God had Mary's heart; whole-heartedly Mary served the Lord God. Now the angel Gabriel has come to her and told her, that first He, the Holy Spirit was going to over shadow her, and secondly, He was going to indwell her. I have prayed that through the pages of this book you would see there are patterns and paths that God places in clear view of his nature and attributes. If only we would see him in the light of His word. God, in the same way as he came to Mary, comes through the ministry of the Holy Spirit to each of us - wooing and drawing us ever so near to Him. He overshadows us, in addition, and it seems everywhere we turn God is around every corner. We can then move toward the knowledge that we are in need of a Savior. If only we ask Him into our heart, He then comes to indwell us, to consume and to infuse Himself within us. A woman, when with child, is one with the child. When she eats the baby eats. When she lies down the baby is lying down. When she is sick the same sickness is flowing through the baby. These two are fused together through an umbilical cord, a lifeline that connects one to the other. This cord is a "life-giving supply" that mingles the blood of each together.

God does not merely want to over shadow us, He wants to dwell in us and make his habitation within us. God does not want a temporary housing arrangement. He wants ownership! God wants the deed to our vessel. It is easy to go in and go out with no commitment and no covenant. No holds barred - let's do it our way and try this Jesus out. However, God's eyes are going to and fro throughout the whole earth looking for someone to bestow His blessing and favor upon. So, why was it that Mary was so highly favored and blessed? What separated Mary from other women? I would like to look a little past the common reading of the angel's visitation. Also, let's take a peek into the nature of her relationship with this God who had come to take up habitation within her womb.

And Mary said, My soul doth magnify the Lord, And my spirit hath rejoiced in God my Saviour. For he hath regarded the low estate of his handmaiden: for, behold, from henceforth all generations shall call me blessed.

*For he that is mighty hath done to me great things; and
holy is his name. And his mercy is on them that fear him
from generation to generation. He hath shewed strength
with his arm; he hath scattered the proud in the
imagination of their hearts. He hath put down the mighty
from their seats, and exalted them of low degree. He
hath filled the hungry with good things; and the rich he
hath sent empty away. He hath holpen his servant Israel,
in remembrance of his mercy; As he spake to our fathers,
to Abraham, and to his seed forever. Luke 1:46-55*

Upon her arrival to visit her cousin Elizabeth, Mary burst
into song after Elizabeth's greeting. When even slightly scanning
over the words of her song, we clearly see that this was a woman
who knew God in a deep, rich personal way. This passage of
scripture is referred to as Mary's song. Unscripted and bursting with
spontaneity she offers up praise to the one whom she knew first
hand. It was out of the depths of her never dying being that she was
able to praise God for far more than just a blessing and showing her
favor. She praises Him then continues by saying, "My soul does
magnify him." *Matthew 12:34 states..." For out of the abundance
of the heart the mouth speaks."*

Out of the bowels of her soul she was able to proclaim, "*Holy
is His name, and His mercy is on them that fear Him from
generation to generation!*" Only a person (a woman in this case)
can speak of God in this manner by having such a close relationship.
This would be possible only if she had previously known Him.
Though she herself had not been alive for an abundance of years, she
had previously witnessed His faithfulness and mercy. *His mercy is
on them that fear Him.* Read the words of *Psalms 111:10* and see a
truth and understanding that she had long before God came and took
up abode within her.

*The fear of the LORD is the beginning of wisdom: a
good understanding have all they that do his
commandments: his praise endureth forever.
Psalms 111:10*

181

She was able to sing from the depths of her heart because He was real to her. She was able to sing with passion because she knew Him intimately, and now what she knew and loved was currently within her. We now have reason to believe that Mary's calling and assignment was divine and relational to her knowledge of God. Peering deeper and reading further, we can see that her understanding was *first taught and then caught*. She speaks of those who had walked with God before her, or those whom shared and taught of God's faithfulness through generations.

> *He hath holpen his servant Israel, in remembrance of his mercy; As he spake to our fathers, to Abraham, and to his seed forever. Luke 1:55*

This young woman was a Jew, a student of the teachings of Moses and father Abraham. As Mary personally reveals, we read that her fathers (biological and spiritual) carried on these teachings. Mary personally made them a part of her life and belief system. She was not unaccustomed to being in the presence of God. Though the angel startled her, she was not troubled at his presence, but rather at the manner of greeting he addressed her with. (See Luke 1:29) The angel of the Lord had come to her and told her that she was blessed among women and highly favored, this is what troubled her.

We can look at it from her point of view: "God I love and know you, but you're telling me that above all women I'm favored." I can imagine even the most modest of Christian women if they received word that the Son of the living God was to be born to them, a hint of pride might have risen up within them. Not intentionally, but rather out of carnality, we tend to take ourselves much too seriously. Mary on the other hand did not. She was in awe and humbled that God would have chosen her for this un-paralleled event. Case in point, this is a very good reason why God was able to use her - she was a woman of low degree as she stated. Not just monetarily, but in humble fashion. God uses those of a low degree or those who will humble themselves and resist any temptation to allow pride, arrogance, or any other self-serving spirit or attitude to creep in. There is nothing worse than to be in a room with someone who thinks they know God better than anyone else and would like to tell you about it. These are prideful, arrogant people who have become un-teachable, thinking themselves to be wise, yet becoming a fool and a snare to themselves.

There is nothing wrong being confident and contending for the faith. However, contending and defending are more effective if you are defending against the refuting of the deity of Christ. Arguing over doctrinal issues has led to countless church, relational, and ministry splits. We are taught to follow the doctrine of the apostles (see 2 Timothy Ch. 3.) Yet, men have and will continue for selfish gain to sow seeds of discord. Many would like to adhere to their supposed God selective personal enlightenment: all knowledge and wisdom. Read what God has to say about these people who have become wise in their own eyes, yet the love of Christ escaping them.

> *Though I speak with the tongues of men and of angels, and have not charity, I am become as sounding brass, or a tinkling cymbal. And though I have the gift of prophecy, and understand all mysteries, and all knowledge; and though I have all faith, so that I could remove mountains, and have not charity, I am nothing. 1 Corinthians 13:1-2*

The Love of Christ keeps us humble; the love of Christ keeps us looking to Him and not ourselves. If we have the love of Christ In our hearts, we understand that Jesus is the center of attention and not us. This was Mary's dilemma: the angel Gabriel had come to her and bestowed accolades upon her, and because of a humble spirit she had a hard time and was troubled. This was not her way. To her, God was the center of attention and now this angel was standing in front of her telling her how great God thought she was, and what He was going to do through her. The love of Christ resists the impulse to take any credit for what God has done or is doing. The Love of Christ will resist pride; pride is not in the equation of God.

> *The LORD is nigh unto them that are of a broken heart; and saveth such as be of a contrite spirit. Psalms 34:18*

We are afforded the right to come before God boldly, but not arrogantly or demanding. God says in *1Peter 5:5* *"God resists the proud, but gives grace to the humble."* Mary was a humble woman and God found a woman among women. Mary was a woman in the middle of many women, one He could use for this perfect event. When we have the love of God in operation in our lives or, better stated, when we are putting to practice the love of God then He can use us. Regardless of our arsenal of spiritual gifting He can use us if we remain humble. *1 Corinthians 13:4* says, *"Love is not vain or puffed up."* We cannot have the love Christ within us and move in power if we are puffed up and full of pride. This does not imply that we are not to be confident; this is not a gray area of going out into the harvest in the power of Spirit of God's might. We know the difference; it is clear and evident when someone has a haughty spirit about him or her. Again, I must remind us we are talking of those who are in the faith. Mary was in the faith, though previously living under the Law of Moses, she now has come to the understanding of the relation to the Messianic Christ. Full and well she was able to receive the light and the seed that the Holy Spirit was to deposit within her. Her heart turned toward God is what made this Immaculate Conception possible.

The same free will we have, Mary did as well. God chose a woman who was humble, who would remain humbled, and whose heart was turned toward Him. What an explosion of truth - "when I put my faith and trust in Christ, when I let the love of Christ spill over and out of me, when I resist the temptation of attaining power and position for self-serving purposes, it is then I set myself up for a miracle." It is not about being perfect. Mary was not, and furthermore proclaimed it. God is not looking for perfect people but a people He can perfect. It would seem that Mary was chosen because she already possessed all the proper attributes God was looking for. To most, it would seem that we could never measure up to the likes of Mary. "I'll never have what Mary had or do what Mary did." If you want to know the truth, "I don't have what it takes to be in the league of Mary, the mother of Jesus." This is not the case: not the case in my opening the scriptures to examine this unordinary woman. So many characters throughout Scripture, good and bad, God uses as examples for us.

God provides many an example of what not to do, how not to handle situations and conduct the affairs of our life. To balance it out, on the other side of the coin, he has the "Marys." One who, like Noah, was perfect in her generation. God is constantly trying to bring to balance in our view of who He is and what He wants from us. It is easy to look at our present life and judge God on what we see. What He is wanting is for us to examine the Word of God and see what He has already accomplished generation after generation; "His faithfulness." Mary said, *"From generation to generation God shows mercy, and beyond generations forever He will continue"*.

I'm sure I will never meet most who read this book; therefore, I will never know most of your stories of where you've come from, what you are in right now, and the battles that possibly lie ahead. Even still, I can confidently say that God is faithful to humanity and those who love, cherish, and fear Him. Furthermore I can reassure all, if we currently do not feel we are the mold as Mary was for God to pour into, we can rest assured that we have something to shoot for. Yes, it is true; God does give us good examples to follow. We are to put our trust, hope, and belief in Jesus. This is paramount. On the other hand, I would like to add that God is looking for some - John the Baptists who would blaze the trail willing to consecrate themselves to a life of purity. This was the life of Mary; we know she was young as stated earlier, and we also know from what we have just read from her song of praise that she was deeply in love with God.

Mary made a choice early on in her life that she was going to serve God!

Though we are looking at the subject of "the woman," this principle is applicable to all. Serving God with a fervent heart from the flower of youth is very fulfilling. Our society has painted a picture through media that the good and pleasurable life is had based on what you can get and what you can ingest. Living by feeling and emotions is what is force-fed to our youth from the time they are old

185

enough to sit in front of TV. I am 47 years of age at the writing of this book. During my childhood I have seen us go from about 10 to 12 channels to endless numbers, as much as you are willing to pay for. Though our family had TV's growing up, a number of those whom my parents were associated with in ministry did not. These ministers believed it to be driven by Satan and would eventually lead to moral decay in the world. I now see just how well these old Holiness people saw into the future. I believe that Media can be used for good or bad, but TV is neither good nor bad. TV is an inanimate object that can be useful or a detriment to society. Unfortunately the norm of the day is that the more rotten the content, the more they sell. We can ask why it is so, with only a brief pause before the truth comes front and center.

We are living in a fallen world with people in need of the same Savior that was born through this little Nazarene young woman named Mary. Mary had set herself apart from the crowd long before the angel appeared in her doorway. Mary had made up her mind that she was going to live for the King of Kings. She had a made up mind and was in position for God to use her life mightily. I would like to make a bold proclamation: God can use anyone He chooses, this is true; however, God can send out into the deep for Him one who has made their calling and election sure.

Therefore, brothers, rather be diligent to make your calling and election sure, for if you do these things, you shall never fall. 2 Peter 1:10

The Apostle Peter exhorts his brothers to be diligent about their calling to Christ. Let me phrase it this way - settle in your heart and mind that you are serving Christ at all cost. If the journey you are on turns south and sour, will you still serve Him and have a tender heart, whether you see success bestowed on your life or not? A position is taken: *"I will not put the fame before God, but in all I do the glory goes to God." I am in the army of the Lord. I have enlisted and I'm here to serve Christ with all my mind, heart, will, and strength.*

Making your calling into the marvelous light sure and secured like: *2 Timothy 1:12, "For this cause I also suffer these things; but I am not ashamed, for I know whom I have believed, and I am persuaded that He is able to guard My deposit unto that Day."*

Mary knew in whom she believed. She had been persuaded before the angel of the Lord arrived. A call goes out from God: *"stay with me, don't leave when times get hard. Don't flee because life has become difficult."* Jesus told us that many are the afflictions of the Righteous. But He did not leave hope in a dismal state, He said be of good cheer for He has overcome the world. Praise be unto the Lord, for every one of my troubles and trials He's already worked out for my good and His purpose. If we could follow the pattern of this passage of scripture, look and know that God will not leave us in a state of disarray. It is this knowledge that we can cleave to.

At times in our life, the situations we find our self in can bring about feelings of shame. The generation that we live in within the Christian circle has said that if we don't have *stuff*, or we can't seem to get ahead, it's because we either don't have God's favor or we lack faith to possess it. Flying in the face of this theology is the knowledge that not everyone will be rich and possess vast amounts of *stuff*. When we have served God faithfully with all the passion and zeal within, and still there is no change in social status, what do you do? I say, keep serving diligently!

If we're not careful to guard our mind the enemy can place in us thoughts of inadequacy or uselessness. Maybe you have gone through trial after trial to the point that you appear to have either sin or major dysfunctions within your Christian walk. Not just the enemy, but also those who should undergird you point accusing fingers or voice unmerited suggestions or accusations. Do not feel like you are the lone stranger and you're the only one to face these types of humiliations. Have you ever read the story of one of the unluckiest man that ever lived?

Job was the most tormented man that ever lived. Numerous unfortunate events came upon the life of Job. I have read the story of his life many times, yet still come to the same conclusion. I am glad that my name is not Job. For no apparent reason it seemed that life itself imploded, and Job was standing in the middle with no understanding. Still, Job remained a man of integrity. Job had been thrown into a tornado of circumstances with no end in sight. He grasped for reasoning. Still, day after day it escaped his comprehension. Somewhere along the way in our service to Christ, we lose that living a life of faith doesn't guarantee a free pass to all things shiny and glamorous here on earth. On the other hand are those who have, in times past and present, served a God in whom they cannot see in spite of all obstacles. Troubles come in seasons - in waves of torrential down pour. Job was a man who lived to see the loss of everything that he worked a lifetime to achieve. Job was no pauper. When in the middle of success everything - and I stress everything - came toppling down. His money went funny, his house and his children in one blast were buried alive under the rubble of his son's fine house.

Maybe you have never experienced loss to this extreme. Maybe you have experienced it on a much smaller scale? Others look at you and it's almost as if you can hear their thoughts - "What's wrong with you, quit you whining, suck it up, it's not that bad." However, to you it is very much real, and at times overwhelming. I am confident that Jesus is as much concerned about your supposed small issue as he was about Job's continuing tragedies. Jesus coming to a house where a wedding party was taking place took concern about an issue to us that seemed trivial. They had run out of wine and with no store for miles, He intervened.

Job's life is a mystery to us. How could a God of compassion and love allow all this mayhem to batter his life? This is a question that we may never know the answer to. Perhaps as an example to us, God's response is, "That I have reserved for myself a people that will have a heart that is turned toward me, and come what may, serve Me." In this passage of scriptures we see that the Son of God came before the Lord and Satan came too. A question was asked of Satan, "Have you considered my servant Job?" God was making reference to one of his servants much like the angel Gabriel did of Mary when he stood before her. God was making a statement that following and serving Me can be done! Serving Me with your whole heart can be achieved. It is a matter of choice. A heart that is turned toward God can be used in ways that far outweigh talents and gifting.

We are living in a time of countless self-help books, seminars, and teachings - as if we can fix our self like we have the power to do so. We can only continue to breathe except that the Father give us the ability to do so. Life is a gift to us. What we do with that life is our gift back to God. Job and Mary made a choice to live for God, a consecrated life rejecting the patterns of the world. Our subject in this chapter is of the woman, yet we as men need to know that God first made man. God redeemed mankind through the death burial and resurrection of Christ. This was not so the Marys or women of the world would have to bear the burden of spiritual responsibility. Front and center, God calls men to lead, and all too often men fail in their God given assignment. It is then that His spirit quickens the weaker vessel and an anointing from on high propels women into areas and levels they never dreamed of.

Either way, God is not limited to whom he bestows his work or delegated duties upon.   After all, He is God, and free to do as he chooses, right? Thank God *we* are not God! God always chooses those whom we would not. Do you think that you would have chosen a little no-name girl named Mary? Would you have thought to entrust such a valuable gift to such a young girl of no reputation? Surely, if we were God then we would have come through the womb of a queen. Maybe a princess in the making, but through a girl such as Mary?   I like that God does His best work through small packages, and his most valued possessions start small. We always want the big shebang or ticker tape parade and the huge payout. God chose to come as a baby through a young virgin named Mary.

I suppose there are tens of thousands of Marys in the world. You might be one. You've done your best to serve God with your best and now you find yourself in a situation that you have no way to explain out of. A situation where all you can do is trust God and let Him work it out. Mary was pregnant with child and unmarried. Job was a loyal and upright man, and both found themselves in a situation that they could not explain their way out of. Job's friends sat in silence until their flesh took over and began to dissect Job's life. They were looking for flaws that would have placed him in the position he found himself in. Joseph had thought of putting Mary away privately but being warned in a dream to follow God. Can you imagine his dilemma? I can hear his thoughts; *"All I want is to get married and start a family. This is not what I asked for!"* Mary told the servants do what He says to do. Joseph humbled himself and did what the angel of the Lord said to do. I wonder, how many of us have been asked to take a step of faith and trust God with a difficult situation - a situation that puts yours and others' reputations at risk. It takes faith to follow and trust the Lord in hard times.

Following Christ will lead you at times down roads you never expected to travel. These roads start out rocky and dangerous; however, if stayed upon for Christ they can lead to unexpected blessings. We always want things to go smoothly and be trouble free. This would be nice, but simply is not the case. Some of the greatest rewards are received just after the most difficult of battles. A woman, when in childbirth, suffers pain that escapes man's comprehension, so I'm told. After all I am a man, however, scripture validates this.

> *A woman when she is in travail hath sorrow, because her hour is come: but as soon as she is delivered of the child, she remembereth no more the anguish, for joy that a man is born into the world. John 16:21*

Jesus was on a mission set in a *marked time* that was ordered by God. Jesus' first miracle was to happen in the Father's time. A woman's deliverance from a pregnancy is set in a period of time broken up into three trimesters. At the time that God has set in order, her deliverance has come. At the end of this siege of her body, the blessing comes through pain.

> *And being found in fashion as a man, he humbled himself, and became obedient unto death, even the death of the cross. Philippians 2:8*

Jesus suffered the death of the cross so we would not have to taste death!

The children of Israel were in bondage for exactly the amount of time that was prophesied, 430 years. Exactly to the day, 430 years after they went into Egyptian captivity, they were delivered.

My friends... do not for one moment think you have missed God and his plan. God is working it out in you, and for his glory. God used Mary, a virgin, to bring about a blessing through adversity. Not only did Mary face, from family and friends, ridicule for being pregnant before officially being married, she also had to spend her time on the run for fear of her life. At times we, as Mary, feel on the run for our lives. I can hear a question asked. *God, if this is what you have given me then why does what you seem to have given put me into the position of having to flee for my life?*

Friend, when I read through my bible I encounter people whose lives were touched by Jesus. Their lives were changed in such a way that they were willing to suffer with Him. Here are just a couple of scriptures to show that this suffering is not such an uncommon thing.

> *Beloved, think it not strange concerning the fiery trial which is to try you, as though some strange thing happened unto you: But rejoice, inasmuch as ye are partakers of Christ's sufferings; that, when his glory shall be revealed, ye may be glad also with exceeding joy. 1 Peter 4:12-13*

God is doing something *in us* when we are going through trials. We feel as if the trying or testing is stretching our limits. However, in actuality it is strengthening us for greater works.

Knowing this, that the trying of your faith worketh patience. James 1:3

When in a difficult situation or tough time, we tend to feel as though we are all alone and no other has gone through our difficulty. This is a deception from Satan that tries to isolate us from the knowledge of the truth in Christ. He said that He would never leave us or forsake us. Hear these powerful words that are covenant statements given to us, the redeemed of the Lord.

> *... for He hath said, I will never leave thee, nor forsake thee. ⁶ So that we may boldly say, The Lord is my helper, and I will not fear what man shall do unto me. Hebrews 13:5-6*

One more passage that really drives home just how much he is involved in every area of our life is this.

> *For we have not an high priest which cannot be touched with the feeling of our infirmities; but was in all points tempted like as we are, yet without sin. Hebrews 4:15*

In every way, in every area, in every emotion and feeling our Savior tasted and was tested just as we are. He knows what we are going through and desires that we allow Him to gain access to our deepest doubts and unbelief. Jesus is after our entire being - mind, body, and spirit. We are the temples of the Holy Ghost; Christ dwells in us and wants us to produce Fruit of the Spirit through us.

I really, really like how Jesus used Mary, His own mother, for His first miracle. It is true that Mary gave birth to this Christ, yet He uses her in such a way that shows two profound sides of His nature while on earth. He first shows His humanity by personally attending a wedding party. This is what we do as a way of respecting and honoring those with whom we have a relationship. We don't just stumble into a wedding; it is something that we share with those whom we care for. Jesus took time out of his schedule of preaching, teaching, and healing the sick to show up at this wedding ceremony. Scripture says both Jesus and his disciples were invited. He wanted to be there; He cared for others more than superficially. We tell others often, "I'll pray for you" when in reality it has become

192

a good thing to *say* in place of stopping what we're doing and do what we've said.

I like the fact that Jesus led by example. He led the way, and those who were his disciples followed. He showed His humanity by being in their midst physically, not "my blessings are on you and my thoughts will be with you." No, this was not the case with Jesus. He went and stood on the ground where they were. We are so busy with life – so much so that I think we fail to realize what is needed is *us*. Not our programs, not the money we can give, or the gifts we can bring - it boils down to us giving an unwrapped package of ourselves. Jesus did just that. He attended the party and gave of Himself while there and after.

Verse 12 of John 2 says that after the wedding He, His mother, His brothers went down to Capernaum and stayed many days. That is relationship at its best; they were a tight knit group of people. Think of the traveling party, not shortages in numbers or personalities. They seemed to move progressively as a group quite well. *Amos* 3:3 says, *"How can two walk together except they be agreed?"(KJV)*

Many, when they achieve a level of success, withdraw and narrow their circle. It is true, Jesus used wisdom many times when to isolate Himself to rest and pray. However, we see that even though the demand of His time was increasing, He still allotted time for those who needed it the most. There is no "I paid my dues and I'm ready for the new crowd," or "now my family and close friends are those on the road to success." No, this was not the case. Jesus was just the center of attention turning water into wine, yet He left the fame of the moment to be with those who were closest to Him.

Secondly, Jesus showed his divinity in dealing with His mother. Mary came to Jesus and informed him of the circumstance at hand. Jesus' response to her was one that appeared harsh and brash. He doesn't address her as 'dear mother' or 'mother '. His response to her was "Woman, what does your concern have to do with me?" He called her 'woman,' not as a means of disrespect, but out of the knowledge of what was to come. God uses His mother as

193

a prelude of what was to take place in the seconds and moments to come.

Jesus is able to be both the respecting son attending and honoring this wedding ceremony, and the incarnate Son of God. Mary comes to Jesus her Son and informs him there is a problem. His response to her draws the line between humanity and divinity. He was not insulting; He was showing her and us that something was about to change. For thirty years He had been her Son, so she obviously knew that this boy was different. After all, lest we forget, an angel announced her pregnancy. Mary had never known sexual relations with anyone; she never compromised, not once, with her espoused Joseph. Certainly, she knew someday it would come. A day she knew, but not the time, has now arrived and no longer does He address her as mother, but *woman*. A profound statement in one word; it is here, now is the time. All the preparation, all the planning for this day has arrived. My Son, the living breathing Son of God, is about to take center stage and change the world.

This woman whom Jesus just addressed never takes offense of His noted lack of concern. His response to her was, "What does your concern have to do with me?" A line is noted and drawn, but He does not leave it there. Jesus uses this as a fulfillment of scripture in so many ways. The mother of Jesus, the woman, has come to Him and brought her and the others' dilemma to the source.

Jesus shows his humanity and now his divinity. We read moments ago how He is our high priest, and He understands our sufferings and problems because He, too, has experienced them. Just a verse later we read that because of this, we can come to him openly, boldly, and confidently.

Let us therefore come boldly unto the throne of grace, that we may obtain mercy, and find grace to help in time of need. Hebrews 4:16

Wow! Exploding from the text is scripture being fulfilled! Mary, the mother of Jesus, the woman of our subject has a problem and she doesn't send for another - she comes to the Son of God, the

194

answer to her and others' needs. We can find grace in the time of need. What is your need? What is it that only Jesus can fix? Jesus is a need supplier. Whatever your problem, whatever situation you find yourself in, you can come to him.

Jesus uses Mary as a perfect model of how it's done. After his response to her she does not hang her head in disdain or discouragement. I don't think so; she knew a season had changed. She turns on her heels and goes straight to the servants of the wedding ceremony boldly proclaiming, "Whatever he says to do, do it!"

If we could get to the place to let faith arise and doubt scatter, we would then see the power of coming in prayer to Jesus. He knows and he understands; however, he does want us to come to him and ask.

> *Ask, and it shall be given you; seek, and ye shall find; knock, and it shall be opened unto you: For every one that asketh receiveth; and he that seeketh findeth; and to him that knocketh it shall be opened. [9] Or what man is there of you, whom if his son ask bread, will he give him a stone?[10] Or if he ask a fish, will he give him a serpent? [11] If ye then, being evil, know how to give good gifts unto your children, how much more shall your Father which is in heaven give good things to them that ask him? Matthew 7:7-13*

The son of the living God had compassion on their need, a need that was important to them. Jesus put off humanity's stepped into divinity and intervened into the affairs of mankind. For reasons much more than supplying wine at a wedding, He did and wants to do. Jesus was not content to just satisfy their thirst for delectable drink! He wanted to go deeper and further than a beverage could go. He was after their hearts. Jesus used this opportunity to show that He was concerned and involved in what concerned them. In a moment, He tells Mary that her coming to him was what concerned her, not Him. Then just as quickly, He gives instruction concerning the six stone water pots. Somehow Mary knew He would care; after all, she knew His concerns for the people. It was she with Joseph, Jesus' father, turning to look for him, and finding Him at twelve years of age teaching and instructing with knowledge from on high the most scholarly of all men in the temple. Jesus cared about imparting love.

Genesis, Chapter 2, gives the account of the creation of woman. Eve was called 'woman' because she was taken out of man. Chapter 2 verse 23   Adam calls her bone of my bones, "Woman". Adam called her woman; the last of God's creation we read of is Woman. However, being the last of his creation he did not fashion her from the dust of the earth. God took out a piece of man and made the woman. Woman, through the blessing of God, completes man. Not competes with, but completes God's plan for humanity.

So the last shall be first, and the first last.........
Matthew 20:16

Though the last created, Women are called into the service of the Lord. There is much debate on interpretation of scripture as to the extent that their service is allowed; yet still God uses them. I like how God does what He wants, when He wants - even against those who think they know best. God uses the least likely of people, and at times they are women. The bible calls them in 1Peter 3:7 "the weaker vessel." This is not to imply that they are not strong in the sense of being *less than*! To the complete opposite, Scripture is defining clearly the husband and wife's role in the family. God created men to be strong leaders, providers, and workers to position their families for success in all aspect of life and eternity. God created man as head of the household, not in a lording fashion as being given supreme rule, but guiding and nurturing them toward and expected end. To all those high-minded men with extreme egos, God brings in a Proverbs 31 woman to show their God given strength.

What a powerful explosion of truth! God uses women in a remarkable way. I grew up in church and many of those years were in churches of less than 100 members. A notable fact during those years was the abundance of women, and at times, the lack of men.

196

Men at times feel as though that 'the religion thing' as it is called, is too touchy feely for them. They leave the church thing up to the women. Flying in the face of this thinking is that God called men to lead their families - especially when it comes to faith. However, when men refuse to lead, God places in the heart of many women to live out a life of faith for the family. This faith many times entails dragging the children to church alone. In the most simplistic and elementary of statements, "it ought not be that way"!

Praise God for women who will step out of obscurity, risk scrutiny, and say as Mary did - "Whatever He says to do, do it!"

It has been said before but it's worth repeating, if more men would stand up and lead, then less women would be forced into callings at times unwanted.

God wants both Men and women who would answer the call; a call to lead screams loudly from the bowels of humanity. Our generation is looking for those who would stand up and lead, charging forward for the cause of Christ. Man or Woman, when God places his anointing and launches them into a world hungry for that, which escapes their understanding, a bridge is built. A way is made and a path shown through God-ordained, blessed and empowered Christian servant hood. A voice is used to proclaim the Gospel of Christ, the good news, through a yielded Vessel. Man or woman, God will, and is, getting his message out - "I love mankind and I gave my son for them."

A notable debate that seems unfathomable to many, and me as well is that of same sex marriage. We currently live in a culture and time where the top leader of our nation has placed his stamp of endorsement on same sex marriage. We do not read were God created Adam and Steve, but Adam and Eve. God created man, and then said, "It is not good that man is alone. I will give him a helper comparable to him." So he created Woman. Man, as he has done since creation, has tried to alter God's creation, creating his own set of standards that fit his desires and not God's laws.

God gave us the Ten Commandments through words written upon stone to show us that we are fatally flawed except submission to the higher and greatest power of all. Elohim is the highest name given for God in the Hebraic language. Its very form is masculine. Representing supreme strength, Satan attacked this supremacy, and then subsequently fell from his place in Elohim's kingdom. Better said, God cast him out and down! This rebellion passed to Eve then to Adam through lust and pride. This spirit says: *God's power is not supreme. His ways are questionable and His laws over reaching.*

We are saved through faith; however, there must be submission of our will that elevates God and decreases man. Our faith must surpass the mere belief in God.

Thou believest that there is one God; thou doest well: the devils also believe, and tremble. James 2:19

Our faith must be in Christ's finished work on the cross as well as His death, burial, and resurrection. Stepping further and reaching higher in our lacking, and Christ's abundance.

Ezekiel 28 gives the account of Satan's stance against God. You could set aside time to read how in verse 2 where pride entered Satan. It says his heart was lifted up against God. The passage goes on to tell how his main desire was to ascend above God. Scripture tells us that the clay shall not say to the potter what it shall become. We cannot forget that Satan was a created being given a measure of power by God. This power given was to magnify God with great talents and gifted leading in the presence of God for the glory of God. However Satan wanted the worship more than he wanted to give. Not to say we are like him, but at times to a degree we fall into this rut of thinking because of our service, we deserve! Listen to what the bible says of our service in his kingdom.

And whosoever of you will be the chiefest, shall be servant of all. For even the Son of man came not to be ministered unto, but to minister, and to give his life a ransom for many. Mark 10:44-47

There is nothing wrong with having high goals or aspirations however if our goals trump God's requests, an impasse is cemented. God will not compete with your will; He wants a submitted willing servant, which, in Romans chapter 12, he calls our *reasonable service*. Jesus came to this ceremony, I feel, for far more than to take part in the festivities of the day; He came to serve. In the same fashion, Mary did as well. She wanted this event to be enjoyable and successful.

I find it fitting as well prophetic the concluding of this chapter on "The Woman "has been written on Mother's Day. Unplanned, yet exciting to know God is right on time, and when we submit to Him, we are as well. Not a day late, God has our course plotted and set. We are His, and in the palm of His hand. Death is even incapable of extinguishing the flame of God's purpose in our life. Let me encourage you today – man, or especially women, to take a bold step in going toward Jesus. Mary was Jesus' mother but she knew He was of royalty. Undaunted, she approached Him without fear of rebuke. You, too, have the same rights. Come into the presence of the King and make your request known to Him. Call on the name of Jesus and tell Him of your need. Jesus is not too busy to hear; He has a desire to help and heal. This desire is to intervene on your behalf, simply because of his love for you. Friend, let him know your need, as small as it might be.

God is surely able!

Chapter 8

The Wine

And wine that maketh glad the heart of man, and oil to make his face to shine, and bread which strengtheneth man's heart. Proverbs 104:15

Turning water into wine... really? Jesus chose His first public miracle to be turning water into wine. It would seem to me that He could have, and would have chosen a much more spiritual miracle to kick off a work of divine intervention in this physical world! However, Jesus is God, lest we forget speaking of His life wrapped in flesh on planet earth. Nothing, and I repeat, nothing He did, that happened to Him, or transpired was anything but ordained by the great "I Am-God!" With this knowledge, let me remind us that He holds us in the hollow of His hand. Also, we are told He has the very hairs of our head numbered - how many we had when we entered the earth, and how many when we departed! Furthermore, he numbered all we had in between. God knows you and knows you well.

While some things are to be taken at face value in life and scripture we cannot neglect the truth - that everything that Jesus did, does, had and has a divine reason for doing so. Let me pause to say this, you're_____ and the _____ and the _____that happened and the_____. - Fill in the blanks with whatever fits for you, it had a reason! It matters to God. Nothing has escaped His sight or is out of reach of His knowledge. God is omniscient, omnipresent, all seeing, and all knowing. You are special and God knows what it will take to get you to your expected end. Let me give us a powerful scripture that trumps all your problems.

And we know that all things work together for good to them that love God, to them who are the called according to his purpose. Romans 8:28

Here's your word - "It's all good"- the good, the bad, and the ugly. God will use it, and get glory out of it. It's hard for us to grasp at times, God getting glory out of the worst of the worst - disease, death, divorce, and murder to mention just a few.

Knowing this vital information, we must also know that His reason for choosing this miracle as his first was for a divine purpose in a physical world. To better state it, God knows what He is doing! To put our trust in God's hands is a hard thing to do at times. Self-preservation takes over and steers us away from God's sovereignty. However, we cannot escape His grasp. God wants us, in our entirety - mind, body, and soul. It was a staggering charge that Mary gave the servants, and it embodies this truth, "Whatever He says to do, do it." Whether or not it makes sense, do it. This is a lying down of your will to do something in obedience that makes no sense at the time. There will be instances where it seems in your own reasoning that if you would do things your way it would turn out better, or faster. We as humanity struggle to trust and obey the voice and commands of the Lord. Not a single time will you obey the leading of the Holy Spirit and not have a long-term outcome that benefits you in some way. To go a step further, if you were to lose your life in obedience to the gospel of Christ, you have not lost but gained even beyond imagination.

According to my earnest expectation and my hope, that in nothing I shall be ashamed, but that with all boldness, as always, so now also Christ shall be magnified in my body, whether it be by life, or by death. For to me to live is Christ, and to die is gain. But if I live in the flesh, this is the fruit of my labour: yet what I shall choose I wot not. For I am in a strait betwixt two, having a desire to depart, and to be with Christ; which is far better. Philippians 1:20-23

Have you ever heard the voice of God? To those who say no, I would have to politely disagree. Jesus shows up all the time for us, but with our enlightenment darkened by carnality we fail to notice. We are told in scripture that true worshippers must worship Him in spirit and in truth. We must approach Christ with the faith of a child. The reasoning of a child is simple! It is a simple faith that just trusts and believes with no big explanation needed – they just believe. As adults we pass through life, we tend to pick up and move from place to place, accumulating baggage. Not a child, he is innocent and pure, untainted by life; he simply believes. Jesus is manifesting His spirit to the inhabitants of this earth at a quickening rate. Peering past all the stuff is Jesus standing with open arms and a loving touch. *Come to me I am here for you, just come to me and trust me.* Yet, at every turn it seems our society is deluged with evil of every kind. As the body of Christ, we are to be *in* the world but not *of* the world.

In the book of John where we extract our text, we find in the 17th chapter a tremendous eye-opening example of what God wants from us.

I pray not that thou shouldest take them out of the world, but that thou shouldest keep them from the evil. John 17:15

Jesus is praying to the Father that He has a desire to fulfill His perfect plan. Here is His plan, God created the earth, He created man and woman, and placed them there to inhabit, rule, reign, and multiply - to love God and love man while we are here on earth. Jesus says, "I pray not that you take them out of the world but that you keep from the evil one. After all, Satan shall not foil my plans. I created this earth and it's mine." Scripture says that the earth is the Lord's, and the fullness thereof (1 Corinthians 10:26). It is God's. He owns it all, and make no mistake about it; He didn't fumble the ball when He created both the earth and man. There is a reason why we are here, and as long as we are here let's make the best of it.

Let's do more than take up space. There is a life that has to be lived. In addition, at every turn there may be the appearance of evil, yet there is a profound work that God wants and desires us to do. Jesus got busy living, and His first public miracle was with the affairs of this earth with a vision for heaven. Yes, He went to a wedding and did the unthinkable - He turned water into wine. I hear gasps from the crowd. Wine? Why wine, and why did He get Himself entangled with the affairs of what seemed to be for the moment? Far reaching and beyond our comprehension, God knows how to take an earthly event to bring about an eternal fulfillment of promise.

Jesus took what we deem to be unimportant and placed it center stage - wine. To some it's a curse, to some it is a passion, to some it means a pleasurable moment in moderation. The substance of this chapter is not to debate the relevance of whether the wine was of an intoxicating nature. Rather, it is to see that God is good and all that He does is good. It sounds generic and real churchy, yet no other phrasing can embody the heart of the truth. Furthermore, nothing rings more true or louder than God is good and wants good for us.

I visited a winery and asked many, many questions until the man I was quizzing asked me, "Are you trying to open your own winery?" I had to laugh and reassure him I would not add to the local competition of wine making. Strangely, he seemed relieved and went about answering further questions I presented him. It seems to me making inquiries of the process and reading on the Internet pertaining to wine making, it *is* a process. It is a process that can occur naturally or with the help of modern techniques, but regardless of the two, one fact remains - it is a process - a process that arrives at a final desired outcome of a distinct flavor, color, and taste of wine. Assuredly we can ascertain that this was new wine that was produced from the miracle of Jesus. Endless arguments have been waged over the subject of wine in the miracle. Was this wine alcoholic? Was it free from the mind and emotion altering chemical that can occur through the process of fermentation from the fruit of the vine? My personal belief is that God is good, and nothing that He does is intended to have the possibility of harming us. As for alcoholic drink consumed by our Savior, just do a quick Internet search and you will overwhelmingly have differing opinions from many biblical scholars arguing for or against. This we know -

our Christ was the spotless Lamb that was sent to take away the sins of World. He never once sinned, or would put anyone intentionally in a position where they would be tempted to sin.

Let no man say when he is tempted, I am tempted of God: for God cannot be tempted with evil, neither tempteth he any man. James 1:13

Let me pose a question since we just read that God tempts no man. Why would Jesus choose his first miracle as an occasion to entice men to drink more once they are already drunk? Think of this logic. I don't think that He took that which was pure and produced that which was impure. It takes three to five days depending on the natural yeast and sugar content of the grape to begin the process of fermentation. Let me ask just one more question, since we are on this journey together. If it was Jesus who controlled the miracle, do you not think that He too could control the chemical structure for it to remain pure without an alcoholic content for the duration of this wedding feast? The miracle was not that the he could produce an alcoholic drink. This happens naturally, and is no big deal. It's done all day long all over the world. On the contrary, He took a supernatural occurrence to produce that which man could not. Listen, I propose to you that we bring God down to our level by holding to the thought that Jesus produced an alcoholic beverage so everyone could have a jolly good time and tie one on.

No, God is much bigger than that. He is not the one who wants to diminish the natural senses of a crowd. We are told to watch and wait, for no man knows the day or hour of Christ's return. God does not want us numbed into a trance to kill our pain. Jesus wants to take away our hurt and our pain. He wants us to cast our cares upon Him. He wants us to give Him our burden and take His yoke, for it is easy and light. He surely does not want a yoke of substance tied around us in the form of drink. Regardless, Jesus the son of the living God had power over all natural elements. After all, He created them. He could, at His own will, show that with His power He could cause men to drink and drink, yet never be fulfilled as long as He was in their presence. Only Jesus can produce that which satisfies a thirsty soul.

All of us at some time or another have been in a place where we felt something was missing. At times we could not place our finger on the problem, a glitch, if we can call it that, in our spirit. There is a void from birth that is looking to be filled in a way that only Jesus the Christ can fill.

I think of the very reason why the wedding ceremony was in need, the reason for a needed invention, and for me writing this book. It's the wine - they had run out. How many times have you run out when in the middle of a very important project? It's possible you run out of money to complete the project. It's possible that you run out of energy to finish what you need to finish. It could be that you're in a marriage and after ten, fifteen, or thirty years you've run out of desire to put anything back into it. The list is endless and we all have been there at times feeling we just don't have anything left to give. It could be that you're in the ministry and you have come to a screeching halt. Things just aren't working for you any longer. Where is the passion? Where is the fire I once had? As far as that goes, where is my desire to do what I'm doing any longer? God, I've prayed, I've fasted, yet I feel nothing. I know I love You and You love me, but I feel so empty and alone. Yes God, I am supposed to get up and smile and encourage your people; however, I'm empty and in need myself.

Lord, where do I go if I'm coming to You, yet feel the way I do? How do I feel? Honestly Lord, it's hard for me to put into words. I just feel I've run out.

If possible I would like to help us out a bit.

In 2 Samuel 7:28. we're given a glimpse into just how important the word of God is to our life.

And now, O Lord GOD, thou art that God, and thy <u>words be true</u>, and thou hast promised this goodness unto thy servant.

Hear the words of King David as he gives an example that we, too, should take note of.

205

Thy word have I hid in mine heart, that I might not sin against thee. Psalm 119:11

It is very critical that we rely on the word of God. The written word of God is a road map. Allow me to help clarify the importance of that road map; a map keeps you on track. Not only does it keep you on track, it helps you get to your destination. It does nothing on its own; however, when you pick it up, read the map, and reread it to ensure you are still on track, it provides a sure win outcome.

When we start to run low or feel we've run out, we too can come to Jesus just as Mary did.

She came to him and he seemed to place no importance on their immediate need. However it never ended there and will not with you feeling you've gotten no answer. We always want God to do the miracle while we sit back and wait until our sparkling wine is placed in front of us in our silver goblet. Countless times in the bible we read where Jesus moves in power yet invokes our participation.

One man named Naaman, who was a Syrian with the disease of leprosy, went to the prophet's house. This man was appalled that he stood at the door and made his petition, and only the servant of the house came. Then if that was not enough, he was told to go dip in the Jordan River seven times. To this man full of pride, it was enough to leave and die in his disease. Naaman was so full of pride he was willing to leave, even though being told what to do to receive his healing. It was only at the urging of his servants did he submit and do what was asked. You can find this story in its entirety in 2 Kings chapter 5.

I submit to you that at times God will ask something of us. How many times are we like this man who is full of pride showing up and feeling as if we deserve to do nothing more? God is after our faith, and when we act in faith according to a word, it sets us up for a miracle.   An exchange happens; a release of God's power is directed to us when we step out in faith.

We read of another man whose eyes Jesus covered in mud and then told him to go the pool of Siloam and wash. We find this account in John chapter 9; the man went and did what was instructed. I like the outcome of his obedience; a healing took place. This man was blind, and Jesus puts mud on his eyes and told him to go wash in the pool of Siloam.   We read this, but read over and through. This man was blind from birth. Get this - he could not see and was told to go wash. This man's reply was not "Jesus I can't see to walk to the pool of Siloam." He went and got his healing. We are not told how he made it to the pool. We don't know if he was led, or if he stumbled to it. What we do know is that he made it to the pool and did as he was told, and from the obedience received his miracle. What a beautiful story of faith in action.

We are looking for answers to our problems and are waiting on God to show up when the answers we are waiting on have already been spoken. Jesus has already given the answers to most of our questions and problems in his word. There are so many directives that the word of God has that we all too often overlook or avoid. They are not comfortable for our flesh to do. We, like Naaman, feel that there must be a better or more pleasant way to get the same outcome. Contrary to popular belief God is not Santa Clause. His gifts to you are not based on whether you were naughty or nice. We are infused with power when we act out of faith in direct relation to His word.

So here is the million-dollar question - What has God told you to do? In a loud or still small voice God gives direction. It possibly could be that you don't need a new word; you only need to keep your hand to what you were previously instructed.

In this chapter we are looking at the wine. The wine is what the outcome of the miracle was intended for. A solution to a problem and a need that was present because there was an absence of wine. If Mary had not come to Jesus and been bold to ask, if the servants had not listened to Mary and heeded her voice then obeyed the command of Jesus, and if they had not run out of wine in the first place there would not have been the miracle for which we extract this book. All participants and circumstances point to the only One who can take the impossible and make something better than what was hoped for. It is an amazing thing that we can be in desperate need and feel we are without strength. We can be at the lowest point and in need of much, feeling that if we just get a little then we would be okay. However, according to Ephesians 3:20, God will do exceedingly above and beyond what we can ask or think according to the power that is at work in us. This power of the Holy Spirit that was at work in the miracle at Cana is available to us as well.

My prayer for you is that you would look at all that transpired and know that if Jesus had compassion on a wedding party to supernaturally produce wine, then he will surely meet your need! God created this universe by a word, and by a word he will not just patch your problem, he will supernaturally intervene.

God more than produced wine, he took what was already there and changed it. More than producing wine he changed the water and *made* it wine. Here is your answer. God will take what is already there and change it for you to be of a better state than you previously were. Whatever your problem is, He will turn it around and the end will be greater than that beginning. What now seems to be turned ruin, God will intervene and not only make it as good as new, he will make it better. We read in the word that it is said that the glory of the latter house shall be greater than the former. What once brought you joy and has now soured, He will change it and bake it better than before.

Where you are at is not as good as it gets. It is not the finality. It will be better if you stay in Jesus. For his mercies are new every day. All too often we reflect on a previous season and have a desire to go back. This should not be. We should have a forward thinking faith that presses forward to an even better day. We are told to look up unto the hills for where our help comes from. This kind of faith walking keeps us looking up. In doing so, it keeps our head and faith from looking down. When you walk long enough with your head down you will at some point trip and fall. Lift up your countenance and know that God is truly aware of your plight.

We are living in a day and time with our advances in modern technology that it appears we are no longer in need of this divine miracle worker. We feel that if we can alter molecules and atoms to fit our desire then we are in control. We want bigger, redder tomatoes so we work our magic and - presto! - there they are. We take pills as an answer to whatever ails us. We write laws to fit our desires, trumping God's sovereign laws. This should not be the case. We can say what we will, but the word of the Lord stands undaunted by man's exploits. All the above and more are washed away in a flash, a flash flood, a storm, and in a moment, an earthquake and fire. We control far less than what we comprehend. We as man can twist and bend whatever to fit what we feel we want; however, we cannot twist the truth of our existence of a Sovereign God. Friend in God and his word, there are absolute and non-negotiable matters!

If we as a church, a nation, and humanity would ever submit to the eternal truth that we need the mercy of, then advances far greater than we had ever dreamed would begin to happen. The wine in this discussion gives indication that we are limited outside of God's intervention. We, in our own power, are limited to what we can achieve on our own. God placed limits on the sea in how far it can travel. There is an unseen limitation that is set in place by God. What has been discovered and invented by man has only been made possible by a loving God allowing us to cross previous limitations set by his design.

There are limits that are set in place in our life that are instituted by God. He is a limitless God who knows what is good for us and sets boundaries for us. We can push and push and then move what was not meant to be moved and in doing so, alter God's best for our life. We must know our limits and what the Holy Spirit is trying to keep us from.

One fact that I personally gleaned from my study into this miracle was the importance of Mary coming to Jesus. A simple fact, yet often forgotten, is that we can do nothing outside of His help.

Having served in the ministry, I've been at the bedside of once strong men, men of great strength and posture who are now gripped by humanity in its final days of life, a shadow of what once was. We may be strong and resilient yet, at any instant that can change. It is then we see the frailty of our stature.

Man was meant to live forever but, due to the sin entering through Adam and Eve, we now must face the certain fate of our earthly tent. Only God can take something and make it completely change. You cannot do it on your own. You do not have the power within yourself to make something change permanently. We must come into the presence of Jesus. I do not imply that God brings about difficult circumstances in our life; however, it is in the tender times when man's will is softened by trial that we tend to lay down our will and lean toward help. In these times, God can do a great work in a short time. When everything is going well we tend to be like the partygoers at the wedding feast. We eat, drink, and are merry from the festivities and the wine. The effect of wine in our well planned out life, which seems to be on track to break records for success. However, pull the plug on the bright lights and we see what remains. When the glimmer and flash is gone we see ourselves for what we are.

God loves to be needed. A proud and pride-filled people He rejects, but his word says He gives grace to the humble. When we have a need and come to Him, His eyes light up and He stands eager to help. Don't let the severity of your dilemma keep you from asking. If your problem is by sin, or not of your own doing, it doesn't matter. Come to Him and ask as Mary did.

I love them that love me; and those that seek me early shall find me. Proverbs 8:17

Scripture goes on to say in Luke 11:10, *"For every one that asketh receiveth; and he that seeketh findeth; and to him that knocketh it shall be opened."*

Very clearly given to us is the knowledge that we can come to Jesus and ask. Maybe you need your water turned into wine. Maybe you need your wine turned into water. Jesus is the source of strength and promise that He will never turn you away. Never will Jesus leave you standing out in the cold of life, empty and dissolute. Never will Jesus leave you in a place where you have nothing to cleave to. It is true that at times supplies will run low in life; yet, He is still Jehovah Jireh, our provider.

Abraham climbed to the top of Mt. Moriah with his son Isaac bound as a sacrifice. What obedience! To us, it is unthinkable that God would even test Abraham in this fashion. He was asked to sacrifice his son, the promise that God made to him, the one he waited years for. Abraham obeyed God to the letter; he took his son and headed up the Mountain with him. If ever was there a question that was asked that had so much volume, the one Isaac asked did.

And Isaac spake unto Abraham his father, and said, My father: and he said, Here am I, my son. And he said, Behold the fire and the wood: but where is the lamb for a burnt offering? And Abraham said, My son, God will provide himself a lamb for a burnt offering: so they went both of them together. Genesis 22:7-8

What was missing in the second chapter of John was the wine - that which is good and pleasurable - that which touched the heart of those attending. Here we find that there is something missing again. God always wants to restore what is missing. If it's joy, we're told to return to the joy of our salvation. If it is provision, He tells us that if He provides for the sparrows He will provide much more for us. He said that if we asked for bread, He would not give us a stone. He said that if we asked for a fish, that He would not give us a scorpion. Whatever it is that we lack, God desires to step into our void and fill our every need.

At times, as God did Abraham, he will test and prove us. At times our lack is even God inspired. He wants our attention. God, according to Exodus 20:5, is a jealous God. Jesus is not into competing for affection, time, or love. No, He wants all that we have. Often He will take away that we might come to Him. How can you give to one who's already full? How can you satisfy the hunger of one who has filled himself with everything except God? Far too much blame is placed on the enemy when at times God will allow a need so you might come to Him. Friends, God will test you. What is the purpose in the test? The test is more for the student than God. He already knows the outcome. When you successfully navigate a trial, it is a faith booster. It becomes a well in reserve that you can draw from in a future season. There will always be a season that will change. No season stays the same. This testing that was accomplished in Abraham's life was also staged in the wedding at Canna.

Think about this. How silly is it to go fill pots full of water at the command of this man named Jesus? There is no record of Him doing anything previously, yet they did what they were told. Because of their obedience we are able to draw from the well they dug. There are many things that you will go through as a Christian that are not about you. One of the hardest things that a Christian can grasp is the fact that your life no longer belongs to you. When you accept Jesus into your heart, you enter into the army of the Lord and He has a plan for you. You can touch others lives by simply walking the life of faith He has paved for you. Out of this entire volume the most important truth I can give is this - you will never go it alone! Not one step, not one minute, not one hour or year will you walk or rest without God by your side.

It seems so trivial and small compared to the larger picture of just running out of wine. The paramount truth is that we are in complete need of everything from God. We need the strength and energy from the sun; we need the rain and all four seasons. At times, we take for granted so much and fail to give God the glory He deserves. He is God and there is none beside Him. He is God all by Himself!

The wine was a drink common to most in the bible times. A quick reminder to us is the fact that we are reading of this first of Jesus' miracles that occurred some 2,000 years ago. Our common beverage luxuries of today were not even thought possible then.

Wine was highly prized and sought after for reasons we will read about.

To arrive at the finished product of the wine you must first understand that it began with a seed, or might I say, a humble beginning. It started as a seed - something small. Have you ever held a grape seed in your hand? Many have, I'm sure. It is very small. Held in the hand, it would appear as just a small round droplet. However, contained and locked within the seed is that which holds the possibility of a vineyard. From one seed, a vast fruit producing vineyard. If properly dressed, it can produce and multiply reaching around the world.

This one seed can grow into countless other seeds that can be carried and replanted. The cutting from the vine can be propagated to grow a vineyard, or carried to be planted anywhere the foot of man can carry them. The grapes of the fruitful planted seed can be consumed by birds and animals and carried great distances and emitted, and a planting can take place by God's natural process.

The next time you see wine, the next time you see a seed, the next time you start with something small, remember this. Far larger and greater is a seed than it appears. Much larger is your dream when planted in the soil of faith. The Lord tells us not to despise the day of small beginnings. What you are doing may seem small and insignificant, but when God is involved it can go around the world almost effortlessly. Let God get involved with your dreams. The truth is that he placed them deep within you in seed form. The seed is only an object until you plant it in the ground. When you do, then you must still give care to ensure a good harvest.

In order to get quality wine, there are factors that are most critical far before the harvest. What takes place during the growing season is critical and at times, uncontrollable. Remember we are at the mercy of God; there is much we can do and even more if the truth be known. However, we must not forget we need the mercy of God and His blessing to have lasting fruit. The soil is critical. All soil is not created equal! I punctuated the last sentence because it is vital you know this truth. What works for one will not work for all.

213

Your seed for your planting may differ from others who have planted and produced. Your seed is unique to you. What God has placed in your possession is again, unique to you. You are not always afforded the luxury of taking soil samples to have them analyzed. So what do you do then? Plainly put, it takes trial and error; it's a process. Things take time in our life. The making of wine takes time and the best of wines are aged. Even this process had to be done and redone to find the best development in order to achieve the greatest results for the best tasting wine.

I'm not trying to speak in code or hidden meaning. I want us to know that our spiritual walk with the Lord is truly a journey. It is a journey that must be lived and our hands put to. The best piece of advice from those who've gone before us could be summed up in this simple phrase. *Our life takes a lifetime to live.* There will be, as there have been, many bumps, turns, bends, and stops. We mustn't forget that if you have breath in you, regardless of the season you're in, there's still a life to be lived.

Let me pause in the middle of this chapter and say, ***LIVE***.

I shall not die, but live, and declare the works of the Lord. Psalm 118:17

Satan, your adversary, would like to take your seeds that God has given and destroy them before you can get them in the ground. A farmer doesn't scatter seed haphazardly; no, he carefully plants them for maximum growth. This life is not meant to be lived in a: "what will be, will be" attitude. Far be it from us to live in such a manner as some do. God created us for a purpose, and just as the grape must go through a process to become wine, so must we. God has us on his potter's wheel and is crafting us into a consumable substance.

I think of the Apostle Paul in the book of 2 Timothy chapter 4. He says that his life has been "like being poured out as a drink offering." Paul's life was a life that went through many seasons. No one that I can think of can compare to the many ups and downs of living for Christ that Paul had. Nearing the end of his life and

214

ministry, he says he is like a poured out drink offering. God crafted a consumable, useable vessel in the life of the Apostle Paul. I pray that we too can come to the place that we allow God to use us in any form or fashion. I pray God use you in such a fashion that you too can near the end of this life on earth and feel emptied of self yet full of Christ's Love.

The Apostle Paul said in Philippians 4:6 that whatever state he found himself in, to be content. Paul lived through all the many things he faced whether being shipwrecked, enduring beatings, hunger, imprisonment, or abounding, he found a way to be content - or better put - live for Christ.

Friends, it's time to live!

Unlike the miracle of Jesus, natural wine had to have a beginning. The seed of the grape had to be placed in the ground. The seed had to sprout into a vine. The vine had to produce branches. All the above can happen, but if the branches bear no fruit, there will be no wine.

The process of the wine mirrors our spiritual life and journey with the Lord. If we are in Christ then we must also know that there is an assignment that we all have. We can have an assignment for a public ministry, or one that is in the shadows of everything and everyone. Regardless of which, both are given by God. The question is asked often, "How do I get there? How do I make this happen?"

God's plan starts with a God given dream or a vision; this is a God given seed. God said that He gives seed to the sower (2 Corinthians 9:10). God gives you seed that you might place it in the ground. You must get it in the ground. You must intentionally, purposely pursue what God has placed within your spirit. If all we ever do is dream, it eventually will become only a fantasy. Go after it with complete abandon, and give it all you've got. After you've given, give some more. You will never give all you've got without God giving back. The Lord said in *Luke 6:38 Give, and it shall be given unto you; good measure, pressed down, and shaken together, and running over, shall men give into your bosom...*

We can dig just a bit deeper and pull back a layer that we might gain a God view on the importance of putting seed in the ground. We can continue to go to his word and find the perfect instruction.

> *Verily, verily, I say unto you, Except a corn of wheat fall into the ground and die, it abideth alone: but if it die, it bringeth forth much fruit. John 12:24*

What seed do you hold in your hand? What has God deposited within you that is ready to be poured out of your hand into the ground? What has God placed within you that is ready to be birthed. There is pain in the birthing process, great pain a woman endures to give birth. However, there is joy after the birth. No longer will she remember the pain, for the joy of the birth of her child far outweighs the pain.

You might be one who has put your seed in the ground only to have a crop failure. You tried and tried again, and still no return. For this group, God is doing a deep work within you. The greater the testing, the greater the assignment can be. I read a Facebook post just the other day on this very subject. It went something like this: *God often gets the greatest glory out of those who have failed, and gone on to do something significant.* If this is you, get up and try again. It is true that coasting, out of fear of failure for the countless time, keeps you paralyzed. I pray today that God, through the power of the Holy Spirit, crushes the enemy's hands that try to hold you. Today I pray you are released from the past and that you go on to greatness.

Get your seed in the ground!

The grape or the fruit of the vine's best possible outcome is dependent upon the soil, rain, and external forces. Rain is vital to the quality of the grape. Too little, and it will be weak and anemic - only a shadow of what it could be, unfit for the transformation into

216

wine. Its state will be unsuitable for service. We also need the water of God's word to make us strong and full of His Glory. I remember a childhood song that embodies this truth.

"Read your bible pray every day, pray every day, pray every day, read your bible pray every day and you'll grow, grow, grow".

External forces can damage the fruit before it can ripen or be harvested. I visited a winery recently to glean as much knowledge as possible. Upon my arrival I noticed they had netting strung the entire length of all the vines. I had never seen this done before. Upon my inquiry I was told it was a must where the vineyard was located. Starling birds can come in masses that cover the entire vineyard and cause irreversible damage. The birds eat the small grapes, and they drop excrement that has toxins and carry disease.

When I saw this, my mind began to race when I applied this to our reading. You as a child of God, intent on serving Christ, can do everything right biblically. However, there are the external forces that can come out of nowhere and swoop down on what you have been caring months for. They are completely out of your control and here they come! Don't let external forces rob your joy. Don't let the pests of life come and roost in your vineyard. You will have to go the extra mile to ensure the pests in your life does not come and rob you of what you are sowing for.

It is true that we can't prepare for everything, but we can prepare for more than we realize. Following God's precepts and principles, we can ensure that He is at the forefront of our lives, and in doing so we allow Him to lead. I'm not sure about you, but I would much rather do it God's way and suffer a washout than do it partly God's way and lose it all.

We have now arrived at harvest time, but where are the laborers?

Say not ye, There are yet four months, and then cometh harvest? Behold, I say unto you, Lift up your eyes, and

look on the fields; for they are white already to harvest.
John 4:35

The grapes, when harvested, are not left alone to just sit and spoil. Care is given to ensure all your efforts are not lost. For wineries, the busiest time of the year is the grape harvest. Anticipation is in the air, an excitement that it is finally time to be rewarded for all our efforts. I believe little thought is given to the importance of this same truth. We can be busy harvesting for the Lord, or simply allow it to remain in the field. Many souls around us within our grasp could come into the glorious harvest if they could see the value they could add. Let us be like those who are now aware that the grape harvest is ready, excited and expectant.

The grapes are harvested delicately to ensure the fruit is not lost in the harvest. It is what is in the fruit that holds the prize. The precious juice that is locked and sealed within the protection of the skin and flesh is what we are after. We must get the grape to the press. I can picture the one that harvests the grapes, as a mother would hold their newborn infant.

We now have the grapes, and they have made it from the field to the winepress. It is here that the true process begins. A crushing, a pressing, and a bruising must occur. Locked within the grape is the precious flow that is waiting to burst forth. The blood of the gape that contains all that is necessary to produce wine. There are modern techniques to make wine more quickly and to produce a wider selection in color and taste. However, there is still a completely natural process that has been, and still is used that uses nothing more than what is given.

Whatever the method used, the desired result is to get the blood of the grape to flow from the grape itself. Contained within the life of the believer is the power of the Holy Spirit. It would be easy if all we had to do were to put on Christ and then do a great feat for him a day later. This is not the case. A bruising and crushing is needed to bring out what Jesus has placed within.

We all too often associate pain, trial, and discomfort in life for being anything other than God's hand at work. Scripture refutes this thought and can empower the believer to help forge a stronger faith through it all.

> *My brethren, count it all joy when ye fall into divers temptations; Knowing this, that the trying of your faith worketh patience. But let patience have her perfect work, that ye may be perfect and entire, wanting nothing.*
> *James 1:2-4*

It is like an escape of the air in the room when you teach on this passage. Our carnal mind cannot process that we are to count it all joy when being tempted on anything having to do with our faith. However, we read that it is working something out in us. We say, "I cannot take anymore or go any further," and God says count it all *joy*!

When we go through trial and testing, the Lord is doing a work in us that at the time, we can't see. If we stay in the faith, if we stay under the shadow of the cross of Christ, we will come into a season where it will all apply. All that you have faced and gone through will be for a purpose. I am all too aware that we can go through spans of time when it appears up is down and down is up. It seems crazy, the thought of counting it all joy when you're faced with a life threatening disease, or when a spouse walks out, or the death of a child.

No one really has an answer as to why we have to go through the difficulties we do in life. However, if we don't allow them to bury us, they will produce, through the power of the Holy Spirit, a flow much like the flow from the grape. This is something that can be used and consumed coming from you. Many that have gone through great difficulties fall between two posts, bitter or better.

What happens to us is not always our choice, but how we respond is. I've found in my life that I can allow flowing from me poison, or the anointing of the Holy Spirit; it is a choice. I myself, like possibly you, have gone through difficulties that attempted to take me under. It is easy to open our mouth and allow things to escape like anger, bitterness, hate, or self-pity. Countering this very easy path is the other, to let God be center and His scriptures take the sting away. It will take effort and is at times difficult beyond comprehension to not live a life based off of emotions after the fact.

It can be done and is rewarding when we chose to not let it bury us, and live knowing somehow there will be something good to come from it. Earlier in this chapter I gave you a scripture, and I want to share it again.

And we know that all things work together for good to them that love God, to them who are the called according to his purpose. Romans 8:28

Whatever your "it" is, God will use it if you don't take flight and leave the faith. You may stay in church, stay giving tithe, but your active faith becomes passive faith finalizing in past faith. You need faith for today as well as for tomorrow. Give it to God and let him do a work and a wonder in the middle of your test.

The wine in Jesus' miracle had more significance than we can even tap into. I ponder the possibilities of what His reasoning might have been. In reality, they are only carefully prayed over and studied conclusions. However, the fact is this miracle was of great importance. It was his first and it produced wine.

All scripture and everything that Jesus did were to point the way to eternal life through his divinity. All the deeds, teachings, and miracles were to paint a clear picture of who he was, and what he was sent to do. They showed us where He was going and how we could be with Him in his eternal kingdom. Jesus said he came to destroy the works of the Devil. This power that Satan held over God's children was to be broken through the death, burial, and resurrection of Jesus Christ.

He shows us that we must follow Him and stay on the path of His Word. Straight is the gate and narrow is the way that leads to eternal life. Not everyone will find it. Not everyone will accept that

Jesus is Lord. Let us not be the one who tries to reason Jesus' deity away and miss the eternal truth. He is God and we are not. Jesus was fully God and fully man on the day he turned the water into wine. He tells and shows that we can do nothing apart from him.

> *I am the true vine, and my Father is the husbandman. Every branch in me that beareth not fruit he taketh away: and every branch that beareth fruit, he purgeth it, that it may bring forth more fruit. Now ye are clean through the word which I have spoken unto you. Abide in me, and I in you. As the branch cannot bear fruit of itself, except it abide in the vine; no more can ye, except ye abide in me. I am the vine, ye are the branches: He that abideth in me, and I in him, the same bringeth forth much fruit: for without me ye can do nothing. John 15:1-5*

Jesus is the true Vine, and was sent by the Father because He loved His creation. Think about this - God so loved us that He gave His only Son for us. For you, for me, and whosoever would believe on Him the promise of eternal life is for them. Jesus turns the water into wine then proceeds to later teach that He is the Vine. I think that when Jesus, God wrapped in flesh, comes back and reinforces a miracle that only He could do, we need to take note. He is the true Vine. No one, nor anything else is capable. No other belief system, and no other program or religion will connect you eternal life.

Jesus' words echo through the corridor of time, crashing head long into the present. He is the true Vine, make no mistake about it; except we, the branches, are connected to him we have no chance at eternal life in his eternal kingdom.

> *If a man abides not in me, he is cast forth as a branch, and is withered; and men gather them, and cast them into the fire, and they are burned. ⁷ If ye abide in me, and my words abide in you, ye shall ask what ye will, and it shall be done unto you. ⁸ Herein is my Father glorified, that ye bear much fruit; so shall ye be my disciples. John 15:6-8*

Oh my! I'm not sure about you but I don't want to wither and be cast into the fire to be burned. We as humanity like all the scriptures that make us feel good. It is our carnal nature to reject most things that do not make us feel a certain way. However, just as a car needs not only the positive side of the electrical system, it needs the negative was well. In order for our life to be balanced we need to know the negative outcome of a life not lived after Christ.

Not that we are to be terrified, but rather a healthy knowledge of the negative outcome of our sowing to the flesh. The bible says that the fear of the Lord is the beginning of all wisdom (Proverbs 9:10). Though not often spoken about these days, a reverential fear of the Lord is needed. Just as if we have a respect for stepping out into oncoming traffic, so too should we fear the outcome of sowing to that which is spiritually wrong.

The Lord, when he turned the water into wine, showed that He had power over the elements. Television and media did not numb the minds of the people of the time. To see and know that once it was water and now it was wine was a miraculous thing. Not much moves us; our senses are saturated with a constant barrage of images. Shootings, camera angles, staged stunts and endless stories that do nothing more than fill the mind with unfulfilling nonsense. Our modern western society has lulled us at times into a trance. This is not so with those in the day of Jesus. What a miracle to not only sees this water changed before their eyes, but they also could taste and see!

O taste and see that the Lord is good: blessed is the man that trusteth in him. Psalm 34:8

Not only did they see the water turn crimson red as it turned from water to wine, they could dip in and draw it out. They were able to validate the miracle by more than sight. It would be easy to say, "Look! It turned red, it must be wine!" However, when it was tasted, little doubt was left as to its authenticity.

God does this in our life when a new birth takes place within us - more than a visual is needed. We begin to produce the Fruit of the Spirit, those around can partake of the fruit, and we are established as a believer. In Galatians chapter 5, we find the Fruit that comes from the Holy Spirit manifesting Himself in the life of the believer. More than just repeating, "I am this or that," but a validation that comes through irrefutable evidence as that which is alive on the inside spills over to the outside. The believer and disciple of the Lord overwhelmingly have a light that resides within and they are unable to hide.

At the end of the day Christ wants to do more than cover, He wants to change us from within - like the wine that was no longer water, it was wine. When we accept Christ, we no longer stay who we were, but live as a new creation. 2 Corinthians 5:17 speaks of this great miracle of change, and be confidant that God can do anything for anyone. Maybe you are in need of a change? Let me challenge you today to come to Jesus and be bold in asking of Him. He is there; He is listening and eager to intervene.

God still turns water into wine!

Chapter 9

The Best for Last

In the culture we live, the thought of waiting has long escaped our way of life. We no longer value investing time, energy, and resources toward a potential harvest that would lie ahead at an undisclosed time. 'Get it now' seems to be the way of life. As I write these words, our country has weathered one of the worst economic times our nation has ever encountered. It would seem banks and loaning intuitions would wane from extending credit toward unworthy applicants, yet we read in the paper how this is the exact opposite. Money that is not secured still flows from resources that have no reserve. Our money is on borrowed time; our financial system is on borrowed time as we sit on the brink of the return of Christ. I feel blessed to live in a generation that has shown as many signs of the times as it has. Prophecy has been fulfilled before our very eyes. Technology has increased at such a quickening pace that society can barely keep up. You can purchase the latest and greatest gadget today, and within a month they are bringing out the new and updated model. All this has set the stage for the return of Christ. Scientists have tried to date the earth; Christian scholars can't seem to agree on a date either. With all this, one truth remains - though God has blessed his people and this earth to yield its fruit, he has saved the best for last.

There are so many things that have caught our attention, distracting us from our needed mind set. This earth is not our home! We are only passing through. We are sojourners in this earth. If we are saved and have become alive in Christ, our citizenship is in heaven. There is nothing wrong with living and prospering on this earth. We need people of influence in the body of Christ. However, when we place all our time and our resources toward building a life here on this earth, it is then we have lost sight of our high calling. When you read the book of Acts, especially toward the beginning, you will find that the early Christians whole heartedly believed that Christ's return was to be within their generation. With this belief, they lived life as if it was going to happen. You read that they had all things in common. They did not hoard all their belongings. They sold what they had and laid it as the feet of the Apostles. Christ did not return within the early church's time, but He will return. Christ will return and split the eastern sky so quickly that the bible says it will be in the twinkling of an eye. Quicker than a nanosecond I suppose, if it was possible to be calculated. Regardless of the measuring, it will happen far too quickly to make ready what was instructed long ago. We go through life in our Christian journey having heard of the possibility of Jesus coming back, but is seems like a fable. I pray that you would take the time to read these ensuing scriptures to better understand the magnitude of ignoring this Prophecy of Christ's return.

This second epistle, beloved, I now write unto you; in both which I stir up your pure minds by way of remembrance: That ye may be mindful of the words which were spoken before by the holy prophets, and of the commandment of us the apostles of the Lord and Saviour: Knowing this first, that there shall come in the last days scoffers, walking after their own lusts, And saying, Where is the promise of his coming? for since the fathers fell asleep, all things continue as they were from the beginning of the creation. For this they willingly are ignorant of, that by the word of God the heavens were of old, and the earth standing out of the water and in the water: Whereby the world that then was, being overflowed with water, perished: But the heavens and the earth, which are now, by the same word are kept in store, reserved unto fire against the day of judgment and perdition of ungodly men. But, beloved, be not ignorant of this one thing, that one day is with the Lord as a thousand years, and a thousand years as one day. The Lord is not slack concerning his promise, as some men count slackness; but is longsuffering to us-ward, not willing that any should perish, but that all should come to repentance. But the day of the Lord will come as a thief in the night; in which the heavens shall pass away with a great noise, and the elements shall melt with fervent heat, the earth also and the works that are therein shall be burned up. Seeing then that all these things shall be dissolved, what manner of persons ought ye to be in all holy conversation and godliness, Looking for and hasting unto the coming of the day of God, wherein the heavens being on fire shall be dissolved, and the elements shall melt with fervent heat? Nevertheless we, according to his promise, look for new heavens and a new earth, wherein dwelleth righteousness. Wherefore, beloved, seeing that ye look for such things, be diligent that ye may be found of him in peace, without spot, and blameless. 2 Peter 3:1-14

This final Chapter of the book you hold in your hands has been fitly titled: "He Saved the Best for Last."

This is the chapter I have waited the whole book to write. I was excited because the Holy Spirit had gently spoken deep within my me that it was to be a chapter of substances. This is a tall statement I know; however, I have spent time in fellowship with God and with Him stirring in me, this subject has been energizing. It's like an impending appointment with greatness. God has so much for us to experience and so much to enjoy. John 10:10 tells of his desire for us; Jesus wants us to have the abundant life. Your gifting was given to you for the body of Christ, and in the process of you walking them out, He infuses you with fulfillment. God created us for worship; He takes great joy when we actively take part in what He has made us to do. You are good at what you do for divine reasoning! The early Churches had passion and zeal for reason. This early group of believers awoke each day surprised to still be on earth. There was such a constant expectancy of Christ's impending return, and they lived as if sitting on the edge of their seat.

When you read 2 Peter the third chapter you see the deep warning we are given as believers in Christ. You can't be lulled into a spiritual sleep forgetting; even though today it was business as

226

usual, tomorrow may not come. We are told to watch and wait for the return of Christ. Examples and parables herald the truth of this impending Second Advent. When reading scripture, it mirrors the likeness of waiting on a ride to take you to an appointment. This ride is your only means of transportation and if you miss your ride, you'll miss your important appointment. In the last days we live, it only takes a surfing through cable channels to know we are in those prophesied days. Many have carved out false paths to eternal bliss, and many say that Heaven is now and there will be no literal Heaven. This same group also would have you to believe there is no literal Hell. Sadly, they will be made believers of both. Jesus said that except through Him, you would not have the possibility of eternal life. People can, as they always have, twist and interpret things, as they desire; yet, they can't explain away the reality of God breathed scripture.

God says what He means and means what He says! He said He would come and He did. He said He would return, and return He will! The paramount purpose of the gospel I cleave to is Christ's good news. You can have eternal life through the blood of Jesus Christ. This is a message that has had its author crucified and nailed to a cross. Just as the cross was not a final resting place for Jesus, neither shall your worst trial bury you.

The miracle we've been examining is one of firsts. Let this be a first for you - a first of finally reaching and grabbing the thought that the truth is, I must be about the Father's business; time is short! We will not pass away into the great by and by; no, we will triumphantly enter heaven or will pass into eternal judgment. I plead with you to know the hope of your calling! Know that you are the called of the Lord. Know you are in the palm of His hand and He has great things in store for you. Know that God is on your side and desires to work with you in your life's endeavors. Know you are not alone in what you're attempting to do. Know He wants to create, through you, a path for others to Christ. You are called to be His mouthpiece in this earth. God desires to speak through you, and wants you to know you are not crazy in the big ideas and big dreams you have for ministry or life.

"A good acidic test of a God dream is one you have the inability to finance, accomplish, or run from." When God puts a dream in your heart or stirs deep within your spirit a God-breathed dream, He will see to it Himself that it comes to pass. Listen, God will not let you quit! You might possibly find yourself at a juncture where you're not sure you can make it through another day. I say you can, and you will! It's possible, as in our text; God has saved the best for last.

I know all too well the desire to see a breakthrough and a moving of what you've been trying to actually make happen. I too have gone through seasons where it seemed each day was no different from the last. There have been times when even years blurred from one to another. What stands just out of sight is the favor of God. God is always watching over his investment. God has invested too much in you to let you quit now. There is a reward waiting on you if you don't quit or retreat. God has saved the best for last - beyond the sweat, at the end of your tears; God has a reward waiting on you. The sweetness of victory will far surpass the happiness had you been given everything upfront.

Catch this; some things are worth waiting on, and some things are worth fighting for. There are times when your faith will come under fire, and it's all you can do to hang on. If it's a fight, then a fight it shall be! Far too many people quit long before their reward.

Tough times don't last, tough people do!

It would be real easy to get super spiritual and say we should all be riding on Holy Ghost cloud nine all the time. In reality, this is not the case. No sir, I beg to differ. Take a stroll through Hebrews the eleventh chapter, and you will encounter those who are on the roll of the Hall of Fame in Faith. These people were battered, beaten, stoned, scorned, accused, and abused. Friend, contrary to popular preaching, the God kind of faith will take you down roads you never packed or prepared for. I can think of no greater honor than to follow Christ down a path others refused to travel. I am aware that across the globe believers are still accosted for their faith.

228

However, they are not persecuted to the degree they once were. This is changing, even in our world of political correctness. As we press toward the end, we are beginning to see the start of what the bible calls birth pains. The name of Christ (Jesus) is the name that Satan and his agents have tried to silence. It hasn't happened yet, nor will it. Employers can threaten employees not to mention His name. Public school systems can deny prayer in school and remove any reference of His name. All this will not eradicate the name that is above every other name - "Jesus."

In our miracle I have mentioned repetitively, Jesus worked a profound supernatural occurrence. He showed up with his disciples as a result of being invited. He does not come in riding a white horse with an entourage of dignitaries. Jesus arrived, walking and unannounced. Jesus' mother Mary comes to Him and tells Him of a huge problem - the wedding party has run out of wine. Jesus never pulls out a magic wand and tells everyone to watch as he performs a trick. To the contrary, he involves others, as an opportunity to build everyone's faith. In John 2:11 we read, after the mighty miracle leaving the house and heading to Capernaum, a noted shift has happened. I want you to grasp this. It reads, "And his disciples believed in Him." Jesus saved the best for last. These disciples already believed in Him to a degree; they were following Him. They followed him to the wedding ceremony. A disciple, as they were called, was one who assisted and spread the message of the one they were following. They were walking with Him, yet after this incredible event, something forever changed.

They believed in Him!

We as believers in Christ can actually believe in Him, yet never fully or whole-heartedly believe in Him. We keep, in reserve, an ace to go to when we run into tough times. We withdraw and go back to our own intellect. To some it seems scary and dangerous to trust fully in the Lord. When you read the bible you read accounts of men who followed God to the end of the earth because of a word He spoke. God told Abraham to leave his family and go to a land He would show him on the way. Most would say, "Okay, I might go, but give me directions and I'll think about it." Not Abraham, he did exactly what was spoken to him to do. A complete abandonment of one's self to follow the Lord is what God is after. I often ponder the degree of reward waiting on obedient souls once in heaven. Scripture says He is God and He changes not. If he asked Abraham and others before him to do the unthinkable, how can we think He doesn't still ask today?

The disciple's spirit within was forever meshed to the Messiah. These men caught the message of the Christ; they received His Spirit within and believed in Him. They put their trust in Him. It's possible that you, as the disciples, have followed Him to different places, but something has yet to happen within you toward Him. I say, let this day be a day of firsts and "believe in Him!" The simplicity of reading this book has stirred deep within you a renewed passion to chase after your calling, to pursue your God dream "then let it be a first."

God is called the Master Builder. He knows the best time to launch you into the deep for a greater use in His Kingdom. It is a time that He has prearranged in His own timing. Scripture says to seek Him while He may be found. This paints a visual that He wants us to pursue Him. He wants us to go after Him. God will not run from you. He is never elusive. To the contrary, He *wants* you to find Him. He is ready and waiting with open arms. Beyond your disbelief, there is a God who will provide evidence for you to walk away believing in Him. I hear the cry from many who feel they have trusted and believed, only to have their dreams dashed and hearts crushed from tragedy. Listen, we as humanity lose sight that God is all knowing and all seeing. Beyond our limited knowledge is a God that sees all. There is so much that you don't see; yet God sees all. Nothing that God does or allows is meant to harm us. Even in His chastening or correcting, He does so to provide for growth. God doesn't save us to set us on a shelf to collect dust. God wants us to be used, and for us to actively participate in what He is doing in the earth - an 'earthly training' if you will.

Our enlistment for Christ's use will not end with our earthly existence.

Do ye not know that the saints shall judge the world? And if the world shall be judged by you, are ye unworthy to judge the smallest matters? Know ye not that we shall judge angels? How much more things that pertain to this life? 1 Corinthians 6:2-3

It is so; we have work to do now and work that awaits us. What a great and exciting mystery that God has awaiting us in a glorious Kingdom. Jesus has truly saved the best for last!

The conception for this book came as I read this powerful account in John and reflected on seasons in my own life. The calling, dreams, and vision God imparts to us at times can frustrate the one possessing them when an extended period of time elapses with no obvious movement. Let me help by sharing a demonstrating scripture.

Hope deferred maketh the heart sick: but when the desire cometh, it is a tree of life. Proverbs 13:12

Living in an earthly tent, we call the flesh, is an issue called the heart, the part of our being that is intertwined with our will and emotions. These emotions and thoughts must be constantly brought into check or placed under control by a renewing of the mind by the word of God. This is only possible by spending time in prayer and bible reading. Not only when spending this time do we discover new truth and revelation, we also are reminded of what we already know or have been told. We need to be reminded of what God has said. Life happens! We are living in a real world with obligations and responsibilities that cannot be overlooked. With this, our mind is constantly being drawn toward everything that is happening and pressing on us. It is then that we simply forget things that we've been told.

It seems so simple yet profound; the accuracy to which our bible has been extended through generations is mind-boggling. God gave us His word and sealed it through time that we might go to it again and again to be reminded of what He said. With all the splendor of this knowledge, still there is better yet to come. We read about the time that God walked with Adam in the Garden of Eden. I glean this book from during the time God was wrapped in flesh and spent it with humanity. Still, there is better yet to come! We, if placing our faith in Jesus, will forever be with Him, living and reigning with Him in his heavenly Kingdom. For us, God has saved the best for last.

Growing up I remember a song that a traveling group sang at my father's church called, *"I'm going to take a trip on the good ole Gospel ship."*

Wow, what a thought to know that one-day the trials and suffering of this life shall pass. A glorious day it will be that we will put off mortality and be wrapped in immortality! I have had an extended pause in the completion of this book. I have had to stop so as to regain my focus and thoughts. My mother, who was a pillar of Christian faith, passed from this life to her reward. She had suffered on and off with different illnesses, and finally after fighting long and hard she breathed her last breath. I had the honor of being in the room by her side when she passed. Just hours before, with labored breath, she was still speaking life over her family and myself. What a glorious testimony to know that she finished in the faith! I've thought many times since, maybe this or that could have helped to keep her here a bit longer.

We naturally, for our own reasons, desire to hold on to what we cherish. This was not to be; my Mom loved God and was ready to go home! Her Father, God, stood with open arms and with a pure robe in hand, wrapped her in his glory. She now knows no more pain. She suffers no more, nor will she ever again. My mother has shed mortality and is clothed in garments sewn from His Majesty on high.

I now would like to turn the clock back some 36 years; I would have been 8 at the time. We were visiting my grandparents who lived in Indiana. I remember even as a child the hush-hush conversations between my parents and them. I overheard the concern in their voice and the earnestness in which my grandmother directed them to immediately get to the doctor. My mother had a growth on the side of her neck that had changed colors causing valid alarm. As instructed, she went to the doctor immediately. After the visit to the doctor, much of my memory seems to be a blur. A blur to me, but it was a reality for my folks. My mother was 26 years old and was now facing a life threatening disease called cancer!

In those ensuing days I can still feel the severity of the doctor's prognosis in the air. I come from a family of faith. Both my mother's parents were preachers. They had lived a life of faith, preaching and pastoring for a number of years. My father, who would become a preacher of the gospel, directly attributes his salvation to their Christian witness. With the faith to move mountains they prayed and they prayed. As a child I felt the disconnect as we were watched over by family members. My mother was in the fight of her life, as was my father. They cleaved to their faith in God and now they faced a very invasive surgery as a last resort. Nearly 40 years ago they did not have the modern techniques of today. I mentioned previously of our advancements in technology; as much as we've progressed, we have still not cured this deadly disease. I remember bits and pieces, and have heard the stories shared of this event. My mother was on the operating table in excess of 8 hours. Afterward she had a scar that extend from her lower pelvic area to the back of her ear, but she made it. My mother, through God guiding the hands of the surgeons, beat cancer. My mother lived another 37 years after having stage 4 cancer. If that is not something to shout about, I'm not sure what is! I grieve with the rest of my family over her passing, yet am keenly aware she is in a much better place.

As a Christian we are not exempt from trials and testing. It does rain on the just and unjust alike. We as Christians suffer with the reality of this flesh we occupy. The difference for being and living in the faith is for us; God has saved the best for last. As I reflect on my mother's life, I can see where she touched many lives. She was the wife of a pastor for over forty years. My mother, though quiet, was always active - teaching Sunday school class, being a youth pastor, or leading a vacation bible school. Mom was busy doing what she did best; she was God's hands and feet behind the scenes. I also think of the lives I know nothing about that were impacted along the way that I will never meet. My mother's ministry extended well past my time in the home. Extending beyond what was accomplished through her life, great ministries lie ahead. She is now is in the presence of Jesus, ministering to Him in worship even as I pen these words. God had better things ahead for mom, better than the illnesses, better than the best day she ever had on earth. While here on earth we have work to do. The catalyst for our service is a glorious fact - Heaven awaits! We have so much more ahead of us, so much that we have to look forward to!

I like that Jesus not only commissioned us to work for Him, but also in doing so, made a promise.

Let not your heart be troubled: ye believe in God, believe also in me. In my Father's house are many mansions: if it were not so, I would have told you. I go to prepare a place for you. And if I go and prepare a place for you, I will come again, and receive you unto myself; that where I am, there ye may be also. John 14:1-3

This to me is exciting; I have a promise that God is preparing for me a place of my own. I admit to not fully knowing the exact vastness of this prepared place; however, I do know whatever God does is good. God is good, and nothing He has ever done is wrong. God is good, Satan is bad. God wants to bless, and Satan wants to steal, kill, and destroy. We cannot twist the truth. God is real and Satan is real. For reasons unknown to us, held in the council of God and His will, He has allowed evil to exist as long as it has. One day this will change, and all that is in opposition to Him will be destroyed. For God's own reasoning, He has saved the best for last!

God is perfect and has many ways to accomplish His will on this earth and in our life. As I read the second chapter of John, it came alive to me. This was Jesus' first public miracle and it seemed so chaotic to me. This was to be the first, yet seemed completely unplanned. If you and I were to set out to make our mark in the world, I believe we would have approached things quite differently. I think it would go along these lines: First we would scout out the location, next we would prep the team, and then we would call all

234

the media and press. I can see flyers and billboards across town saying, "Come see the great miracle to be performed!"

It's almost comical, the degree to which we set the stage. Jesus' approach was and is the opposite. Jesus was always stepping into the middle of a mess to make things better. We as humanity tend to wait until the dust settles or the air is cleared before we want to move in and set up shop. Down deep, I feel this is why He chose to accomplish His mission in the manner as He did. Jesus wanted to show that the way to act in His service is "*now!*" Jesus found a problem and acted. Jesus was the answer to their problem. Jesus was the master of Intervention, he led the way.

We read the heart of the message of the gospel in John 2 verse 9-10. I would like for you to read it one last time.

When the ruler of the feast had tasted the water that was made wine, and knew not whence it was: (but the servants which drew the water knew;) the governor of the feast called the bridegroom, And saith unto him, Every man at the beginning doth set forth good wine; and when men have well drunk, then that which is worse: but thou hast kept the good wine until now. John 2:9-10

Jesus has kept the best for last! As absolute and with clarity, I purpose to show what God has shown me in this final mile of our reading.

The ruler of the feast tasted the water turned to wine and had no clue it had been water. The servants knew because they had taken part in what Jesus had accomplished. I've heard it said many times, "it's the small things in life that matter." Maybe you are living a life of stature and have no clue what is it is to struggle. These servants knew all too well what it was like to fight to stay alive. Both parties were not excluded from the miracle; each had a specific role to play. I'm not sure where your social status places you currently. Want I need you to know is you are where you are for a reason. God has positioned you for divine reasoning. God chooses where we are to be in life for His purpose. God does not exclude us from his plan; He includes both prosperous and poor. In whatever place you find yourself, know that you should work in the field where He has planted you.

What an honor to know, firsthand, that Jesus had accomplished this mighty miracle. They may not have had a lot of money and a fancy house, but what they did have would be forever cherished. We overlook the obvious; these people were able to pass to their children this great and mighty feat. We can't lose our heritage as believers; we must pass down to our children and our children's children what it means to walk with Jesus.

Tell ye your children of it, and let your children tell their children, and their children another generation. Joel 1:3

This wedding feast was about the joining of two people who were to spend the rest of their lives together. A family setting is where Jesus chose to perform his first miracle; hopefully, children would come from this union. What a powerful thought to think that these two unnamed people would have the power of a living God being a part of their marriage. The stories that could be passed from generation to generation as a direct result of God being a part of their marriage are an awesome privilege. I mentioned previously of my mother's victory over cancer, and eventually over the grave as a part of my heritage. I have shared, and will continue to share with my adult children, of these great feats of God. It is our testimony that we carry that is meant to be shared of God's faithfulness and mercy that He shows His children. The disciples would carry this mighty miracle and be empowered from its impact. The servant's lives would forever be changed as a result. The bride and groom's marriage carried a special blessing. The ruler of the feast had a distinct privilege of declaring a truth, that "God saves the best for last!"

If you would allow me to go just a bit deeper and reach further, I feel that together we can grasp the message God is speaking.

For now we see through a glass, darkly; but then face to face: now I know in part; but then shall I know even as also I am known. 1 Corinthians 13:12

God has not granted us to see all that He is doing and will do. I dare to say, had God showed you all you would face along the way you would not have been so eager to accept the challenge. Even so, you did and have made it this far. It's only going to get better from here. I think of the Apostle John exiled to the Isle of Patmos, with God speaking mysteries to him. A faithful servant to the end, obediently he recorded the words of the Holy Spirit as they were spoken to him. A certain fate he faced, yet he held his fear in check and dictated as the Spirit of God shared His plan for the end of times. This man could not possibly comprehend all that God was speaking; yet he obeyed. John saw through a glass part darkly. He could see the risen Savior, but not all that was to happen in detail. It took faith in Christ to continue in persecution, yet he did.

You too are not afforded to see all that will happen along your journey. However, this one fact you can take to the bank - you play a part in the kingdom of God. It may seem like all that either has or has not happened is for no good. I hope and pray you can receive an encouraging word. "It will all work out for your good!" Read this very uplifting passage, and when you do, believe what you are reading.

And we know that all things work together for good to them that love God, to them who are the called according to his purpose. Romans 8:28

Jesus performing the miracle at the wedding in Cana was no random act. He knew in advance when it was to take place, what would happen, and how it would unfold. Nothing in your life is a mystery to God. You, looking through that cloudy glass, have a difficult time seeing what God sees. Friend, this is where faith comes into play - trusting when you can't see a positive outcome, trusting during a difficult season, or continuing to believe when all seems to have fallen apart. It's all going to work out for your good somehow, some way. From the beginning, the wedding seemed to be doomed for failure, but God stepped on the scene and changed the outcome.

God saved the best for last; can you wait until the end? Can you wait past the storm to receive a greater reward? Can you stand the trying of your faith to receive a crown of life for your service to Christ?

I feel the central theme that the Spirit of God keeps reminding me as I share with you is as follows: While you are here on this earth, pursue Him and pursue His Kingdom. I can hear the desperate plea of many who would ask, "What does that look like?" I can sense the frustration of many who have shouted out in the night to Him saying, "God if you would just show me, then I would know!" I can hear many others who are screaming loudly, feeling no one hears them. "God, I don't know what to do, and I don't know where to go!" This is difficult to hear and difficult to accept because we want the voice of God in the whirlwind. However, I need to tell you this - you're doing it. You are fulfilling the mandate of God by continuing to come to Him. Many quit coming, many quit speaking to Him, and many simply quit asking Him for help.

I can't proclaim it loud enough through this printed page to be pleased. If it were possible I would, however as desperately as I can, I want to tell you, "Never quit!" Just don't quit - whatever you do, don't turn back or cast off your faith. God will see you through, and even though it has been rough and difficult, God will bring about change that will be better in the end than in the beginning. I hope you can hear the encouragement expressed in this most blessed passage.

Behold, I will do a new thing; now it shall spring forth; shall ye not know it? I will even make a way in the wilderness, and rivers in the desert. Isaiah 43:19

We can go through periods in life where it seems the best days are behind us. When we read this passage of scripture we see that God is doing new things. If you notice, when you read part way through this passage He says, *"Shall ye not know it."* Stated more clearly, "You will know and you will see." It will be no mystery to you when it happens. Every day God is doing something new, things will not always appear at first to be what you had hoped for. However, you will see that when God does something new, it is always better than what we had thought, and more than what we hoped for. Here is the key - it takes time for it to grow. We want the instant and immediate, but God more often saves the best for last. If more people would be willing to weather the harshness of certain seasons, they would be overwhelmed at the blessing of the next.

This scripture should help us.

Be patient therefore, brethren, unto the coming of the Lord. Behold, the husbandman waiteth for the precious fruit of the earth, and hath long patience for it, until he receive the early and latter rain. James 5:7

The farmer waits patiently; he has done what he has to do. He has prepared the ground, and he has planted and fertilized it. He must wait patiently, and his labor and effort shall be rewarded. There is a time where we must wait and endure until it springs forth.

For the earth bringeth forth fruit of herself; first the blade, then the ear, after that the full corn in the ear. Mark 4:28

There are stages we go through in any given effort, whether realized or not. First the blade, then the ear, then the full corn in the ear - it takes time. Whatever you are tackling or facing right now, regardless of how difficult it seems, see it through, keep moving toward the prize. See it through until the finish! At first you may only see a tiny blade begin to emerge, but it is something, right? I shared earlier Isaiah 43:9, *"Shall ye not know it?"* You will begin to see with your own eyes as it begins to turn in your favor. Repeating once again I would like to say, "Just don't quit."

The Master of the feast called the bridegroom and told him a tremendous truth. He told him that most people give the best first, and then when all have drunk much they bring out the inferior. The

Master of the feast told him, "But you have saved the best for last." Many have tried to apply the numbing of alcohol to his passage; however, this is not an argument worth entertaining, nor is it relevant. What I want you to see is the relevance of to the "end of things." Most don't give the best they have toward the end. People tend to veer off track once they get started. They start off good and ready to give their best, but something happens along the way. They get board, tired, or discouraged and give only a portion - or that which is inferior. This passage refers to drink; yet the same principle can be applied to our service.

Marriages can start out the same way - full of passion, love, and devotion only to fade out for a lack of long-term commitment. Many good business ideas are positioned for success only to fail because of a lack of long-term determination. We are not to start out in a flame of fire only to go down in a puff of smoke. This life is a race, but it's not a sprint. It's a long, steady, mostly uphill journey - so settle this fact within.

Our mindset is the most vital key to our success in Christian living. In Romans 12:2 we're told to be transformed by the renewing of our mind. We do this by an application of the word of God directly to our life. The more we spend in time and fellowship with God, the more He fills our heart and mind. As a direct result, we become full to overflowing; allowing God's word to take precedent in our decision making process. In doing so, we allow the word of God to even trump emotions that once ruled our life. Get in the word of God and watch Him work in your life. As crude an analogy as it is, it mirrors this principle.

Do you remember the cartoon of the rabbit and tortoise? That poor little rabbit ran himself ragged trying to outrun that slow turtle. I like the fact that in the end, the turtle always won. It was humorous to watch but I've seen it repeated by those who have gone out long before, only to allow life to sideline them. Broken, busted, and forever discouraged, their faith is shipwrecked by the tidal wave of life's trials. Friend, there is enduring faith available that seems to strengthen with each steeper hill and heavier load. This faith is

240

fanned by the flames of the Holy Spirit, like a believing coach and loving father standing on the sideline screaming. "Yes you can"!

I echo them. "You can do it, and you can accomplish that which seems impossible!" If God didn't think you could, He wouldn't have tasked you with it. You will see a better end than you thought. You will see advancement that you only dreamed of. If you don't cast off your hope, God will cause you to catapult into your divine destiny. All your prayers, all your fasting, all your meditation and efforts are going to pay off. God has been keeping a record and just at the right time He is going to release you. I believe the right people hold in their hands this book, if only for me to tell you this - many people have written you off and said you never will. They say you will never recover. They say you will never go to where you said you will for God, or will do what you've said you will do for Him. This same group says you have made one too many mistakes. They also say that too much time has passed; you are too old to achieve what God has said you'll do.

The biggest rebuttal that could be used is, "You don't know my God! For you, it came easily, but for me God has saved the best for last! If you stick around long enough you will see His hand move in a mighty way!" I wonder how many of those who showed up for the wedding feast left when word came that they were out of wine. I feel it is safe to say that more than a few did. Can you see them leaving in disgust? *"You mean we came all this way and you weren't prepared?"* But there were those who were willing to see this through. They didn't need all the Ritz the party could offer. They were happy to be there, if for nothing more than to be a part of the ceremony. It's funny how blessings show up unexpectedly. I'm not sure about you, but I like unexpected gifts. Most people are no different. They like to be blessed without warning. Think of this group who was willing to ride out the storm of need that received greater in the end than in the beginning. God reserves the right to save the best for last.

God saves the best for last!

Gideon said, "Who, me?" in Judges 6:15 *And he said unto him, Oh my Lord, wherewith shall I save Israel? Behold, my family is poor in Manasseh, and I am the least in my father's house.*

You know the story of how God called him to save Israel from the hands of the Midianites. He first tells the angel of the Lord how lowly and poor his family is, and then proceeds to tell Him how of all those in his father's house, he is the least of the lowly. I like that God likes those who other don't. God will call you at the end of your family tree and raise you up higher than the highest. God did it with Joseph. He was second to the youngest, yet God spoke through a dream that he would lead his entire family.

So, the story of Gideon continues with the army of Israel being dwindled to just three hundred men to fight against a vast army of the Midianites. This small, leftover army got the victory. God uses the least to accomplish greatness. God uses six pots of water, turning them to wine to continue the wedding feast. God took two fish and five loaves of bread to feed five thousand people. God causes a widow woman's oil and meal to not run out through supernatural multiplication. It seems that God likes that which is left to bring about the best. Jesus always seems to get glory from saving the best for last.

It's possible you find yourself today with only pieces left over from previous dreams and endeavors. You gave your best and your life only to see it crumble before your eyes - broken, shattered dreams. It is you I want to speak directly to. You do have something left. You have breath, you have the gift of life and regardless of the battle, you've made it. If you can read this book, if you can listen to this on an audio file, you have the chance of a mighty comeback. It is not in what you have lost, but in what's left over. The widow woman I mentioned earlier told the prophet that she only had a little meal and oil left and she was going to make one last meal for herself and her son and then die. However, God had a different plan. He had a minister of his own that was going to come on the scene and change things forever.

Her leftover that would only sustain for a fraction of time fed her, the prophet, and her extended family. It may seem that you have only a small portion left, and as soon as it runs out you're as good as gone. I beg to differ with you; God would have me to tell you that He is here to save the day. He will send an angel, He will send a man, He will use a woman, or He will send a prophet. God is not in the business of letting you die needing or wanting. God is an abundant God who can take a little faith and move mountains.

Do you believe this can happen for you? If so, share your faith! Speak your testimony to others of God's faithfulness, and watch the hand of God not only multiply your life, but also other lives in the process.

Have you ever noticed that it seems God lets things get really bad at times before He acts? I think of his friend Lazarus that died. Scripture says Jesus wept at the news. His sisters came to Jesus and complained and accused that ultimately it was His fault. They knew He had the power to heal, and yet He waited until Lazarus was dead to go to him. How many times have we bemoaned the Lord that He never showed up, and it's far too late now? Our child, our life, our spouse, our dream is dead. "Jesus, there is no sense in coming now, it's too late. Had you been here just a few moments sooner, this would not have happened." Where Jesus is center, death is no limit! I want to encourage you; Jesus can bring about good out of any situation, and at times can exceed previous joyous seasons if you allow Him to be Lord of all. Let God be Lord of all, Lord of all the good and the bad.

In the bad, Jesus is still there. He has never left us. When his friend Lazarus died, scripture says He wept. I feel He wept for many reasons. I feel He genuinely wept at the passing of His friend; Jesus felt the power of emotions. Though he felt the power of emotions, He never let those emotions control Him. Scripture says He was tempted in all ways, yet was without sin. Also, He wept at the lack of faith of those who knew Him the best. When Mary, Lazarus' sister, came and told Jesus Lazarus was sick, His response was one of confidence. Jesus told her, "This sickness is not unto death, but for the glory of God, that the Son of God may be glorified through it" Mark 11:4.

Often it is hard to discern, at the time of God speaking to us, the extent of his final meaning; or should I say when God speaks to us, we hear and try to establish His exact meaning when, at times, He has more than one meaning. Rest assured, God will allow you to understand His desires and directives. God does not want, nor does he allow, us to wander around aimlessly with no direction or plan for our life. He will seem to hide Himself for a season, only to manifest His meaning toward the end. He saves the best for last. There is a season where He wants us to search Him out. He wants us to search Him; He wants us to look to Him. God wants us to look into His word to examine what He has already said; He wants us to know what He has already spoken.

It is the glory of God to conceal a thing: but the honour of kings is to search out a matter. Proverbs 25:2

The great thing about the search is the reward at the discovery of the treasure! The search is fun and exciting, yet pales in comparison to the spoils of the reward. Friend, God saves the best for last, and at the end of your searching, God is there. Many spend a lifetime searching and looking around every corner for that one thing that would bring fulfillment. God is the only one who can fill the void, heal the hurts, and right every wrong. I am aware this book will make its way into the hands of people from every walk of life, position, and circumstance. Knowing this fact, I am confident to say that no matter where you are, God is there. At the end of you and your life, God is still there. Nothing has, nothing can, or nothing will remove His love from you! God has been arranging and rearranging all your life to get you to where He wants you. The life you lived was of no accident; the life you are living now is no accident. God is going to use it all, and in the end God has saved the best for last. He wants you to commit everything to Him. God wants the success story; God wants the story of your biggest blunders in life to be handed over to Him.

I've met so many who don't feel they will or ever recover from what has happened in the past. I can give testament that these seasons are most difficult to climb out of; however, you can, and I want you to know, you will. The central them of the gospel we cling to is of God's redemptive work through the death, burial, and resurrection of Jesus the Christ. The central theme of this title is that God has saved the best for last in your life; no matter how good or how bad it has been up to this point. We read in the book of Ruth a story of God's redemption toward women that mirrors His work toward his church and all mankind.

A woman by the name of Naomi walked a path that seemed to be of her ruin. Ruth, whom the book is titled after, married a son of Naomi's. Naomi had followed her husband to the land of Moab; while there, he died, leaving her to care for her two sons. By providence, both her sons married women from Moab. This would seem to be a lifesaving matter for Naomi, but this was not to be. After ten years both of her sons died. What a picture of destruction. She left her homeland to follow her husband. In the process her husband and two sons died - what a tragedy. To lose your support and your livelihood, and being a woman in a foreign land was a certain death sentence. She found herself at the end of her options in her current place of occupancy. She now knew she either pick herself up and return, or face a horrible fate. Famine had gripped the land and she had heard God had visited his people by giving them bread. There was no time to delay; she knew it was time to leave. Making this decision, she was granted a traveling partner she never expected. Ruth, her daughter-in-law, refused to return to her own family upon Naomi's suggestion. Ruth wanted to stay with this woman whom she now considered to be her mother.

I can think of the fear mixed with dedication and loyalty that Ruth felt. All she had ever known was her homeland of Moab, and now she had made a decision on her own against the advice of her Mother-in-law. However, her mind was made up. She cast all to the wind and told Naomi her people would be her people, and her land and God would be hers as well. To me this is an incredible leap of faith. Long before she was to understand Naomi's God and the faith available to her, she acts on it. To some this would seem blind faith;

to those who know God, they would agree this is the God kind of faith. This is a faith that shows up and is activated under pressure. We look for faith to show up in big, burly men and yet God shows His faith in the smallest and lowliest of women. If you have read the bible, you would have taken note of the many stories of women just like Ruth. I believe and am unwavering in my confidence that God strategically allowed these women to encounter the difficult situations they did in order that our faith might be built. God wants us to glean from their lives and know that if He can show himself strong in the life of these vulnerable ladies, He can for you as well. God wants you to know that no matter what you face, He has a way of bringing about good from your circumstance.

Naomi and Ruth shared a life experience, they lost their livelihood, both of their husbands had died, and now they had no way to support themselves. There are times when we are faced with making tough decisions. There are times in life when we would much rather keep doing what we were doing. Life will take us by surprise and not give us many options. It is in these perilous times we feel as if God has left us. However, it is in these times that God makes drastic changes. In God's allowing of these seasons, the outcome has a very positive end. I know all too well the drastic, difficult seasons I speak of. I also would have liked if I had never had to walk through them, but on the other side, I am much better for having faced what I did. I think the Psalmist said it best in Psalms 119:71, *"It is good for me that I have been afflicted; that I might learn thy statutes."*

No one when in a trial or facing a difficult situation thinks that any good will come out of it. God really does save the best for last. There is a blessing from having stood in tough times. When we look back, we can see how God was with us all the time. We can reflect and see the times that He intervened and how, the time we did not perceive it. I believe He does this so we will know that if times like this come again, we can stand positioned with a faith that has been strengthened by experiencing His faithfulness.

I do not imply by this passage that all trials are as a result of God's correction; I want this to be clear. However, this passage will

246

give us insight into a principle of God bringing about a good work in your life after the fact. There is always an end to everything, and the end of all things for God is Love! In the end of everything in your life, God loves you and desires that we settle that fact.

Now no chastening for the present seemeth to be joyous, but grievous: nevertheless afterward it yieldeth the peaceable fruit of righteousness unto them which are exercised thereby. Hebrews 12:11

When we are faced with tough times, it seems they will never end and no good will come from them; but, more times than not, God uses these for His glory. Ruth and Naomi, her mother-in-law, had a tough way to go and both had made a decision - for them there was no turning back. Awaiting them was a divine occurrence that neither expected. Under Jewish law there was a right as a close relative to request to be redeemed by the one who was in a position to do so. This right involved the relative buying back for the other relative their right to property sold in times of need, or when they had fallen into debt and sold the property as a result. This right could be exercised to buy back the right of freedom of a relative who had sold himself or herself into slavery as a result of indebtedness or poverty. There were more provisions under the institution of the kinsman redeemer institution, see Leviticus the 25th chapter.

The story of Ruth and Naomi is one of God's redemptive work and saving the best for last in their life. Naomi had a close relative that was a property owner who had servants working in the field. It would almost appear by chance that as Ruth set out to glean from those working the fields; she would glean from the very field that Naomi's relative owned. Friend, we don't just stumble into things! God orders our steps; and even though it seems by chance, we are guided by the Holy Spirit into the right place at the right time. This rich landowner takes notice of this young lady and sees her humility. Ruth gains favor in his eyes and the man named Boaz sets out to provide and protect her. He gives special instruction to his workers not to harm her and to purposely lay barley so she could pick up what appeared to be dropped. When I read this again and again I was amazed to see this principle at work in our lives. We

247

seem to stumble upon promotion and provision, an unexpected raise, or a refund check in the mail you never knew you were entitled to. All these are the goodness of God and reminders that He is there and He is our kinsman Redeemer. God desires to bless His children and all He asks in return is that love be returned to Him! What a trade; He blesses us unexpectedly, and all we have to do is love Him. Wow, what a God we serve!

Ruth comes home with what looks more like a bunker harvest than picking up scraps and Naomi questions her as to her success. Ruth shares everything with her and it is then she informs Ruth the very man you speak of is our kinsman redeemer. Ruth was in the right place at the right time for the purpose of saving herself, and many others to come. What looked like certain doom was, in turn, divine aligning of lives for the fulfillment of scripture. It was through this connecting of lives that Jesus the Messiah would ascend though the linage of Boaz and Ruth.

Naomi learns who owned the field was the man who showed Ruth kindness, and immediately formulates a plan for Ruth to follow.

Then Naomi her mother in law said unto her, My daughter, shall I not seek rest for thee, that it may be well with thee? And now is not Boaz of our kindred, with whose maidens thou wast? Behold, he winnoweth barley to night in the threshingfloor. Wash thyself therefore, and anoint thee, and put thy raiment upon thee, and get thee down to the floor: but make not thyself known unto the man, until he shall have done eating and drinking. And it shall be, when he lieth down, that thou shalt mark the place where he shall lie, and thou shalt go in, and uncover his feet, and lay thee down; and he will tell thee what thou shalt do. And she said unto her, All that thou sayest unto me I will do. And she went down unto the floor, and did according to all that her mother in law bade her. And when Boaz had eaten and drunk, and his heart was merry, he went to lie down at the end of the heap of corn: and she came softly, and uncovered his feet, and laid her down. And it came to pass at midnight, that the man was afraid, and turned himself: and, behold, a woman lay at his feet. And he said, Who art thou? And she answered, I am Ruth thine handmaid: spread therefore thy skirt over thine handmaid; for thou art a near kinsman. And he said, Blessed be thou of the Lord, my daughter: for thou hast shewed more kindness in the latter end than at the beginning, inasmuch as thou followedst not young men, whether poor or rich. And now, my daughter, fear not; I will do to thee all that thou requirest: for all the city of my people doth know that thou art a virtuous woman. Ruth 3:1-11

My heart burst with joy when I read this truth that Boaz spoke to Ruth. He told her in verse 10 that she showed her more kindness in the end than in the beginning, in that she never went after the young men, but now has come and lay at his feet. Boaz was much older than Ruth, yet for both Ruth and Boaz God saved the best for last. For Ruth it was a second man that God has blessed her with to raise her from the depravity of widowhood. For Boaz, the best was saved for last for God brought a young woman who was known to be virtuous in his old age. When I read this account, coupled with our subject matter in John, I am amazed at the kindness of God. I can write it no clearer than to say, "Even when it's over, it's never really over!" God can bring life out of death, He can bring back to life or he can create new life. You cannot count God out. When things look as dark as they possibly can get, know this one thing - God has not forgotten you. He is there and wherever He leads you, He will bring about good from your life and your situations.

We can't forget that there is a real enemy that is trying to steal from us. Comprehending how God allows this is not fully understood. Many have reasonable theories for this; many are viable and help us understand. With all these circumstances understood, and those not, I feel compelled to say that no matter what happens, life or death, God has saved the best for last! If you go on to overcome all the earthly obstacles and challenges, or if you lose your earthly life for any reason, if you are in Christ you win! Not only do you win, but also God saved the best for last! You will rule in a heavenly Kingdom that will far surpass your earthly existence. We have a life to live while here, which is true and cannot be ignored. Yet, God wants you to know that He has you covered. Whether you have a life or death victory, or feel like you lost the battle to a struggle, friend, you win. God has saved the best for last. I know of no other religion that has a message as good as the gospel we live by. The Gospel is good news, and this good news is what you need for an eternal existence with Christ by placing your faith, trust, and hope in Him - repenting of all sin and surrendering your existence to Him.

What an awesome word of encouragement and hope! - Believe in the Lord Jesus Christ and you shall be saved!

I am aware that many reading this book are saved, but have gone through, or are in a difficult season. I know you feel as if nothing good can happen from this point on. I beg to differ with you. Let me be the first to tell you – "Not only will God bring good from it, He has saved the best for last for you. This is a new day and a new time. What was yesterday is not today. God is the God of yesterday, today, and forever. He knows where you are and where you are headed. Don't get in a panic; slow down and don't be anxious because He has it worked out. Stop and take a deep breath, bend your knee, and bow your head. Utter a simple acknowledgment of His supremacy over you and your life. God loves a humble heart; now commit your life to Him. Give the past, present, and your future to him. Let God take you to a place; a place He desires to bless and prosper you is where He wants you." For some, this will not be a geographic relocation, but rather a spiritual one. In one prayer prayed, and in one instant, God can change everything.

It changed for Ruth in a foreign land with foreign people. He did as well for Boaz, a wealthy landowner, who had money but lacked a wife - Ruth. He changed it for Naomi too. If you were to continue reading the book of Ruth you would be amazed how God blessed her through the union of Ruth and Boaz. God changed it for Daniel in the lion's den. He changed it for David when Saul repeatedly attempted to take his life. God changed it for the wedding party in Cana and He wants to change it for the better in your favor! Reject the voices that would try to drown out God's voice that says He will not for you as well. You are an heir and joint heir with Christ. This means that what is entitled to Jesus is to you as well. What a thought to think that what God has laid up for his children is far greater than anything we can be given on earth. If that is not God saving the best for last, I'm not sure what is.

The master of the ceremony told the bridegroom that most put the good out first, and then bring out the inferior later when everyone is well drunk. It is my hope that you have seen that God has so much more that lies ahead for you. When we apply Ephesians 3:20 we learn of God's desire and willingness to surpass any previous blessing, dream, or hope. No matter how good or bad, there is a season of blessing in which God will overwhelm you.

I have witnessed this in my life, and God placed it in my heart to share it with you. I feel He wants the same for you - to share of His goodness and mercy in the many seasons of your life. Share it; tell others of the faithfulness He has shown to you. If you're honest, you can reflect on the difficult times and still see that as bad as it was, it could have been much worse. God is faithful and wants to bless His children. If you have ever tasted of the goodness of God, it would be hard to keep quiet about His loving kindness. The master of the ceremony tasted the water that had been turned into wine and could not keep quiet about it. He called the bridegroom and told him how blessed he was. With all the turmoil and negative news we endure on a daily basis in our society, the gospel of Jesus Christ is still "Good News!"

> *O taste and see that the Lord is good: blessed is the man*
> *that trusteth in him.* Psalm 34:8

This book is one of firsts, Jesus chose an obscure wedding party to work His first miracle. This miracle changed all those who were present. Jesus came to the party upon being invited. Invite Jesus into your life, heart, and house today. Let Him see your willingness to allow Him to occupy all that you have, and with what

He has already given you. In doing so, more and better from Him is to come.

God saves the best for last.

This is the last chapter and the last sentence in this book but not in your life; the last chapter has yet to be written.

"God saves the best for last!"

I would love to hear from you. If you have enjoyed reading this work I desire to hear from you. If this book spoke to you or ministered to you in any way please contact us via email – or connect with us conveniently on one of the many media outlets listed below

Email: thewaterthewomanandthewine@gmail.com

Gabrielbeadyministries.org

John2.org

Twitter: PastorGabrielB

Facebook: Gabriel Beady